THE
New Jewish Cuisine

THE
New Jewish Cuisine

GILA BERKOWITZ

Illustrated by Mona Mark

1986
DOUBLEDAY & COMPANY, INC,
GARDEN CITY, NEW YORK

Library of Congress Cataloging in Publication Data
Berkowitz, Gila.
  The new Jewish cuisine.
  Includes index.
  1. Cookery, Jewish. I. Title.
TX724.B464   1986   641.5′676   84-25949
ISBN 0-385-19091-3

Acknowledgments

In literature as in life, my husband, Arvin Levine, gets top billing. No one has done more, given more, to help me reach my goals. Cooking was just another chore until Arvin taught me its joys. Before marriage, any place I laid my head was home, but with Arvin a true House of Israel has become a reality. He awakened me to the wondrous possibility of a home where "the face of a guest is welcome as the presence of the Almighty," where "the poor are members of your household," and "the wise and learned gather."

The life of my father, Mendel Berkowitz, is proof that the spirit and the letter of the Torah are one. I have never known him to rationalize the laws of kashrut for his own convenience; indeed he once refused a gift of nonkosher meat—in a concentration camp. Nor have I ever seen him eat the smallest morsel of food without thanking God. His integrity and his great intellectual grasp of Judaism make him an awesome model.

My mother, Miriam Berkowitz, is a brilliant Hungarian cook, but her contribution is not limited to the recipes that pepper this book. Her unfailing optimism, energy, and faith have fueled me all of my life, and her openness to new ideas and her eternal youthfulness are an inspiration to a lesser mortal.

I doubt that even my parents could have predicted the extent to which my brother Ivan would follow their dictate to "be good to your little sister." He has always been my biggest booster and most useful adviser. May my work be worthy of his generous admiration.

My son, J.J. injected this work with joy. At the age of three it already gave him great pride and delight to know about the dietary laws, and his pleasure in them grows with his growing intelligence. My daughter Livia was born in the midst of this writing. The sweetness of her nature allowed me to continue working without a substantial break and without guilt. Thanks, kids!

Among my earliest memories are those of the hospitality of my uncle and aunt, Moshe and Emma Klein of blessed memory. My uncle, as part of a righteous and humble life, was often to be found busying himself in the preparation of a simple meal for friend or stranger. My aunt was probably the first chef in America to cater traditional kosher dishes with light, healthful ingredients. Her cooking ideas in the postwar period were quite visionary.

Even the richest cake can be crowned with frosting and even the most wonderful family can be enhanced with great in-laws. Saul and Pauline Levine have been marvelously supportive throughout every stage of the making of this book. Brother-in-law Myron Levine has contributed in both delicious substance and warm spirit. Both of my sisters-in-law have expanded the vistas of the New Jewish Cuisine. Francesca Berkowitz has shown just how sophisticated and subtle kosher food can be; Gavrielle Levine has shown how luscious vegetarian foods can be.

The Palo Alto Orthodox Minyan has provided an extraordinary setting in which to explore Judaism. This book could not have been written outside that special, loving community.

Innumerable friends have affected my cooking, and thus this book. I am especially grateful to Steffi Sussman, Jodi Kassorla, Bracha Weiss, Penny Katz and Esther Aumann.

While no rabbinic authority has reviewed this book, and its inaccuracies are those of a Jew who has sipped mere droplets from the bottomless spring of Torah, Rabbi David Grossman of Los Angeles and Rabbi Hayyim Kassorla of San Francisco answered all my questions about kashrut with speed and warm wisdom. They are exemplars of the idealistic breed of young rabbis who can truly be labeled progressive.

Contents

Whenever a recipe is mentioned in initial capital letters, instructions for making it may be found by consulting the Index.

Introduction

Mr. Schwartz: Hi honey, what's for dinner?
Mrs. Schwartz: Hello dear. Why, we have p'tcha (peppered calf's foot jelly), krupnik (mushroom-barley soup), flanken (boiled beef), and then, why don't we catch a movie off the videorecorder while we have our prune and quince compote?

Is this the script for an antacid commercial? A scene from an addle-brained situation comedy? Mrs. Schwartz's menu is parody today, but not so long ago it was a standard dinner in most Jewish homes.

Jewish life has changed dramatically in this century, and Jewish cooking, too, has undergone a revolution. Staples such as kishke (stuffed derma), tzimmes (carrot stew), and gefilte fish are cooked at home on special occasions only, if at all. Caterers and take-out shops specialize in Old World dishes that once simmered on every kosher stove. The staff of life has become the stuff of nostalgia. No matter how fond a Jew is of his or her tradition, the taste buds seem to take on a progress of their own. Even that black-frocked Hasid on the streets of Brooklyn or Jerusalem is much more likely to make a quick lunch of pizza or falafel than of schmaltz herring.

Great-grandmother would feel strange indeed in today's kosher kitchen. Yogurt has replaced sour cream; light vegetable oil has taken the place of animal fats; turkey and tofu have edged out goose and goat. Meat and fish are broiled and baked instead of boiled; exotic vegetables are lightly cooked or eaten raw; desserts are sweet, not tart. The contemporary cook makes daily use of herbs and spices that poor Bubby could not even pronounce! How and why, she might wonder, did kosher cooking undergo such radical change in only fifty or so years?

The change in Jewish cooking styles is part of the dramatic and poignant upheaval of Jewish life in this century. What most people mean when they refer to "Jewish food" is the cooking of the Jewish communities of Russia, Poland, and Germany. At the turn of the century, these countries were home to the overwhelming majority of the world's Jews. With the great migration to the United States, the extermination of millions in the Holocaust, and the founding of the State of Israel, the centers of population shifted with unprecedented speed. Today most Jews live in the Greater New York area, the American Sunbelt, and Israel. The robust cuisine of Northeastern Europe is simply too heavy for these temperate and subtropical climes. You can't expect a liver and kasha knish to tempt in San Diego as it did in Minsk. Consequently, Jewish cooking is veering to styles more typical of warmer areas; it is lighter and spicier, and it makes use of the grains, fruits, and vegetables grown in these areas.

Geographical changes coincided with industrialization and modernization and the changes of life-style that inevitably accompany them. Jews, like other people, do less physical work today. Yesterday's housewife expended hundreds of calories a day on physical labor. She hauled wood and coal, pumped water, lifted and beat carpets—to list just a few typical tasks. Today's homemaker uses managerial skills more than physical ones. Yesterday's merchant lifted his own bolts of cloth or kegs of beer or sacks of wheat. Today's merchant has machines to do such labor. It stands to reason then, that those who spend most of the day sitting behind desks or steering wheels would prefer food lower in calories, and the new Jewish cuisine came to reflect that preference.

Another reason that the quality of the cuisine has changed is that the quality of available foods has changed. Improvements in modern agriculture and transportation have given the cook a cornucopia of seasonal fruits and vegetables to work with. The long winters, the lack of refrigeration and quick-freezing in Northern Europe, necessarily meant that only the hardy root vegetables could be eaten regularly. A kosher meal today is more likely to include steamed broccoli rather than sauerkraut, because winter vegetables are available year round; they need not be pickled to extend a short harvest.

There is a negative side to the story, too. Kosher meats, for example, are of poorer quality today. In the small towns of Europe livestock was locally raised and the *shochet* (ritual slaughterer) and butcher were directly accountable to the consumer. Today slaughtering, butchering, and packaging of kosher meat and poultry are done in central processing plants. The products are then shipped to buyers far away. Even in some large Jewish communities many meats are available only in their frozen state. Our ancestors also enjoyed exquisitely fresh dairy products from their own cows or nearby farms. The products we buy from giant dairy concerns are several days old when they reach the stores, and often "improved" with fillers and additives.

Social, psychological, and medical shifts in standards of beauty and health are important factors in the development of the new Jewish cuisine. Kosher cooks and diners are increasingly weight-conscious and aware of the health-related aspects of diet. Few are aware that the rich foods we commonly associate with Jewish cooking were often specialty items eaten once a week on the Sabbath, or even less often. Only the rich could afford to eat meat and pastries every day. (Everyone could tell they were rich because they could afford to be fat!) Now that everyone can afford these foods at any time, obesity has come to be considered a social and medical disaster. Jews are as keenly aware of the importance of slimness as other Western peoples—and if the number of weight-loss diets by Jewish authors is taken into account, perhaps more so. (Diet empress Jean Nidetch thought up the Weight Watchers program while preparing for Passover.) The past few generations have voted with their plates: they prefer fashionable figures to Grandma's cooking.

Traditional Jewish cooking isn't just rich in calories. It is also rich in cholesterol, salt, and refined carbohydrates. It is rather low in the nutrients provided by green vegetables and fresh fruits. Little wonder, then, that so many of those treats of yesteryear are on the nutritionist's blacklist today. In 1900 a typical Jewish mother would send her kids to school with a midmorning snack consisting of a thick slice of bread covered by a slab of chicken fat. That mother could be arrested for child abuse today!

Judaism has been concerned, almost from its beginnings, with the health-related aspects of food. The Talmud gives much advice on the foods that were then thought to cause or cure various illnesses. Back in the twelfth century the great philosopher and physician Maimonides advised against excessive consumption of white bread and sweets. Throughout history, however, rabbis urged compliance with the dietary dictums of the best physicians of the age. One can follow contemporary nutritional advice and easily remain in the framework of the Jewish dietary laws. Indeed, kosher dining and self-discipline provide one with extra help in designing a nutritionally sound diet for the average family. However, for a diet considered healthful today, one would have to depart substantially from the traditional Jewish cuisine of Northern Europe.

There were bound to be repercussions from the explosion in the variety of foods and food information that became available to the kosher cook in the last few decades. Not only are more fruits and vegetables available, thanks to advances in agriculture and transportation, but processed and prepared foods are now accessible, too. Most of the nation's largest food companies provide rabbinical supervision for many of their products and an increasing number of specialty items are being produced by manufacturers aiming at a kosher market. In short, both producers and consumers are enjoying the advantages of a growing population of kosher food consumers.

Information about different foods and cooking techniques is now available to everyone. Newspapers, magazines, and books have brought the cuisine of the entire world and its finest restaurants right into the home. Jewish cooks are culling the best of these, modifying them to suit the dietary laws and coming up with a unique cuisine of their own.

Much of traditional Jewish cooking—like the traditional cooking of other peoples—is based on frugality. Above all, the Old World cook had to be able to make do with what her family could afford from the limited supply of foods and flavorings that were available. Modern affluence means that cooks can now experiment freely. Today, most foods, including exotic ones, are affordable most of the time to most of the cooks. Serious eaters will scrimp elsewhere rather than actually tighten their belts. Indeed, experts on the gourmet food industry have called that business "recession-proof."

Greater financial comfort means that more Jewish homes are the scenes of casual and formal entertainment. Indispensable to these parties and gatherings are glamorous, decorative, and original foods.

Affluence has also brought about more traveling. The Jews, always a well-traveled people, are being exposed to a wider range of cuisines than ever before.

In the old days if a cook heard of some exotic recipe, and if she had the ingredients available to her, she still might have shied away from trying it out. The reason: techniques and utensils also differed from country to country. Technology has helped to break down the barriers. Now the miracles of the electronic age admit difficult and time-consuming recipes to the repertoire of even the novice cook. He or she can knead, purée, shred, grate, and crush at the touch of a button, thanks to food processors, blenders, mixers, and other electrical appliances. Thanks to the freezer and the microwave oven, the home chef can prepare complicated meals when there is time to concentrate, rather than when the family is clamoring for dinner.

In the past two decades, Jewish women responded enthusiastically to the feminist movement and avidly rose to the challenge of careerism. New types of food were necessary to accommodate the millions of Jewish women who went to work outside the home. Gone is the time when soups and stews simmered on the stove all day, for there is no longer anyone at home to give them an occasional stir. Many traditional Jewish foods fell out of favor as working women replaced them with dishes that require only minimal preparation time.

A corollary to this trend is that Jewish men—with no cooking tradition—are taking over more and more of the cooking chores in kosher homes. Today it is both chic and expedient for men to do the cooking at least part of the time. Nevertheless, few men were trained by their mothers in the kitchen arts. When a man cooks, he is likely to use a recipe rather than depend on the wisdom of generations. Even when men have fond memories of traditional dishes, their own food is likely to be more contemporary.

An unexpected influence in the development of the new Jewish cuisine is that many Jews are cooking kosher for the first time. These cooks have no culinary tradition to continue. A significant proportion of kosher cooks come from families where the dietary laws have not been observed for one or more generations, and in becoming observant, they feel an obligation to adhere to religious laws, not nostalgia for a "home cooking" they have never known.

Jewish cuisine has its ironies. Most of the new kosher restaurants serve exotic fare, such as French, Chinese, Japanese, Israeli, or vegetarian cooking. Most of the delicatessens serving Jewish-style food throughout the United States are, in fact, *not* kosher.

Which all leads us to the question at the heart of the new Jewish cuisine. What is true tradition, as opposed to passing and superficial aspects of culture? Which elements of the Jewish culinary heritage are worth preserving and elaborating upon, which ones merit incorporation in our everyday lives? And which are merely mementoes of history to be cooked up once in a great while in quaint remembrance of times and places gone forever?

According to manufacturers of kosher foods, more people observe the dietary laws today than at any time since World War II. Half of the world's 12 million Jews observe some form of kashrut, if only to keep pork out of their homes, while three to four million maintain strictly kosher kitchens. A great number of people—sometimes for surprising reasons—keep a four-thousand-year-old tradition alive and vigorous. Ancient and unyielding as this tradition is, it allows for infinite variation, innovation, and play within its eternal parameters.

This book explores the new horizon of Jewish cuisine as it exists *today.* It will concentrate on but not limit itself to dishes that are light and healthful, and are easy and quick to prepare. I hope it inspires every reader to adapt and create wonderful life-giving foods for happy times and joyful celebrations.

> *Hearken diligently unto Me and eat ye that which is good!*
> —Isaiah 55:2

NOTE: Terms basic to Jewish cuisine and used throughout the book are defined below. Each recipe in this book is designated *M, D,* or *P.* This means that the dish may be used for, respectively, meat, dairy, or (Pareve) either type of meal.

Kashrut: the dietary laws of Judaism.

Kosher: in compliance with Kashrut; acceptable.

Meat: containing the flesh of any of the permitted animals or fowl or their derivatives.

Dairy: containing milk.

Pareve: containing neither meat nor milk; compatible with either meat or milk.

THE
New Jewish Cuisine

Kashrut:
Core of
the Jewish
Cuisine

There are dozens, perhaps hundreds, of distinct cuisines that can be legitimately called Jewish. Spicy or bland, meaty or vegetarian, rich or lean, what they have in common is adherence to the dietary laws of Judaism, or kashrut. What is remarkable is not that this set of laws has influenced the cuisine of the Jews, but that it has had a major role in shaping their history, society, and consciousness. It has done so for four thousand years, and continues to do so today.

For Jews and non-Jews alike, kashrut, more than any other form of religious expression, is the hallmark of Judaism.

What an unlikely candidate for the honor! The dietary code seems almost trivial compared to dramatic, immutable rituals, such as circumcision. It lacks the clear spirituality of the Sabbath and festivals, or the moral grandeur of the codes of justice and ethics. It doesn't even appeal to curiosity, as do the more exotic rites of purification. Why, then, is it such a powerful symbol?

Several reasons suggest themselves. First of all, no voluntary act is done more frequently than eating. This means that of necessity those who abide by kashrut must do so at least three times a day, every day. This is no charming little ritual to celebrate from a sense of nostalgia. Kashrut demands constant commitment.

Secondly, kashrut is quintessentially Jewish in that it is a physical, concrete expression of spiritual and moral values. It is one thing to give lip service to the idea of compassion, quite another to eschew cheeseburgers because of the remote possibility that the milk for the cheese came from the cow that mothered the steer that was ground into patties and sent to McDonald's.

Third, it can be argued that the dietary laws are irrational so that their observance is a test of faith. Indeed, Jewish philosophers from ancient times to the present have raised the possibility that they are largely arbitrary. Thus observance of these commandments became a true measure of the altruistic service of God.

The prohibition against pork is the best known of the dietary laws, but its fame is due to the universal popularity of that meat, rather than to exceptional

A priest and a rabbi were seated next to each other on a long airplane flight. The priest watched, fascinated, as the rabbi was served an elaborately packaged kosher meal.

"Truthfully, Rabbi, have you ever tasted pork?"

"Actually," the rabbi confessed sheepishly, "as a young man I once gave in to my base appetite and polished off a ham sandwich."

Emboldened, the rabbi ventured to ask, "How about you, Father. Did you ever sleep with a woman?"

The priest blushed. "To be honest, as a youth I once succumbed to temptation and did, in fact, experience sex."

The rabbi smiled and nodded. "Sure beats ham, doesn't it?"

condemnation by Jewish law or a special horror of the pig on the part of the Jews. Insects, for example, are even "less" kosher than pigs, yet this is rarely remarked upon because most people around the world would rather not eat insects, divine commandment or not. Misplaced emphasis, inaccurate observation by outsiders, and ignorance among many Jews have resulted in common distortion of this aspect of Judaism. It is illuminating to go back to the sources and trace the historical development of kashrut.

All the laws of kashrut are biblically based. Verses in the first five books were interpreted as commandments. These commandments were interpreted according to an oral law. More than two thousand years later the oral law was finally written down in the Talmud. This massive encyclopedia of Jewish thought included more than simple traditional explanations. It also described the cuisine of its time (from the years 200 to 500), speculated on possible applications of the dietary laws, made suggestions regarding health and medicine, defined appropriate dining etiquette, and reflected on thousands of issues dealing with food.

Ever since then Jewish law, halacha, has built upon the Talmudic law. Succeeding generations of scholars made new rulings. These were never completely novel—deciding something was kosher or unkosher on impulse. Nor did scholars ignore previous rulings, say by skipping the decisions of the Talmudists and interpreting the biblical verses by their own lights.

In the Middle Ages scholars found it helpful to codify Jewish law in a systematic fashion. The Shulchan Aruch (set table) was the most important of these codes, and part of it deals with kashrut. It is the chief workbook for preparation for the rabbinate. Even today thorough knowledge of the laws of kashrut is necessary before a student can become an Orthodox or Conservative rabbi.

In the sixteenth century a condensation of the Shulchan Aruch became popular as a guide for the layman. This book is available in English as the Code of Jewish Law. However, some of its content is outdated—much stress is put upon food preparation in a European household without modern conveniences and is of more historical than practical interest. And of course it does not discuss important factors in modern kashrut, such as the freezing process or food additives. A well-versed rabbi is an essential resource for those who intend to observe kashrut conscientiously. Even well-informed laymen will have cause to consult with a rabbi about matters of kashrut at least once or twice a year.

THE DIETARY LAWS

The following are fifteen biblical laws, listed according to their appearance in the Five Books of Moses. It might well be argued that the list is overinclusive (e.g., food that has not been blessed, as in Law number 12, is still kosher) or deficient (e.g., stolen food may not be eaten). The rationale of the list is that those laws are included which deal directly with the preparation or consumption of foods.

The many laws of agriculture and animal husbandry are omitted, as are the laws of the sabbatical year. For the record, it is forbidden to cross-breed plants, but permitted to eat hybrid fruit. It is forbidden to castrate animals, but permitted to eat capons. It is forbidden to eat food grown in the Land of Israel during a sabbatical year, but permitted to eat tomatoes grown there hydroponically.

It is also worth noting that many Talmudic and later rabbinic rulings about food derive from biblical laws that do not deal specifically with food. For example, the injunction "Verily, guard your souls" was interpreted as meaning "Be scrupulous in guarding your physical health." The rabbis thus forbade serving dishes which combined meat and fish (because the diner would be lax in watching for fish bones and might choke). They also forbade eating rotten or dirty food. And they strongly advised following the medical wisdom of one's own era in formulating one's diet.

(1) It is forbidden to eat the thigh muscle of an animal's hind legs.

Genesis 32:33 *The Israelites therefore do not eat the sciatic nerve on the hip joint to this day. This is because (the angel who wrestled with Jacob) touched Jacob's thigh on the sciatic nerve.*

The nerve, as well as the two tendons extending from the rear hip and thigh are forbidden for food. Because it is difficult to remove these parts from the slaughtered animal, the entire hind quarters of kosher-slaughtered animals are sold to nonkosher distributers. This part of the animal includes the sirloin, tenderloin, and filet mignon. In recent years specialty kosher butchers have offered to do the painstaking task, for a considerable fee, of extracting these parts, so now you can get kosher filet mignon at some kosher restaurants and caterers.

The rabbinic scholars derived important lessons from this commandment. In Jacob's ability to overcome a supernatural opponent they saw proof that God would side with Israel against all its enemies. In times of crisis throughout the ages, Jews saw in this law divine assurance that they would not be annihilated. Another derived lesson: a Jew must not let a physical handicap be the cause of despair.

(2) It is forbidden to eat leaven on the Passover.

Seven biblical verses pertain to the Passover dietary laws, including Exodus 12:19 *Seven days shall there be no leaven in your houses,* and Exodus 13:3 *And Moses said to the people, "Remember this day in which you came out of Egypt, out of the house of slavery, for God took you out with a show of power; leavened bread shall not be eaten.*

See the Chapter, Passover: The Taste for Freedom, for Passover laws and foods.

(3) *Terefah,* the flesh of injured animals, may not be eaten.

Exodus 22:30 *Be holy people for me, do not eat of flesh that has been prey in the fields; throw it to the dogs.*

The word *terefah* means "victim of a predator"; however, it has come to be used for any food which is not kosher. (The word kosher itself does not appear in the Books of Moses. It appears rarely in the later books of the Bible, but never in reference to food!)

This prohibition has come to include many injuries other than those caused by predatory animals. Also forbidden are animals killed by human hunters; animals injured by falls and other natural causes; diseased animals; animals with birth defects; any animal that could not be expected to survive for another twelve months.

The ritual slaughterer examines the carcass immediately after slaughter for many possible defects that would render it unsuitable. These include perforated organs, underdeveloped organs, organs of abnormal size, absence of an organ, internal cuts or bruises, internal hemorrhage, hernias, fractured bones, dislocated limbs. There are more than seventy defects of which the slaughterer must be aware. Kosher slaughter goes far beyond the most exacting government requirements in such matters.

The ban on terefah seems like a classic example of health legislation. However the biblical verse itself goes out of its way to deny this theory. It begins with the assertion of Jewish holiness, indicating that the following commandment is meant to underscore that mystical condition. The verse ends with the suggestion of throwing the terefah to the dogs. This says that the herder dogs should be rewarded by a windfall of meat that their human masters may not eat for spiritual reasons. It is implied that the meat is not physically harmful.

(4) It is forbidden to mix meat and milk.

Exodus 23:19 *You shall not cook a kid in its mother's milk.* Similarly, Exodus 34:26 and Deuteronomy 14:21.

Perhaps the most thoroughly explicated of the kashrut laws, this commandment has many implications. All methods of cooking and mixing are equally prohibited, as is the eating of meat and milk. Not only goats but all of the food animals and fowl are included (but not fish). A waiting period is necessary between the time meat was eaten and a dairy meal or snack. Most traditions declare a six-hour wait, while certain traditions of European Jewry accept three or even one hour as adequate. The six-hour wait is due to the fact that it takes about that long for the body to digest meat. After a dairy meal it is necessary to clean the teeth and mouth before meat may be eaten.

This law defines the "kosher home." To comply with it, two sets of dishes are needed, meat and dairy. Separate utensils, pots and pans, dishwashing equipment, and tablecloths are also necessary.

The prohibition against mixing meat and dairy foods has spurred great originality in Jewish cuisine, since all but a few nationalities combine meats and poultry with cheese, cream, butter, and other dairy products.

(5) It is forbidden to drink the wine of gentiles.

Exodus 34:12,16 *Take care to make no covenant with the inhabitants of the land, for it will be a trap for you. And you will let their daughters marry your sons and their daughters will go whoring after their gods and make your sons go whoring after their gods.*

And Deuteronomy 32:38 *Who ate the fat of their sacrifices and drank the wine of their libations.*

In the ancient world the ceremony of libation was virtually universal. All drinking, unlike all eating, was religious in nature. The dedication of wine to a deity has passed down to the present in the still-popular form of toasts. To prohibit idolatry it was necessary to forbid the drinking of wine in the presence of non-Jews, or to drink wine produced by idol-worshipers who had dedicated their wine at various stages of its production.

When idolatry disappeared from among the peoples with whom the Jews lived, the rabbis acknowledged that there was no longer any such thing as libation wine. However, since Scripture makes a point of tying an ominous course of events to the drinking of wine with gentiles—frivolous socializing leading to intermarriage and the subversion of Judaism—they extended the prohibition, although there is no concern that the wine may have been dedicated to pagan gods.

Kosher wine is made exclusively by observant Jews from the time the grapes are crushed through bottling. By extension, grape products such as true brandies, juices, jams, and grape-flavored candies, must also be kosher. Table grapes and raisins, however, need no supervision. Spirits made of grains or other fruits are kosher. Liquors that contain any grape products, however, such as Cognac, Grand Marnier, and Chartreuse are not kosher by Orthodox standards.

(6) It is forbidden to eat the abdominal fat of an animal.

Leviticus 7:23   *You shall not eat the fat of the ox, the sheep, or the goat.*

The prohibition extends to the fatty tissue covering the stomach, kidneys, and flank of animals. This was the part of the animal most commonly used for sacrifices in the ancient world. Kosher butchers always remove this tissue.

It is interesting that the earliest biblical commentators already noted that fat is unhealthful.

(7) No blood may be eaten.

Leviticus 7:26   *You shall eat no manner of blood, whether of fowl or beast;* Leviticus 17:14   *For it is the soul of all flesh, the blood is the life of it* . . . Also, many other verses.

The Jewish abhorrence of consuming blood was unique in the ancient Middle East. Secular scholars have noted that it does not resemble any other cultic rite and have concluded that it is not a derivative custom but a deliberate expression of the Jewish reverence for life.

The removal of blood from meat is a key element of kosher food preparation. Immediately after ritual slaughter the carcass is hung, neck down, so that the major blood vessels can drain. The animal is then butchered in the desired cuts. Within seventy-two hours of slaughter the meat is subject to the kashering process. Either the butcher or the homemaker can do this procedure of extensive salting and soaking, or direct-fire broiling.

It must be emphasized that kashering is not a magic formula for making meat kosher. It is merely the removal of the blood. Kashering is pointless in the following cases: (a) when the meat is from a nonkosher animal; (b) if the animal has not been ritually slaughtered; (c) if the slaughtered animal is injured in one of the specified ways; (d) if the cut of meat is from a prohibited part of the animal; (e) if more than seventy-two hours have passed from time of slaughter—unless the meat was frozen—and the blood has had a chance to congeal in the muscle tissue.

Blood is also prohibited in cases other than meat. An egg with a speck of blood in it may not be eaten even if it is not fertilized. Nor may any food on which blood has dripped, including blood from an injured finger or gums of the diner himself, be eaten.

(8) Designated species are permitted for food.

Leviticus 11:3   *Of the mammals you may eat any that has both true cloven hooves and that brings up its cud.*

Leviticus 11:9   *You may eat any creature that lives in salt water or fresh water, as long as it has fins and scales.*

Leviticus 11:22   *Among the insects you may eat only the red locust, the yellow locust, the spotted gray locust, and the white locust.*

Deuteronomy 14:4   *Among the mammals that you may eat are the ox, the sheep, the goat, the gazelle, the deer, the antelope, the ibex, the chamois, the bison, and the giraffe.*

Deuteronomy 14:11   *Of all the pure birds you may eat.*

A strong case can be made for vegetarianism as religiously desirable. Nevertheless Scripture is clear about permitting the consumption of many creatures. Included by name are most of the common domesticated animals, as well as the deer. Don't expect to find venison in the kosher butcher shop around the corner, though. Since hunting is forbidden, it would be necessary to capture a deer without injuring it, so that it could be ritually slaughtered. On very rare occasions, however, the persevering and well-heeled kosher gourmet can obtain such exotic meats as venison, beefalo, and reindeer. Giraffe, although specifically listed in the Bible, cannot be offered as a kosher entree. The size of its neck makes it impossible to slaughter with the instant, deep incision that is ritually required.

The Bible identifies kosher fish as those that have fins and scales. Because fish need not be slaughtered ritually they are easier to prepare than meat. Fish have always been a favorite food of the Jews, even in those communities which are located in landlocked countries. They frequently symbolize fertility and success and are a staple of the holiday table. The Bible mentions no fish by a specific name, but there are over twenty different terms used for fishing implements.

Insects come in for especially pejorative treatment, except for four kinds of locust which are permitted for food. Only the Yemenite community has a tradition of eating them, however, and they identify only two permissible kinds.

The nonkosher birds are listed rather than the kosher ones. The Talmudists constructed a set of characteristics by which kosher birds can be identified, including the shape of the talons and the structure of the alimentary canal. This was fortunate because in later years many species of birds unknown in biblical times were introduced to the Jews.

Doves and quail were the first fowl to be cultivated for food. Since birds are subject to the same rules of preparation as meats, it was difficult to eat many permitted birds because they could not be raised in captivity and were easily injured in trapping. Of course it was forbidden to hunt them in any manner. All this changed in Talmudic times with the introduction of the chicken from India. It soon became the favorite meat of the Jewish people. This is partly due to the fact that the kashering process of salting and soaking seems to improve the flavor of poultry, an effect opposite to what it does to red meats. To this day, kosher chickens enjoy a good reputation—*Consumer Reports* consistently rates Empire brand kosher chickens as the best of all frozen chickens—no such praise greets kosher beef.

Other fowl were brought from the Far East to enthusiastic reception. Ducks and geese were much loved for their fatty meat in the calorie-starved populations of Europe. Today, these fowl are appreciated in different, less fatty dishes, such as those prepared in Chinese or French styles.

The turkey, which the Jews of Colonial America identified as kosher, took a while to be properly appreciated by the larger Jewish communities. Today, however, turkey has become the most popular meat in Israel.

The milk, eggs, and roe of kosher animals are kosher. However, their fetuses and fertilized eggs are not.

(9) Designated species are forbidden as food.

Leviticus 11:8 *Do not eat the flesh of any of these animals.*

Leviticus 11:10 *All creatures in seas and rivers that have no fins and scales, whether invertebrates or mammals or other creatures, are an abomination to you.*

Leviticus 11:29 *These are the smaller animals that breed on land which are unclean to you* [list of rodents, reptiles, and mollusks].

Deuteronomy 14:19 *All the winged, swarming things are unclean to you; they shall not be eaten.*

Those mammals that have only one of the signs of kashrut, cloven-hoofed or cud-chewing are not kosher. The Bible gives four examples: the camel, the hyrax (a small desert mammal), the rabbit, and the pig. All of these animals were relished by most of the peoples of the ancient Near East. It is sometimes argued that the Jews acquired their prohibition against pork from the Egyptians, who also did not eat it. However, the four described animals all make up an important part of the diet of the peoples of the region. There are Bedouin tribes in

Saudi Arabia today whose diet consists solely of dates, camel's milk, and occasional camel meat. This prohibition alone must have drastically changed the lifestyle of the ancient Hebrews.

The prohibition of seafood other than those with fins and scales was also harsh. Israel has a long coast on the Mediterranean, access to the Red Sea and the freshwater lake known as the Sea of Galilee. Even in these polluted times there is an abundance of crab, shrimp, scallops, and other seafoods that are relished by the Lebanese to the north and the Egyptians to the south. They were an important source of protein in ancient times—yet were forbidden to the Jews.

To modern sensibilities the prohibition of rodents, reptiles, and mollusks seems unnecessary—they meet with near-universal revulsion. But these animals were important supplements to the diet of desert nomads, whose protein sources were scarce. Too, those who have tried some of these as food tend to grow fond of them. Various lizards have their aficionados in Mexico, some Texans adore fried rattlesnake, and the gourmet Cajuns of Louisiana relish alligator. Mollusks are considered delectable, properly dressed, with the French paying dearly for snails and the Chinese reserving slugs for their most elegant dishes. What is repulsive on the hoof is often appetizing on the menu of a glamorous restaurant.

(10) Insects and crawling animals, such as worms, are not to be eaten.

Numerous verses, including five in Leviticus, such as 11:43   *You shall not make yourselves abominable with any swarming thing that swarms.*

The repeated warnings against eating insects, which, one assumes, are not nearly as seductive as pork or shellfish, are a true mystery. Why does Scripture protest so much? In addition eight of the "creeping things," besides being unkosher, have the status of arch-defilers in the purity cult of the Temple. The entire rite is one of the deepest mysteries in Judaism. The singling out of these creatures as "abominations" is an added puzzle.

(11) The *challah* portion must be separated from bread dough.

Numbers 15:18–21   *When you come to the land to which I am bringing you, and you eat of the land's produce . . . you must separate the first portion of your kneading as a dough offering . . . In all future generations you must give the first of your kneading as an elevated gift to God.*

Strictly speaking, the dough offering is a commandment which pertains only to the Land of Israel at such times as the priests are performing their temple offices. It was one of many religious agricultural taxes. One twenty-fourth of the dough of a home baker and one forty-eighth of the dough of a professional baker were given to the priest for his own use.

After the destruction of the Temple in the year 70, the rabbis decreed that the practice be continued in the following manner: The baker removes an olive-size piece from any dough made of wheat, barley, buckwheat, oats, or rye. This includes any bread dough or dough for yeast rolls. It does not include cake batter or sweet quick-bread batter. If the volume of the dough is 73 fluid ounces/9 1/8 cups/131.8 cubic inches or greater, a blessing is said: "Blessed are You, Lord, our God, King of the universe, who has sanctified us with his commandments and commanded us to separate the challah." The removed dough, called challah, is given to a priest or burned and discarded. If the volume of the dough is less than this amount, the challah is treated in the same manner but the blessing is not said. If the baker neglected to remove the challah at the time of kneading, she may remove a piece from the baked bread.

The origin of the word challah is obscure. Its use today to designate the elegant Sabbath bread is relatively recent, probably in commemoration of the unleavened sacrificial breads of the Temple, which were known by that name.

(12) God must be blessed for all the food that is eaten.

Deuteronomy 8:10   *And you will eat, and be satisfied, and you will bless the Lord your God.*

All meals must be followed by the Grace. By rabbinical amendment snacks are also followed by declarations of thanks. Furthermore, a blessing must be said before partaking of any food, even a drink of water.

Since one is blessing God so profusely, it is important to be "satisfied" and truly enjoy one's food.

Because of the number of blessings said over food, the ordinary table was declared the equivalent of the Holy Altar. Thus high standards of cleanliness, manners, and conversation were demanded. A truly kosher home is characterized by a table that is the center of its religious life. The meals, especially the Sabbath meals, become the chief occasions of hospitality, charity, and education. Each course achieves holiness as it is followed by talk of Torah and the singing of special mealtime songs called zemirot.

(13) All animals to be used for meat must be ritually slaughtered.

Deuteronomy 12:21   *Then shall you slaughter of your herd and of your flock.*

Ritual slaughter is not described anywhere in the Bible. Nevertheless, it has always been accepted as a cornerstone of kashrut. An interesting aside: the

Samaritans are a tiny sect dating back to ancient times, who consider themselves the only true Jews yet are not considered Jewish at all by any Jewish community. Their faith is based on literal interpretation of the Bible, without any rabbinical addenda whatsoever. The Samaritans practice ritual slaughter anyway, though it has no resemblance to that practiced by mainstream Jews.

How is ritual slaughter performed? First, the slaughterer or *shochet* examines his special knife. It must literally be sharp enough to split a hair. It must also be completely smooth; a single nick in the blade renders the animal unkosher. The shochet recites a blessing and then cuts the animal's throat, instantly and cleanly severing both the trachea and the esophagus. The following are among the deviations which render the slaughtered animal unfit for kosher butchering: a hesitation of the shochet's hand in the act of severing; the pressing of the knife heavily on the animal's throat; if the point of the knife is caught between the trachea and the esophagus; if the cut occurs outside or mostly outside the prescribed small area; the dislocation of the trachea and esophagus from their normal position during slaughter.

Because of the intricacies of kosher slaughter, a shochet must be specially trained. He receives a type of ordination upon completing his studies. Traditionally, the shochet was the second most learned man in a community, while his piety came under closer examination than that of the rabbi. Many old-timers will point proudly to the presence of shochtim on their family trees, considered a sign of aristocracy. On the other hand any sign of religious deviance on the part of a shochet renders the animals he slaughters unkosher, even if they were slaughtered within all of the legal requirements. To do the act properly the shochet must have great physical strength and dexterity. For this reason women almost never enter the profession, although, according to the Talmud, they may do so. In the postwar period the shochet's place has changed drastically, while his duties have remained exactly the same. Instead of being a community employee, the shochet is now almost always situated in huge meat-processing plants. Pennsylvania is the center for kosher slaughter in the United States. Almost all of the beef consumed in Israel is slaughtered in Argentina, frozen, then sent halfway around the world to its consumers. Israeli shochtim, who slaughter mostly fowl, are government employees, as are the few who are permitted to work in Eastern Europe. Because today's shochet is removed from the eyes of the community, his work must be diligently supervised by rabbis.

A rather large proportion of animals slaughtered according to Jewish law turn out to be nonkosher, as one can imagine from all of the above specifications. The result is very expensive meat, usually priced at several orders of magnitude above nonkosher meat. Periodically, kosher meat companies and butchers—private enterprises—are rocked by scandal, since unscrupulous types are tempted by such large sums of money. There have even been accusations of mob infiltration in some kosher-meat enterprises. The consumer must be on constant alert. Any ethical taint on shochet, packinghouse, or butcher strongly indicates that the meat they are selling is not kosher.

Kosher meat has always been very expensive. Many traditional communities put an additional tax on slaughtered animals to help finance the charitable institutions of the community. This was considered fair because the major consumers of meat were the rich. Jews have always considered meat a necessity for the main Sabbath meals but, until this century, meat was a rarity on the weekday menu of the average Jew.

Most rabbinic commentators point to the necessity of kosher slaughter because it is humane. Many see it as a concession to human frailty. It is essentially indecent to kill animals for food, but since humans have a base passion for meat, let them take utmost heed of the animal's feelings.

Is kosher slaughter truly humane? Several objective agencies have examined this question, including a British royal commission and the agricultural departments of many American states. Every one of the unbiased investigators has found that kosher slaughter is as humane as or more humane than any other form of slaughter in modern use. Meat workers who have worked in both kosher and nonkosher slaughterhouses have testified that the animals definitely indicate greater pain in the latter. Electrical stunning and tranquilizer injection (commonly used in modern slaughter) are actually forbidden in kosher slaughter because it has been observed that the animals frequently experience greater nerve sensitivity and muscle rigidity than when they are instantly slaughtered by the ritual method. Under the banner of humane kindness, anti-Semites periodically attempt to ban kosher slaughter in various locales. These "humanitarians" were most successful in the 1930s in countries that would later become Fascist or collaborate with the Nazis. At this time three countries ban kosher slaughter: Norway, Sweden, and Switzerland. To meet their requirements, Jews in these countries must import all of their kosher meat supplies. Recently, an international human rights organization has complained to the government of Sweden, which poses an import tax on kosher meat.

(14) It is forbidden to eat the flesh of a live animal.

Deuteronomy 12:23 *You shall not eat the life with the meat.*

Of all the laws of kashrut, this is the only one that is considered binding on gentiles as well as Jews. It is one of the Seven Laws of the Sons of Noah, basic standards of decency without which civilization would fall into chaos. The law has little direct application today, except, perhaps, that thinking people everywhere might reconsider eating live clams on the half-shell or boiling live lobsters. In the ancient world the application was direct indeed. The Mongols who overran much of Asia and Europe spent most of their lives mounted and on the move. Their strength and mobility were enhanced by the custom of cutting slices of meat from their horses and pack animals. They were adept at this and the injuries would often heal. In this way they avoided carrying large amounts of butchered meat and coping with spoilage.

From this law the rabbis derived general principles of kindness to animals. Corollary rules include the one that enjoins a Jew who owns animals, whether they are barnyard animals, watchdogs, or pets, from sitting down to his main meal of the day before feeding the animals theirs. It is forbidden to kill animals for any reason other than food or self-protection. No one has a true sense of humility unless he shows respect and responsibility for the lower orders. The prohibition against eating "the life with the flesh" provides yet another reason for forbidding hunting, an activity repugnant to the very spirit of Judaism.

(15) It is prohibited to eat any animal that has died a natural death.

Deuteronomy 14:21 *You shall not eat of any carrion.*

This law, in addition to the prohibition of terefah, eliminates from consumption any animal that has not been ritually slaughtered.

Many theories have been posited as to the "reasons" for the kashrut laws. Many Jews believe that the way of life prescribed by these laws will lead one to a heightened awareness of a universal *morality*. Certainly, the laws show an acute sensitivity to the welfare of animals. They go even further in demanding, for example, that the Jew see the intrinsic horror of bloodshed—in the prohibition of eating so much as a drop of blood, and in insisting that the Holy People steer clear of cruelty—in the plethora of details explicating the commandment "You shall not cook a kid in its mother's milk."

In modern times some Jews have taken the liberty of declaring as unkosher the foods produced by those they see as unethical. Pepsi-Cola was so declared by Soviet Jewry activists when the company that produces it became one of the first to trade with the Russians, over the pleas of dissidents. (Pepsi was already on the outs with many Jews for refusing to franchise in Israel—it provides cola for much of the Arab world, while Coke sells in Israel but cannot sell to its neighbors.) In the early seventies, when lettuce and grapes were being boycotted because of labor disputes, there were those who declared those foods unkosher. And there are some who will not dine on German china or drink from German-made crystal, declaring the food served on such ware to be unkosher. (Ordinarily, bone china is permitted and does not affect the status of food served on it.)

While such examples of self-imposed restrictions of diet may be commendable, they are not essentially concerned with the issue of kashrut, because the latter by definition implies a divine commandment that is assumed to be ethical in nature rather than a commandment to act ethically, which is covered elsewhere.

It has been pointed out that kashrut is an *ecological* system. It places humans on a viable rung of the ladder of living things. That is, it asks people not to consume those creatures that are on the same link of the food chain, i.e.,

A couple we shall refer to as Mr. and Mrs. Katz took a trip to the Soviet Union. They hoped to make contact with dissident Soviet Jews and provide them with any aid they could. But when the Katzes got to Moscow they found that the contacts they had been told about could not or would not meet with them for fear of informers. After a week of futile attempts they gave up on their mission and decided to just sightsee for the remainder of their trip.

One evening they entered a restaurant, one of those spots frequented only by Western tourists and Party officials. The waiter recited a list of the available dishes. The Katzes' faces fell—all of the dishes contained meat.

"Do you have any salads?" they asked the waiter.

"No."

"How about eggs?"

"Not today."

"Fish?"

"Sorry."

"Fruit?"

"Not this time of year."

"Well, I'm afraid we're vegetarians," they mumbled.

Disappointed and a little embarrassed, they left the restaurant.

A few blocks away someone whispered to them from an alley. To their surprise it was the waiter. He had followed them from the restaurant! The waiter turned out to be a Jew and he led them to other refuseniks. The Katzes were finally able to get on with their mission.

Later they asked the waiter how he could identify them as observant Jews, rather than strict vegetarians.

"Easy," said the waiter, "after I recite the menu, the vegetarians always sigh and say, 'Ah well, just this once,' but a kosher Jew will never break the commandments just for a bowl of borscht!"

According to *Fortune* magazine, the most profitable pork products company in the United States is Frederick and Herrud, whose chief stockholder and officer is Henry Dorfman. Mr. Dorfman himself keeps kosher, and none of the company's products is ever served in his home.

---

carnivores, nor those that are much farther down the chain, such as shellfish, which act as scavengers and filters of the waterways.

Of course, kashrut has a strong *mystical* resonance. Biblical verses on which the laws are based frequently mention "holiness," and "purity," terms which always deal with a spiritual state. Jewish metaphysics has maintained that the soul is deeply influenced by what the body consumes. There is at least one mystic, in the city of Jerusalem, who, it is claimed, can tell at a glance whether a person keeps kosher or not.

Health has been cited as an important reason for kashrut. In the early years of the Reform movement in Judaism, health was implied as the only reason for the kashrut laws, which led to the rationale that they could, in the superior light of modern science, be abandoned. For example, it was assumed that the reason for the prohibition of pork was that the ancient Hebrews had observed that those who ate pork often fell sick. By the time Reform rabbis considered the issue, scientists had already identified trichinosis in pigs and proved that thorough cooking would eliminate the problem. The Reform theologians then saw no obstacle to permitting the consumption of pork. Orthodox rabbis have also maintained that health is a major benefit of the kashrut guidelines. Today, however, this theory is enjoying less of a vogue. While kashrut promotes cleanliness, freshness, and moderation, those who keep kosher do not seem to be protected from the major alimentary diseases of modern times.

Trichinosis is not the only intestinal worm disease to plague humanity. Another parasitic ailment is popularly called "Jewish grandmother's disease." The worm inhabits fish, and while it is killed in cooking, some gefilte-fish makers have become infected by tasting the uncooked fish mixture before correcting the seasoning.

Another benefit of kashrut, it has been argued, is the strengthening of *self-discipline* in the individual. The ability to postpone or modify gratification has been proposed as the major reason for the extraordinary achievements of Jews in many fields.

And kashrut has been an important means of achieving a sense of *national character*. This way of eating proves to a Jew, over and over again every day, that he or she is part of unique and cohesive community.

Yet after all the theories have been posed, most practitioners of this difficult discipline maintain, kashrut must be considered as the commandments of a God who, in his goodness, sees that they offer a variety of advantages, but whose *ultimate reasons remain unknown.*

Orthodox ruling usually determines what is kosher. In some states and countries this is so by law, elsewhere by convention. Conservative Judaism has much the same standards of kashrut as Orthodoxy, with a few exceptions. Using a centuries-old ruling which had previously been accepted only by Sephardic Jews, the Conservatives permit the consumption of sturgeon—and its caviar—and swordfish. Orthodox rabbis do not permit it. These two fish have fins and scales, as the Bible requires, but do not have those organs throughout their lifecycles. Conservative ruling also permits ordinary cheese. The Orthodox forbid hard cheese, which is made with rennet, an animal-derived enzyme, and permits only cheese made with kosher rennet. Conservative Judaism also permits the use

Mention "kosher" and the image that invariably pops into everyone's mind is the prohibition against pork. Oddly, the Bible does not single the pig out for special scorn, listing it with other animals that are prohibited because they lack one of the two requirements for a kosher animal. The pig has a split hoof but does not chew its cud.

It is the prominence of the pig in the world's cuisine that makes its absence in the Jewish one so conspicuous. Pork is the most widely consumed of all meats. Only since the advent of the fast-food chain has beef consumption surpassed that of pork in the United States. In many ways the pig is an admirable creature. It requires less care and less expensive feed than any other animal raised for its meat. It adapts easily to many environmental conditions. And it can be used very efficiently—everything, as the saying goes, but the squeal.

Certain critics of kashrut used to claim that the Jews outlawed pigs because their meat tended to spoil in the warm Mediterranean climate. Actually, pork was probably the first meat to be preserved and it has been preserved in a remarkable variety of ways. Pork is the favorite meat in most of the tropics and subtropics.

Pigs were not unknown to the ancient Israelites. Wild boar is native to the land of Israel, and the Canaanites were fond of its meat. The Greco-Syrians who conquered Judaea about 300 B.C.E. (they're the ones who were overthrown by the heroes of Chanukah) discovered that sacrificing a pig at the Temple was the ultimate insult to the Jews, and since then the pig has represented all that is alien to Judaism.

There is no validity to the myth that the Easter ham was introduced as a way of distinguishing early Christians from Jews. Ham was part of pagan spring rites in some parts of Europe from pre-Christian times.

It is interesting that while almost everyone eats pork (Moslems are a notable exception, but they frankly borrowed their taboo from the Jews), few have kind words for the pig. To call someone a swine is to insult him in almost every language, often more terribly than in Hebrew and Yiddish, in which the epithet merely means "glutton."

Jews may use pork products in any way except for food. They may wear pigskin leather and use lard-based lubricants, soaps, and toiletries.

of ordinary wine for all but ritual purposes, while the Orthodox forbid it in all circumstances.

Reform Judaism originally overthrew kashrut with a vengeance. For the first time in Jewish history, Jews abandoned kashrut on principle, claiming that it was a vestigial observance of rules of behavior that were no longer relevant. Historically, the Conservative movement was born in 1885 when American

Reform rabbis introduced the Pittsburgh Platform, which declares all laws of kashrut to be dispensable. Some historians also found support for the new movement at a turn of the century commencement exercise of the Reform rabbinical seminary. Several newly ordained rabbis split away from the Reform body when they protested the serving of shrimp at the graduation buffet.

Today, however, a growing number of young Reform rabbis are advocating a return to kashrut, if not always in the traditional manner. They see important cultural and ethical values in the dietary laws, values that are worth preserving and promoting. Reconstructionism, the branch of Judaism least likely to accept nonrational commandments because it does not believe in a supernatural "divine," does, however, support the idea of kashrut, because its value in preserving Jewish integrity throughout history is undeniable.

Those who choose to keep kosher, whatever their affiliation, will want to choose a rabbi who is both qualified and caring, able to assist in this important road to Jewish self-fulfillment.

Because so much of what we eat today is already processed before purchase, it is important to look for symbols of kashrut supervision on the packaging of all foods other than pure grains, vegetables, and fruits.

The supervisor need not be a rabbi. Any observant man or woman trained to look out for kashrut problems can give certification. Kashrut organizations offer the services of a supervisor for a fee. Foods produced under such supervision may bear the seal or certificate of the organization. The most common seals are the ⓤ and the Ⓚ, and there are numerous others, sometimes under the aegis of the chief rabbinate of a city, where such an institution exists. The mere appearance of the letter *k* on a label means only that the manufacturer of the food claims it is kosher. The manufacturer may have hired a private supervisor or simply affixed the letter himself. There are no legal requirements for including this symbol on a package.

Why should a product require certification when the law requires that all ingredients be listed? There are many reasons. The law in most states is not as exhaustive as Jewish law. For example, the lard used to grease a baking pan might not be listed if the brownies baked in it contain no animal fat. Yet these brownies would not be kosher. In addition, many additives in use today can be of animal, vegetable, or mineral origin without specifying which is used. And, of course, mistakes will happen and substitutions will be made where food is being produced by those who are not conscious of kashrut. Certain items need special care in their selection.

• All meat and poultry and related items. Example: meat "flavoring" is the reason that one spaghetti sauce has no certification while all the other products of that brand are kosher.

• Any food prepared with oil or shortening. Example: french fries are usually deep-fried in vegetable oil, but animal fats are sometimes dispersed in the oil for added flavor.

• Baked goods. Lard and other nonkosher fats are often used in baking breads, cakes, cookies, and pastries. Example: lard is almost always used in pie crusts.

 • Foods containing additives such as emulsifiers or stabilizers. Example: the ubiquitous mono- and diglycerides may be synthesized from either animal or vegetable fats.

 • Food containing gelatin or other thickeners. Gelatin is derived from animal bones and kosher gelatin must be derived from kosher, ritually slaughtered animals—and is usually expensive. Example: gelatin is used as a short cut in thickening sour cream, yogurt, and cottage cheese. (Natural cultures are kosher and make tastier, more wholesome dairy products.)

When products are made for a specifically Jewish market they often have kashrut information on the packaging. Some of the terms used:

Cholov Yisroel. "Milk of Israel" (Hebrew). Until this century milk was one of the most commonly adulterated foods. Some farmers and dairies added the milk of nonkosher animals to extend their supplies of cow milk. Today government regulations are quite strict in this regard, and Jews, in general, trust that the milk and dairy products they purchase (except for hard cheeses and products with additives) are kosher. However, some Orthodox Jews insist on dairy products that have been supervised by observant Jews from milking to packaging.

Glatt. "Smooth" (Yiddish). In ritual slaughter the slaughterer is required to check certain internal organs and make sure they have no lesions on them that would disqualify the carcass. In Glatt slaughter, additional organs are checked and the qualifications are stricter. Because modern slaughtering plants are so rushed and the general level of kashrut is not what it used to be, many Orthodox Jews insist that Glatt is now a minimal rather than an extraordinary level of kashrut quality control. The term is derived from the condition of the lungs of a kosher animal.

Hashgacha. "Supervision" (Hebrew). Unlike manufacturers who bestow a *k* on themselves, producers of truly kosher products contract for responsible supervision. Those held accountable are either supervisory organizations, such as the Orthodox Union (Ⓤ); individuals, such as Rebetzin Rosa Ziemba of Chicago; synagogues, such as Khal Adath Jeshurun of Washington Heights; or a rabbinical body, such as the Chief Ashkenazic Rabbinate of Jerusalem.

Mehadrin. "Glorified" (Hebrew). Indicating that a product more than meets the minimum requirements of kashrut, or is supervised with exceptional care.

GETTING KOSHER

Many thousands of Jews are approaching the age-old customs of kashrut for the first time. The rules and equipment sometimes seem so complex that they put off this essential part of a truly Jewish life. The following suggestions are meant for persons who wish to take that first step. While these rules are not comprehensive, they do meet the standards of what most informed authorities consider kosher.

Six Steps to Keeping Kosher

1. Eat only meat and poultry which has been slaughtered, butchered, and packaged according to the laws of kashrut.
2. Purchase meat and poultry which has been soaked and salted, or do the kashering process yourself.
3. Eat, prepare, serve, and clean up after dairy products and meat products separately.
4. Drink kosher wines only and eat kosher grape products only.
5. Eat only those fish that have fins and scales.
6. Look for kashrut supervision on all processed foods and baked goods.

The kosher kitchen has been so vital a part of the Jewish home that one can hardly imagine a truly Jewish home without it. Making a kitchen kosher is almost a rebirthing experience; it touches the core of a person's life and the life of his or her family. Yet the physical reality of making and maintaining a kosher kitchen can seem so awesome that newcomers to the Jewish experience might hesitate to begin. Indeed it is demanding and expensive to embark on this course but most people who do so find it personally rewarding even in the short run.

Organization is the key to the kosher kitchen makeover. Remember that meat and dairy meals must be (a) prepared separately; (b) eaten separately; (c) cleaned up separately. A competent rabbi should be called upon when there are questions of how to make something kosher—and there will be. In some communities volunteer crews are available to come in and help you with the actual kashering process and attendant cleanup. The Chabad organization is especially helpful in this regard. They have branches in many urban and suburban areas and are listed in the phone book.

Ready all surfaces on which food is to be eaten and prepared by thorough cleansing with strong detergents and scouring brushes or pads. Tables and counters made of glass, glazed tile, stone, or Formica can be made kosher. Carefully pour scalding hot water on all clean surfaces. Those of some materials cannot be made kosher because they have irreversibly absorbed nonkosher food or both meat and milk. Tabletops can be made kosher by refinishing the surface.

THE KOSHER EGG

The egg has been used extensively in the cooking of all Jewish communities, and is an important symbol in many Jewish rituals. It is considered pareve (neutral) and may be used freely in both milk and meat dishes. The Talmud claims that it has mild laxative and aphrodisiac properties.

The biblical prohibition against eating blood is so strict that an egg containing even a speck of blood is rendered nonkosher. Moreover, food that touches on any part of a nonkosher egg is customarily discarded. Prudent cooks always use a separate cup or bowl in which to break each egg and inspect it for blood spots. A wide-mouthed juice glass is handy for this purpose. If the egg is found to contain blood, it is discarded and the glass is washed out.

Today, blood in an egg does not mean that it has been fertilized. On modern egg farms the hens and roosters have no access to each other. A blood spot in an egg indicates that the hen that laid it is diseased. Most commercial egg farms candle their eggs for blood before they are packaged for market. However, some are apparently more careful than others. Individual examination by the kosher cook will show that eggs from one supermarket will have blood drops far more frequently than those from another. He or she will thus find it more economical to buy eggs from the latter grocer because there will be fewer wasted eggs.

Truly fertilized eggs, sold mainly in health-food stores, are *not* kosher.

Or the table can be used with tablecloths at each meal. Slabs of butcher block can be purchased to replace old countertops and are both attractive and useful.

Remove all nonkosher foods from the house. If possible, give them to a non-Jew. However, do not give them to a Jew, even if that person does not choose to keep kosher. Clean cupboard shelves and lay fresh shelving paper.

The stove must be thoroughly cleaned. Sometimes it is easier to purchase new replacement parts for small parts that are removable. The burners should be left on maximum heat for sixty minutes. The oven, too, must be thoroughly cleaned. Self-cleaning models should be run through their cycles twice, while standard types must be cleaned and left on maximum heat for two hours. Microwave ovens should be cleaned, then their floors covered with a layer of water, then turned on to their maximum setting.

Dishwashers are made kosher by turning water heat on to maximum and running through on the longest cycle three times, using detergent twice. They must be designated for either meat or dairy use.

Refrigerators and freezers should be cleaned. If ice trays have been used for freezing anything other than plain ice (such as baby food), they should be replaced.

Sinks must be very well cleaned. If you have two sinks you should kasher them by cleaning and filling with scalding water. Then designate one dairy and one meat. A single sink should be cleaned. However, it will always be a nonkosher surface, since dairy and meat utensils will both be rinsed in it. Separate washtubs (in different colors) should be used for washing dishes, flatware, and other utensils, and dishes may not be placed directly into the sink to be washed later.

New sponges or dishrags, draining racks and trays, and any other items used for dishwashing, must be bought. You will need two of each, color-coded so that meat and dairy are easily distinguishable. Be certain that all cleaning agents used for dishes and food-preparation items are certified kosher. This includes dish detergent, scouring pads, dishwasher powder, silver polish, and many other cleansers. Many of the national brands, generics, and supermarket brands are so certified.

All pots and pans, china, flatware, and any other utensil must be designated either meat or dairy. If you have two of the same kind, use indelible marker or colored electrical tape to identify the dairy one. It is a good idea to have very different patterns of dinnerware and flatware to distinguish meat from dairy.

Metal flatware can be made kosher by submersion in scalding water. A red-hot iron or stone is added to a pot of boiling water before the clean utensils are submerged.

Do you have expensive china that has been used for nonkosher food? As long as it has no cracks and food was not actually cooked in it, it need not be thrown away. Clean well and store it for one year. After that time, designate it meat or dairy.

True glassware, but not tempered glass like Pyrex or Arcoroc, may be used for both meat and milk, although you may feel more comfortable with two sets, to avoid confusion.

In addition, you may wish to have some pareve items. A bread knife, cutting board for vegetables, peeler, paring knife, perhaps an entire set of bakeware, measuring cups and spoons, and mixing bowls. Such pareve items must be rinsed off individually, or else a third set of washing utensils must be provided. These utensils may never be used for either dairy or meat, as they then become permanently dairy or meat.

Designate tabletops either meat or dairy. The latter is often favored, since meat meals tend to be more formal and you will want to use a tablecloth anyway. Either way, a simple change of tablecloth converts the table to the opposite category.

Kosher meat

The greatest care must be taken in the purchase and preparation of meat and fowl. Buy from a butcher of impeccable reputation, or the packaged meats of reliable firms. Here again a rabbi and a supportive community are the best sources of up-to-date information.

Some kosher meats will be familiar, others are cuts that are traditional to Jewish cuisine—such as brisket or flanken. All must come from the front of the steer. Cuts from the twelfth rib and back are not kosher.

Some popular kosher cuts: chuck, pot roast, London broil, breast, "filet mignon"; shoulder, rib, rib-eye, Delmonico, and minute steaks.

These must be substituted whenever a recipe calls for nonkosher cuts such as: loin, flank, rump, round; sirloin, T-bone, and porterhouse steaks.

All the usual parts of poultry are kosher.

The kosher parts of kosher animals that have been ritually slaughtered must still be kashered—soaked and salted. It cannot be overemphasized that this is not a magic rite; it will not render kosher any meat from a nonkosher animal, from an animal that has not been ritually slaughtered, or from a nonkosher part of a kosher animal. The purpose of kashering is to remove as much blood as possible from the meat.

Nowadays virtually every kosher butcher performs this service for the consumer, either routinely or on request. All meat and poultry must be kashered within seventy-two hours of slaughter, after which the blood becomes so coagulated that it cannot be properly removed. Freezing suspends coagulation so long-frozen meat can be kashered. However, one must remember not to refreeze raw meat. Such meat loses much of its flavor and nutritional value. Once meat has been defrosted it should be cooked before freezing again.

Years ago kashering was always done at home, and meat was a much more important—if not more frequent—part of the Jewish diet. Kashering meat was the most important part of the training of a young bride. Today one hesitates to recommend this messy, time-consuming procedure when it is so universally available at the butcher's. On those occasions when it is not, most would prefer skipping the meat and having fish or dairy instead. However, with the price of kosher meat being what it is, and the sin of wastefulness as serious as it is, one should at least be aware of how to kasher meat in an emergency.

The following equipment is needed: a large bucket, for completely submerging the meat in water; a grooved, slanted board on which to place the meat while it is draining; kosher salt, which is sold as "coarse salt" but which is actually medium ground (fine table salt may not be used as it dissolves on the meat, nor may true coarse salt—the kind used on icy driveways—which falls off the meat); a pan or other receptacle into which the meat drains. All of these may not be used for any other purpose.

The meat is rinsed in cold water and completely submerged in cold, clean water for thirty minutes. It is then removed from the water and placed on the board. Kosher salt is liberally sprinkled on all sides of the meat, as well as into the cavities of birds. The meat is left to drain for a minimum of one hour. It is then washed three times in cold, clean water.

Liver, which is especially rich in blood, must be kashered in a different way. A large liver, such as that of a calf, should be sliced. The liver is sprinkled with kosher salt and pierced with a fork, as for tenderizing. It is placed on a rack that permits draining over or under direct flame. The liver is seared until the color changes or a crust forms. The knife, fork, rack, and any pan into which the liver drains, may not be used for any other purpose.

Persons who have been advised by their physicians to eliminate all salt from their diet can kasher all of their meat in the above manner but without salt.

Fish is not kashered. However, it is desirable to obtain fish that is not cut with the same knife used on nonkosher seafood. Some fish markets keep a separate knife for cleaning fish, which they will use at the request of kosher customers.

While few of us will eat insects on purpose, the prohibition against eating them goes further than mere aesthetics. The salad maker is duty-bound to carefully inspect lettuce, spinach, and other leafy vegetables. If insects are found, the vegetable should be washed and may then be eaten. Grains and flours should be kept in canisters or plastic bags to prevent infestation. Check these each time you use them.

Eating spoiled food is forbidden by Jewish law. Of course, Western standards of food freshness are very high; however, certain time-hallowed customs are worth following. Among them: a food that has been cut, such as half an onion or a cut salami, is not entirely eaten. Even if it has been kept in the refrigerator and wrapped in foil or plastic, a thin slice is taken from the cut end and discarded.

Even in the most carefully kosher kitchen, accidents will occur. What happens if, say, a meat utensil is used on a dairy dish, or a shred of cheese falls into a stew? The variables are so great that a rabbi must be consulted. The user should not be tempted to either ignore the event or wastefully discard food or utensils. Rather, a good rabbi will be pleased to decide on a kosher and sensible course of action. And remember, kashrut has been observed for more than four thousand years, during which they've heard sillier questions than yours!

There are very poor people who can afford no meat, and vegetarians who choose to eat none, whose kitchens are uncomplicated places. And there are wealthy folk who maintain separate kitchens, each with a full array of appliances and utensils, for meat and dairy. For the vast majority, however, keeping a kosher kitchen involves frequent decision making. Among the most important: which appliances are worth duplicating, and among those for which doubles cannot be accommodated, which is more practical, dairy or meat. Here are some suggestions.

Baby-food equipment

Infants eat everything mixed with or followed by milk or formula, so keep it all dairy. When they begin eating meat, get a plastic placemat and a baby-sized spoon for meat meals. If you are making your own meats, you may wish to get a hand mill or inexpensive blender that will be meat—but don't expect to get a lot of use out of it, as infants outgrow this stage quickly. No need for a baby to wait after meat for formula or milk. Just clean up the meat things and the baby and serve the milk. When kids reach the age of three or so, they are ready to learn, and take great pride in knowing, simple rules of kashrut.

Blender

In most homes with other small appliances the blender is generally used for making milk shakes and other drinks, so make it dairy.

Cleavers and quality knives

One or two good knives are indispensable for carving meat. Consider a cleaver for dicing vegetables and at least one paring knife for fruits and vegetables. These should be pareve. For dairy, a good cheese knife or plane is handy.

Cutting board

Two cutting boards are ideal, one for meat and another (pareve) for vegetables. To avoid confusion, purchase boards made of different kinds of wood, or one of wood, one of Lucite.

Deep-fryer

If most of the things you fry, like french fries, are served with meat meals, you can make it meat and also be able to do things like meat-filled fried wontons. However, if you eat mostly dairy meals, make it pareve.

Electric skillet

It's almost always worthwhile making this appliance meat.

Food processor

The most difficult appliance to decide, because it is so handy; yet it is expensive and takes up considerable counter space. The processor can make quick work of cutting up meat. On the other hand, it eases the chore of grating cheese, so either choice is reasonable. A pareve choice can be justified because so much cutting, grating, chopping, and slicing are done on vegetables. An alternative is to buy one food processor and then get an extra bowl and set of blades. Be sure to mark these clearly.

Juicer

An ordinary juicer can easily be pareve, but if it is one of those multijob machines, it may be worthwhile to make it dairy. In that case the juice will have to be used for dairy meals only, but if most juice is drunk at breakfast that will pose no difficulty.

Kitchen counter or dinette table

It is practical to make small eating areas dairy, as most small, on-the-run meals are dairy. A small cloth or a few placemats convert it to meat for an occasional meal or snack.

Mixer

As with all baking equipment, best left pareve. However, an extra set of blades is useful for occasional dairy cakes and whipping cream. Heavy-duty mixers for kneading, along with their bowls, should be kept pareve.

Popcorn popper

Don't melt butter in with the popcorn, as popcorn makes a great pareve snack after a meat meal. You can use margarine, and on those occasions when you want butter, melt it in a separate dairy saucepan.

Pressure cooker

Should be meat for all but the strictest vegetarians, who will find occasional use for it.

Slow cooker

Same as for pressure cooker.

Steamer

The small ones that fit into most pots are inexpensive and so convenient that you may want one for both meat and dairy. A large pot steamer is best made pareve as vegetables and rice are the most frequently steamed foods. Try steaming fish as a delicious and healthful alternative to other means of preparation.

Toaster oven

Convenient for small meals such as melted cheese sandwiches, so dairy may be the best bet. Alternatively, a good way to heat up individual-portion frozen meals, which are often meat.

Wok

Chinese food just about never uses dairy ingredients so this should be designated meat. It is excellent for frying, as it uses less oil than other utensils for that purpose, so those who eat very few meat meals may wish to leave this pareve.

Traditional
Foods
for Today

At a recent, community-wide celebration of Israel Independence Day in San Francisco, a young man was interviewed by a local newspaper. He was described as struggling with the burden of balancing numerous plates of foods sold at the celebration: falafel, knishes, and snack foods galore. But, he complained to the reporter, he was disappointed. "Where's the bagels and lox?" he asked. "They were supposed to have traditional Jewish food."

That man is not alone in assuming that the sliced bagel, slathered with cream cheese and embracing tender slices of smoked salmon, is a dish so traditional that Moses himself might have refreshed himself with it on Mount Sinai. However, the fact is that this sandwich is unknown except to Americans. And American it is, having spread far beyond its Jewish roots to the point where you can get a reasonable bagel-and-lox without much difficulty in places like Youngstown, Ohio, and Salt Lake City, Utah.

Lox is all-American as a symbol, too. When Jews emigrated from Russia to the United States in the early years of this century, they sought the most expensive delicacy to express their newfound prosperity. Gone was the humble herring that had sustained them for centuries. Paper-thin sliced lox, then as now selling for two or three times the price of the best cuts of beef, became the rose-colored membrane through which the "Golden Land" could be viewed.

Other luxurious foods were adopted as well. Sturgeon, the parent of caviar, became a Bar Mitzvah staple—it isn't even kosher according to much rabbinic opinion. Old-country staples like noodles with pot cheese were thrown over as everyday fare. Their place was taken by holiday specialties incorporating fried dough and rich dairy products: blintzes with sour cream, knishes, cheesecake. Back home a family might drool all week in anticipation of Friday night's chicken soup, followed by the boiled chicken removed from it. In America free men chose to sip the soup and let their wives disguise the bird as they could. They ate meat every day—not just any meat but highly seasoned pastrami and corned beef. And that was just lunch!

In short, what most people think of as traditional Jewish food is actually the cuisine—and let us not underrate its deliciousness—of *nouveau-riche* Russian immigrants of the first half of the twentieth century.

There are other well-known dishes that are ancient and near-universal among Jews: gefilte fish, chopped liver, chicken soup. These have their origins in Jewish law and custom, in the Sabbath and festival celebrations.

Many of these excellent foods deserve a place on today's menu. Clearly, however, we cannot simply cook as our grandmothers did.

How can we put new life into traditional foods?

1. By cutting down on the amount of fat, especially such fats as chicken schmaltz, goose fat, sour cream, and butter.
2. By reducing the amount of smoked, pickled, salted, and preserved meats and fish.
3. By reducing cooking times and easing preparation, so that working women and men can enjoy them.
4. By using fewer starches and more vegetables.
5. By taking advantage of the many excellent traditional foods available through take-out delis, in frozen, canned, and prepackaged forms.
6. By returning to authentic old-time recipes previously rejected as poor people's fare.

JEWISH RYE BREAD

Great everyday bread was a given in Europe, and crusty, zesty rye and pumpernickel loaves were produced in America as soon as the first immigrants got off the boat. If you live near a Jewish bakery worth its salt, you will not need to bake your own bread—it was almost always the province of the professional baker in the old country, too. But if you must make do with the soft and soggy breads available in a supermarket, homemade rye will be a real treat.

Makes 1 large loaf.

2 packages dry yeast	*1 teaspoon instant coffee*
1 1/2 cups warm water	*1 teaspoon dried minced onion*
1 teaspoon sugar	*1/4 cup cocoa*
1/2 cup molasses	*2 cups rye flour*
1 1/2 teaspoons salt	*2 1/2 cups all-purpose or whole*
3 tablespoons oil	*wheat flour*
2 tablespoons caraway seeds	*2 tablespoons cornmeal*
1 tablespoon vinegar	

Dissolve yeast in 1/2 cup of the warm water to which the sugar has been added. When yeast begins to bubble, add rest of warm water, molasses, salt, oil, caraway seeds, vinegar, coffee, minced onion, and cocoa. Stir well and mix in rye

flour. Add all-purpose or whole wheat flour until a smooth dough is formed—
more flour may be needed. Knead well, at least 5 minutes. Place in a greased
bowl, cover with a towel, and let rise in a warm place until doubled, about 1½
hours. Punch down and knead lightly. Remove ritual challah. Spread the cornmeal on the bottom of a pie plate or cookie sheet. Shape either a round or
oblong loaf, place on cornmeal-covered pan, and let rise 45 minutes. Bake at
375° for 40 minutes or until tapping the loaf with your knuckles produces a
hollow sound.

HIGH-PROTEIN BLINTZES   [D]

Blintzes, like crepes, palacintas, and their other delectable relatives, make
scrumptious desserts, especially when topped with fruit preserves and sour
cream. The calorie count should make this a rare treat for most modern weight
watchers. But the idea of blintzes—a filling wrapped in a light pancake, finished
with a creamy topping—is retained in this low-cost, low-calorie, nutritious main
dish. Use a pan or griddle with a nonstick coating so that frying oil is kept to a
bare minimum.
Makes about a dozen pancakes, 3 per person.

BATTER	FILLING
3/4 cup flour	*1 small can salmon*
1/4 teaspoon salt	*1 cup cottage cheese*
2 eggs, well beaten	*1 egg, beaten*
1 cup milk	*1 teaspoon sugar*
	1/2 teaspoon salt

Mix batter ingredients together with a fork until large lumps disappear.
Pour a small amount on a greased pan or griddle, forming a thin pancake. Cook
only until top is dry. Repeat for remaining batter. Mix filling ingredients together. Fill pancakes, browned side up. Place about 2 tablespoons of filling in
center of blintz, flatten filling sidewise. Turn in sides, then roll blintz. Fry blintz,
loose edge down. Turn and fry other sides.
Serve with horseradish and plain yogurt. Garnish with sprigs of dill or
parsley.

NOODLES AND CHEESE   [D]

Plain, honest food that satisfies hunger and a sweet tooth without over-doing richness. Precede this with a homemade vegetable soup.
Serves 4.

1 (10-oz.) box medium egg noodles	1/4 cup sugar
2 cups pot cheese or low-fat cottage cheese	2 teaspoons cinnamon

Cook noodles in boiling, salted water until tender. Drain. Toss with cheese. Sprinkle each serving with sugar and cinnamon.

KASHA-CHEESE CASSEROLE   [D]

Kasha (buckwheat groats) is an important crop in Russia. Jews of Russian descent enjoyed the high-protein grain as a side dish; indeed, for many it was a staple. Nowadays, kasha is neglected, which is a pity, because it has a distinct, nutty flavor that many people savor, and it is very nutritious.

This dish is quickly prepared, especially if you have a large cast-iron frying pan that can go from stove to broiler.
Serves 4–6.

2 onions, chopped	1 cup cottage cheese
3 tablespoons oil	1 large can corn, drained
1 cup kasha	1 (8-oz.) stick Cheddar cheese, grated
1 egg, slightly beaten	
2 cups water	1/2 cup fine bread crumbs
1/2 teaspoon salt	1 tablespoon butter or margarine

Sauté onions in oil until translucent. Stir in kasha and egg, mixing vigor-ously with a fork until each grain separates. Stir in water and salt and bring to boiling. Lower heat, cover, and cook for 5 minutes. Remove from heat and mix in cottage cheese, corn, and one cup of the Cheddar cheese. Combine remain-ing cheese and bread crumbs and spread on top. Dot with butter or margarine. Place under broiler until cheese melts and topping begins to brown. Serve with lettuce and tomato salad.

HUNGARIAN CHEESE SPREAD [D]

A very flavorful alternative to cream cheese, at a fraction of the calories.
Makes 3–4 cups.

1 (8-oz.) package farmer cheese
1 (8-oz.) package Neufchâtel
  cheese
4 scallions, green parts only,
  minced

1 teaspoon paprika
1 teaspoon caraway seeds
1/4 teaspoon salt

Mix all ingredients together thoroughly.

MUSHROOM SAUTÉ [P]

The forests of Europe provided a delicious treat—wild mushrooms that
even the poorest Jew or peasant could savor. Urban life now denies this pleasure
to even the richest, while wild mushroom hunting is restricted to the very
knowledgeable. However, in the Soviet Union, it is still customary to pick cham-
pignons. The ability to distinguish the poisonous from the edible is wisdom
handed down from parents to children.

Supermarket mushrooms are rather bland, but many ethnic markets, particularly oriental ones, offer unusual fresh and dried ones. All edible funguses are
kosher, so this is a good opportunity to expand the scope of the kosher diet.

Soviet Jews who have managed to get to Israel or the United States have
brought a number of imaginative mushroom recipes with them. This one makes
a wonderful brunch or light supper dish.

Serves 4.

1/4 cup margarine
4 large onions, sliced and broken
  into rings
1 lb. fresh mushrooms, sliced or
  4 oz. dry, reconstituted, sliced

1/2 teaspoon salt
Freshly ground black pepper
4 eggs, beaten
1/4 cup snipped parsley

Sauté onions in margarine until tender. Lower heat, add mushrooms, cook
5 minutes. Add salt and pepper and eggs. Stir until eggs have set. Stir in parsley
and serve hot.

GEFILTE FISH

Gefilte fish is a truly Jewish dish with origins deep in Jewish law and history. The separation of undesirable things from desirable substances—such as chaff from wheat or fishbones from the flesh of the fish—is a labor forbidden on the Sabbath. Thus, as early as Talmudic times, Sabbath recipes featuring filleted fish were devised.

Gefilte (stuffed) fish is the form most popular among Jews from the largest European populations. It consists of coarsely ground fish mixed with chopped onions, matzoh meal, and eggs. It is seasoned with salt, pepper, garlic, and sugar according to regional custom, as well as to taste. The mixture is shaped into oval, hamburger-sized patties and poached in a fish court-bouillon.

Elsewhere in Europe other forms of fish appear on the Friday night table. Slices of cold carp in aspic are classic, as are whole fish stuffed with a fish forcemeat. The latter is also favored among Sephardim. All Friday night fish dishes are flavored with garlic. According to ancient tradition garlic is an aphrodisiac and fish a symbol of fertility. Sabbath Eve is considered a special time for marital relations, as well as for the mystical union of Israel and the Sabbath Bride.

GEFILTE FISH QUENELLES WITH HERB SAUCE   [P]

Guaranteed to infuriate gefilte-fish purists! This is an airy French version of gefilte fish that is too delicate to be eaten with horseradish, but can be served with any light sauce.
Serves 4–6.

1 lb. fish fillets, preferably pike
1 clove garlic, peeled
1 tablespoon flour
1/2 teaspoon salt
1/4 teaspoon nutmeg

1/4 teaspoon hot pepper sauce
Freshly ground black pepper
1 tablespoon brandy
2 cups pareve whipped cream
2 egg whites

In a food processor, purée the fish and garlic until smooth. Add flour, seasonings, and brandy, mixing well. Fold in whipped cream. Cover bowl and place in freezer for a few minutes. Fill a large pan halfway with water and bring to a boil. Lower heat to simmer. Meanwhile beat egg whites until stiff. Fold egg whites into fish mixture. Gently drop tablespoon-sized quenelles into the simmering water. Cover, and cook for 20 minutes.

HERB SAUCE
1/2 package Israeli vegetable soup
  mix
1 cup water

1/2 cup dry white wine
1/2 teaspoon chervil
1/2 teaspoon tarragon

Bring soup mix, water, and wine to a boil. Lower heat, add herbs, and simmer for 10 minutes.

GEFILTE FISH BOUILLABAISSE [P]

Hearty, aromatic French fish stew, so complex and intriguing, is amazingly easy to make with that old standby, a jar of gefilte fish. Serve bouillabaisse as a meal, accompanied by garlic bread.
Serves 6.

1/4 cup olive oil
2 onions, sliced
2 cloves garlic, minced
2 stalks celery, sliced
1/4 cup snipped parsley
6 carrots, sliced
1 green pepper, sliced
1/4 lb. mushrooms, sliced
6 cups vegetable broth
3 tomatoes, diced

2 tablespoons tomato paste
1 tablespoon lemon juice
2 teaspoons grated orange rind
1 teaspoon salt
1/4 teaspoon thyme
1/4 teaspoon hot pepper sauce
1/8 teaspoon saffron
1 small bay leaf
1/2 cup dry white wine
1 large (6 pieces) jar gefilte fish

In a heavy pot or Dutch oven sauté the onions in olive oil until very tender. Add garlic, celery, and parsley, sautéing briefly. Lower flame; add carrots, green pepper, and mushrooms. Cover and simmer 5 minutes. Add broth, tomatoes, tomato paste, lemon juice, orange rind, salt, thyme, pepper sauce, saffron, and bay leaf. Bring to boil, then lower flame, cover, and simmer for 30 minutes. Stir in wine. Cut each piece of gefilte fish into three and drop into soup. Cover and simmer 15 minutes more. Remove bay leaf before serving.

MARINATED SALMON WITH MUSTARD SAUCE   [P]

A nice change of pace from lox, and considerably more healthful. Excellent with buttered pumpernickel.
Serves 6–8.

1 (3-lb.) salmon
1 bunch fresh dill, chopped
4 tablespoons white peppercorns,
  crushed

1/4 cup kosher salt
1/4 cup sugar
Mustard Sauce (see below)

Cut salmon in half and debone. Place one half skin side down in a shallow pan. Combine dill, peppercorns, salt, and sugar and spread on salmon. Cover with other half of salmon. Cover all with foil and place heavy dish on top of foil to compress the fish. Refrigerate. Every 12 hours, turn the fish over and redistribute the marinade. Fish is done 3 days later, but may be marinated up to a week. Skin the salmon and slice thinly on the diagonal. Decorate with mustard sauce and sprigs of dill.

MUSTARD SAUCE
4 tablespoons Dijon mustard　　　　*1/4 cup vinegar*
1 tablespoon mustard powder　　　　*1/2 cup oil*

Blend all ingredients together until smooth.

CHICKEN SOUP　[M]

Better than ever cooked the modern way—with plenty of vegetables and herbs. The amount in this recipe is a suggested minimum. Almost everyone of every generation loves chicken soup, but few today will have anything to do with boiled chicken. After cooking, skin and bone the chicken and cut into bite-size pieces. Use in Chinese and Indian recipes with plenty of seasonings and vegetables.
Serves 8.

1 chicken, halved　　　　*1 tomato*
3 quarts water　　　　*1/2 onion*
2 teaspoons salt　　　　*1 parsnip with top, scraped*
6 carrots, scraped　　　　*1/2 bunch parsley*
2 stalks celery, with leaves　　　　*1/2 bunch dill*

Place the chicken in a large pot. Add water and salt. Cut carrots, celery, tomato, onion, and parsnip in halves. Tie parsley and dill together with a string. Heat all ingredients to boiling. Lower heat, cover, and simmer for 1 1/2 hours. Cool and remove chicken and all vegetables and herbs. Place soup in freezer. All fat will rise to the top; remove fat with a spoon. Reheat soup and return carrots to pot, if desired. Serve with salted radishes.

AN ALL-AMERICAN BREAD

What can be more Jewish than your basic bagel? Well, it happens that the Iron Doughnut, the ambassador of the People of the Book in Wyoming and Mississippi, is a native of America! While the word bagel is a generic term for roll in Yiddish, the boiled-and-baked roll with the distinctive shape was apparently invented in New York sometime around 1910. Millions of new immigrants adopted it enthusiastically.

Food histories, even Jewish ones, ignore it—or assume that the Jews always ate this bread. A visit to Israel, with its representatives from every Jewish community in the world suggests that no one but Americans have ever sunk their teeth into this earthy delicacy. Ask an Israeli for a bagel and he will politely hand you a pretzel.

The Arabs of East Jerusalem blithely call the following snack a bagel: a large, soft roll with an indentation in the middle, much like a giant bialy (itself an authentic European roll). The crater is filled with a coddled egg and herbs. It's all sprinkled with sesame seeds and baked in a hearth oven.

I'll have it with an egg cream, Ahmed.

MEAL-IN-A-KNISH　[M]

Instead of a fattening snack, a knish can make a hearty main dish. This one makes a fine dinner, accompanied by a cooked vegetable and a fresh salad. Serves 4.

FILLING
1 lb. lean steak, cut in small
  cubes
2 cups diced potatoes
1 large carrot, diced
1 large onion, chopped fine
1 teaspoon salt
1/2 teaspoon pepper
1/4 teaspoon thyme
1/2 cup dry red wine

PASTRY
3 cups flour
1 1/2 teaspoons baking powder
1/2 teaspoon salt
1/3 cup vegetable shortening
1 egg, beaten
1/4 cup ice water

For best results, prepare filling and pastry the night before or several hours prior to assembling and baking the knishes.

Mix ingredients for filling and let marinate in the refrigerator in a covered bowl.

Make pastry by combining dry ingredients, cutting in shortening, then blending in egg and water. Divide in four, wrap in plastic, and refrigerate.

Assemble knish by rolling each portion of pastry into a large circle or rectangle. Cover half of each pastry with a fourth of the filling. Fold the other half of the pastry over the filling and seal the ends by pinching with wet fingers. Place on greased baking sheets and bake for 1 hour at 350°.

MOCK KNISH   [M]

Pita bread is a good substitute for the time-consuming knish dough. As a knish, pita is best when stuffed with a highly flavored filling, such as meat, rather than a bland one, such as potato.

Makes 8 knishes.

1 large onion, chopped	*1/2 teaspoon paprika*
1 lb. ground beef	*Freshly grated black pepper*
1 tablespoon oil	*8 small pita breads*
1 cup mashed potatoes	*1 egg yolk, beaten with 1*
1 egg, well beaten	*tablespoon water*
1/2 teaspoon salt	

Brown onion and beef in oil. Pour off excess liquid. Combine with mashed potatoes, egg, salt, paprika, and pepper. Slit about 3 inches of a pita's circumference. Stuff with meat mixture. Seal with egg yolk. Place filled pitas on a lightly greased baking sheet or pan. Brush tops with egg yolk. Bake in a 350° oven 30 minutes.

PICKLES   [P]

Fresh pickles are easy, and you can avoid the excesses of the store-bought kind—too sour or too salty.

Small pickling cucumbers	*4 cloves garlic, peeled and split*
1/4 bunch fresh dill	*2 teaspoons salt*
6 peppercorns, whole	*1 slice stale bread*

Wash cucumbers and score the top and bottom of each with an inch-deep X. Pack them tightly into a 2-quart jar. Press in dill, peppercorns, garlic, and salt. Fill almost to the top with water. Place bread on top and screw on cap. You will have good half-sours in 3 days, or wait longer for desired acidity. To stop pickles from further souring, simply refrigerate them.

> Few peoples can best the Jews as popularizers of food styles. Their dispersion in the Diaspora meant that they alone could spread the use of a regional product, such as sugar, to the point where it would appear on virtually every table in the world.
>
> Some food historians credit the German Jews with introducing the hamburger to the United States. (Old-fashioned European versions usually contain at least some pork.) Food was usually supplied on board the better ships from Germany to America in the middle of the nineteenth century. However, as Jews could not eat the nonkosher meat, they brought along seasoned ground meat, which could be conveniently fried as patties aboard ship.

CHOPPED LIVER

Chopped liver is a uniquely Jewish food because liver requires special broiling to remove all excess blood. Early on inventive Jewish cooks doctored the dry, seared organ meat with tasty additions such as chicken schmaltz, fried onions, hard-boiled eggs, and spices.

Chicken livers are preferred over beef or calf livers, as their taste is more delicate.

Years ago, goose livers, or, in their absence, chicken livers with goose fat, were the most desirable for this pâté. The best livers came from geese that had been force-fed corn—the liver of an obese goose is enormous. Sharp controversy arose between a rabbinical faction that considered the practice of force-feeding to be cruel, and forbade eating goose livers, and another faction that maintained that the geese did not suffer. Indeed geese being force-fed sometimes complain, but at other times they seem to be enjoying themselves.

The Jews of medieval France and Germany ate chopped liver in a pie. They and their Christian neighbors, whose pâtés were composed largely of pork, pig livers, and bacon fat, adapted the custom from the ancient Romans. The French infatuation with pâté de foie gras was for many years serviced by Jewish farmers in Hungary. Some claim that the Jews introduced it to early French gourmets. Today, Israeli goose livers form an important export to France.

CHOPPED LIVER EN CROUTE   [M]

You've seen chopped liver in the shape of a menorah, with carved-carrot flames. You've seen chopped liver as a portrait of the Bar Mitzvah boy. Now for something elegantly different.

2 cups flour

Pinch salt

1/2 cup margarine

1/2 cup water

1/4 lb. turkey loaf, sliced

1 lb. chopped liver

1 tablespoon Worcestershire sauce

1 tablespoon brandy

1/2 teaspoon allspice

1/4 lb. salami, sliced

1 egg yolk, beaten with 1 tablespoon water

Place flour and salt in food processor or bowl. Cut in margarine with cutting blade or pastry knife until a fine meal is formed. Add water until a soft dough is formed. Wrap tightly in plastic and refrigerate for 2 hours.

Roll out 3/4 of dough into a rectangle. Fit it into a greased loaf pan, so that bottom and sides are covered with dough. Line bottom with turkey-loaf slices. Mix chopped liver with Worcestershire sauce, brandy, and allspice. Place in pan. Cover chopped liver with salami slices. Roll out remaining dough and place on top. Pinch the ends to the dough from the lining and trim the edges. Use little bits of remaining dough to make designs, such as flowers, and press them on top. Prick the top with a fork in a decorative pattern. Brush with egg-yolk mixture.

Bake at 375° for 45 minutes or until crust is golden. Let cool, then refrigerate. Unmold and present on a decorative platter. Slice and serve at the table.

CHICKEN WITH RAISINS AND ALMONDS   [M]

Raisins and almonds were a delicacy much prized by Jews everywhere, especially in Eastern Europe where they reminded a people impoverished and exiled of the produce of the Land of Israel. In much of Europe these products of a Mediterranean climate were very expensive, more dreamed about than tasted. The haunting melody of "Rozhinkes mit Mandlen," perhaps the most beautiful of all Yiddish lullabies, testifies to the evocative powers of what was so much more than a delicious snack.

This dish, with its complex sauce is considerably more exotic than the chicken recipes Grandmother made. Such a use of precious raisins, almonds, and spices would have horrified her as wasteful and frivolous, if indeed she could have obtained them at all. Fortunately, our bountiful times allow us to luxuriate in this abundance.

Serves 6.

1/3 cup raisins
1/4 cup brandy or rum
1 tablespoon margarine
3/4 cup almonds
2 tablespoons oil
1 large onion, thinly sliced
1 large green pepper, diced
2 cloves garlic, minced
6 chicken legs with thighs

1/4 cup flour
1 teaspoon cinnamon
2 ripe tomatoes, diced, with juice
1 (8-oz.) can tomato sauce
1 cup water
2 teaspoons curry powder
1/2 teaspoon thyme
1/2 teaspoon salt
Few grinds of fresh pepper

Soak raisins in brandy or rum. Melt margarine in Dutch oven or large pot, preferably with a nonstick coating. Fry the almonds quickly; they will start snapping when they are done. Remove with a slotted spoon. Heat oil and sauté onion, pepper, and garlic until tender. Remove vegetables from pot and add a little oil if necessary.

Skin the chicken pieces and remove any additional fat. Combine flour and cinnamon in a plastic bag and shake each piece of chicken in it. Brown the chicken well and remove from pot.

Heat tomatoes, tomato sauce, and water to boiling. Lower heat and add seasonings. Return vegetables and chicken to the pot and cover, cooking for 1 hour. Remove cover and cook 1/2 hour longer. Just before serving stir in raisins and almonds. Serve on a bed of rice or noodles.

In the Holy Temple, in a darkened room
Sits the Widow Zion
Rocking to sleep her only son, Judah
Singing to him this sweet song

Under Judah's cradle
Lies a pure white kid
This kid is your only inheritance
You will travel so far with it.

Raisins and almonds
Raisins and almonds
Sleep, little Judah, sleep.

ROAST BEEF WITH HORSERADISH SAUCE   [M]

Boiled flanken was the classic meat dish of Eastern Europe. Today most diners prefer less fatty meat prepared in some other way. But horseradish sauce, *chrain,* the traditional accompaniment, is still a great condiment for a good slice of meat. Extra-hot prepared horseradish is good—but not as good as homemade. Serves 6–8.

1 (3–4 lb.) lean roast
1 teaspoon garlic powder
1 horseradish
2-inch piece of fresh ginger root

1/4 cup vinegar
1/2 teaspoon salt
1/4 teaspoon white pepper

Place the roast in a shallow baking pan. Rub garlic powder on all sides. Roast at 375° for 2–3 hours. Prepare sauce by peeling and grating horseradish and ginger root. Mix with vinegar, salt, and pepper. Serve roast hot or cold.

PASTRAMI SALAD   [M]

"Pastrami with heartburn to go," begins the stand-up comic's ancient routine. But pastrami need not be served in gigantic portions, its richness uncut by anything with more roughage than a pickle. Makes 1 serving.

3 leaves romaine or other leaf
   lettuce
1 hard-boiled egg, sliced
1 tomato, sliced
3 radishes, sliced
1 scallion

1 carrot, cut in sticks
1 stalk celery, cut in sticks
1/2 cup raw cauliflower
3 oz. pastrami, cut in strips
Thousand Island dressing

In a large bowl arrange lettuce leaves. Place egg slices and vegetables in a circle. Pile pastrami in center. Serve dressing on the side.

TZIMMES   [P]

Carrots were a mainstay in Europe, where they grow easily and keep well in a cold cellar. Sweetened carrots, stewed to softness, combined with other vegetables and fruits, thickened with a flour-and-schmaltz roux, and cooked until none of the ingredients were clearly identifiable, was a treat, especially at the time of the New Year. Chunks of fatty meat were considered an essential ingredient of tzimmes in some parts of Europe.

This recipe is not a *gantse tzimmes* (a big messy bother) to prepare, and fats and flour are eliminated.

Serves 6.

4 large carrots, scraped, sliced in
   2-inch pieces
4 sweet potatoes, peeled, cut in
   thick slices

1/2 cup Chinese duck sauce
1 cup canned baby peas, with
   liquid
1/2 lb. mixed dried fruit

Steam carrots and sweet potatoes until they are tender. Heat the duck sauce on a low flame. Add peas and dried fruit, heating through. Stir in carrots and sweet potatoes. Simmer for 5 minutes.

FRUIT COMPOTE   [P]

In Europe, where the fresh fruit season was short, the harvest was often put up in the form of compote—stewed fruit. Today, fresh fruit is available year-round and we need not cook fruits so thoroughly because they don't need to be preserved for such a long time. The flavor, texture, and vitamin content of this compote is enhanced by its short cooking time.

Serves 6.

1 cup sugar
3 1/2 cups water
1 teaspoon cinnamon
1/4 teaspoon ground cloves
Juice of 1 lemon
6 firm, large fruits (apples, pears,

peaches, or quinces), peeled,
   cored, and quartered
2 teaspoons vanilla
1 tablespoon amaretto or fruit
   liqueur
3 oz. chocolate chips

Combine first five ingredients in a large saucepan. Bring to a boil, stirring constantly. Boil for 5 minutes, reducing the syrup. Lower heat to simmer and add fruit. Cook for 5 minutes. Remove from heat and stir in vanilla and liqueur. Serve hot or cold. Sprinkle each serving with chocolate chips.

EDIBLE REMEDIES

The medicinal properties of chicken soup have long been remarked upon. But there are other folk remedies that date back to the days when Jews were excluded from medical schools and the nearest doctor was a day's sleigh-ride away.

Each of these makes 1 serving.

GOGEL-MOGEL (for sore throat and cough)
1 egg yolk
1 cup hot milk
2 tablespoons sweet red wine

1 tablespoon sugar
Few drops vanilla

Place the egg yolk in a large mug and beat in milk a little at a time. Stir in wine, sugar, and vanilla.

A LITTLE GLASS TEA (for colds and flu)
1 cup hot, dark tea
2 teaspoons lemon juice

1 jigger Scotch whiskey
1 teaspoon honey

Stir all ingredients in a tall glass.

RICE AND MILK (for upset stomach, second day—first day, tea and toast only)
1 cup cooked rice
1 cup hot milk

2 teaspoons sugar
Cinnamon

Stir rice, milk, and sugar together in a bowl. Sprinkle with cinnamon.

NEW WAYS WITH OLD-TIME FOODS

Frozen blintzes are of excellent quality. To keep calories down, brush a nonstick pan with just a few drops of oil, and fry blintzes as usual. Serve cheese blintzes with vanilla yogurt and fresh berries. [D]

Wild strawberries were a delight our ancestors knew that we, alas, are unlikely to taste. But this still makes a fine breakfast: 4 or 5 ripe strawberries, mashed with 2 tablespoons sour cream, on a slice of fresh rye bread, sprinkled lightly with sugar. [D]

For a refreshing and pretty summer soup, mix equal parts borscht and pineapple juice. Serve chilled. [P]

Wontons (Chinese knaydlach) are a pleasing appetizer. Fold a sheet of phyllo dough in quarters. Place a teaspoon of chopped liver in center and fold over to make a triangle. (No need to pinch ends together.) Fry in deep, hot oil for just a few seconds. Drain on paper toweling. Serve with hot mustard and sweet-and-sour sauce. [M]

Chopped liver Italiano: stir 2 teaspoons chopped capers, 1/2 teaspoon sage, and 1 tablespoon anisette into 1 lb. chopped liver. Serve with marinated vegetables. [M]

Another chopped-liver canapé idea: stir 1 tablespoon soy sauce, 1 tablespoon grated ginger root, and 1/4 cup chopped water chestnuts into 1 lb. chopped liver. Stuff into celery stalks. [M]

Milk and Honey:
The Food
of Israel

*"And you shall eat and be satisfied and bless the Lord for the good
land that he has given you."*
                                                    Deuteronomy 8:10

A visit to Israel can be the gastronomic event of a lifetime. No, you will not
find the perfect pastrami sandwich there—nor the quintessential couscous, for
that matter—and you will not dine in the kosher equivalent of Maxim's for
mere pennies. But you can eat superbly at every meal, experiencing tremendous
variety and striking originality of cuisine—and you can do it on any budget.

The key to good eating is understanding just what Israeli cuisine is, taking
advantage of its strong points and sidestepping its limitations.

The cooking of Israel is not, as the cliché will have it, a happy blend of
dozens of cuisines brought by a nation of immigrants. Nor is it a crazy quilt of
dishes from far-flung cultures thrust indiscriminately upon the blank slate of the
land. Rather, it is a constantly changing menu, a result of the following influences, which are always in a state of flux: the ethnic food history of the population; the climate and natural resources of the land of Israel; the life-style and
contemporary culture of the Israeli people; and the innovations of chefs and
other leaders of the food industry.

• *Ethnic origin.* Israel's population is composed of immigrants from almost
one hundred countries and their descendants. About half of these are Sephardim, or oriental Jews from North Africa, the Baltic, and the Middle East. The
other half are Ashkenazim, or Western Jews from Europe, the Americas, Southern Africa, and Australia. It is probably fair to say that Israeli food is 50 percent
Sephardic and 50 percent Ashkenazic, but the subgroups are not represented
proportionally. For example, Jews of German origin, who have had such a powerful impact in most areas of Israeli culture, have hardly influenced its cuisine at
all. Many German Jews themselves concede that their cuisine is uninspiring.
Hungarian Jews, on the other hand, while holding a less exalted social position,
have had a greater influence on Israel's cookery, since Hungary's piquant season-

ings are appropriate to the climate, and its carefully composed pastries are a delight to a nation of cafe habitués.

One finds, also, that while the majority of Sephardim hail from North Africa, the cuisines of smaller communities, such as those from Syria and Turkey, have made greater inroads in the eating habits of the nation at large. And there are always influences that come in from left field. When, in the late seventies, the Israelis accepted a group of Vietnamese Boat People whom no one else would have, they surely did not expect that this small group would find employment in its food industry and would inject the distinct flavor of Southeast Asia into Israel's culinary portrait. Whether an ethnic cuisine or a particular dish is accepted by the average Israeli depends on whether it measures up in other ways: if it suits the climate, exploits available resources, fits in with the life-style, and appeals to an already sophisticated national palate.

Visitors often wonder why so little of the local Arab cooking has been adopted by the Jewish population. Palestinian food is, of course, well suited to the climate and it uses locally grown products for the most part. However, it is simple peasant fare, and thus has not found a niche in the highly urbanized life-style of almost all Israelis, including the farmers. Too, local Arab cooking is identical with the basic rustic cooking of Syria and Lebanon. Those countries had highly refined cuisines in their cities, and these more sophisticated dishes were incorporated and further elaborated by the Jewish communities of those cities, which have now relocated in Israel. Few prefer conservative Palestinian food to the Syrian and Lebanese-style delicacies that are widely available in Israel.

• *Climate and resources of the land of Israel.* Most immigrants had to adjust their cuisines to Israel's climate. European immigrants found it necessary to lighten their food and season it more pungently (hot weather requires fewer calories for the body to maintain its temperature; spicy foods cause thirst, insuring greater fluid intake).

But even Sephardim from similar subtropical climes changed their eating habits. All Israelis eat a great deal of fresh vegetable salad, a habit new to both Sephardim and Ashkenazim. Those from northern areas rarely had fresh lettuce, tomatoes, cucumbers, and green peppers, and thus did not develop a taste for them. Those from warmer parts of the world tended to cook or marinate most of their vegetables, perhaps because poor hygienic conditions made fresh produce a likely source of dysentery, cholera, and other dreaded diseases.

> Israel's life-expectancy is one of the highest in the world—higher than that for Americans—despite the toll of continuous wars. The World Health Organization attributes this phenomenon to the fact that Israelis eat more fruits and vegetables per capita than any other people in the world.

This is not to say that Israel's climate precludes hearty foods. Winter is brisk in many areas, including the Galilee region, Jerusalem, and the Golan Heights. The expense of heating households also means that, throughout the country, hearty, filling soups and stews are welcome fare November through February. Also, the massive reforestation of Israel has caused its average temperature to decline. Israelis can enjoy a varied range of dishes, rather than limit themselves to those suited to a "hot" climate.

Israel's farms and their produce are remarkable phenomena, even in a land of, as Menachem Begin put it, unlimited impossibilities. At first glance the land does not exactly look like a prime candidate for agricultural excellence. Water for irrigation is extremely scarce, and the soil, not naturally rich, has been further eroded by being worked for longer than any other place on earth. In addition Israel is simply too small to support many crops. Its perennial place in the news leads many people to forget just how tiny Israel is. In fact, Israel is one of the few nations that cannot afford to grow its own grain or graze its own cattle—it simply hasn't got the plains and grasslands to do so.

Taking all this into account, it is simply astonishing that Israel produces an extraordinary variety of foodstuffs, and that agricultural exports form the backbone of its economy. Israel holds all sorts of world agricultural records in both quantity (most eggs per hen) and quality (best foie gras).

The Bible colorfully describes Israel's traditional wonders. Moses's spies to Canaan returned to their desert camps with clusters of grapes so huge two men were needed to carry each one. Israel will always be known as the Land of Milk and Honey. Indeed its dairy products are superb and its candies have a devoted international following. Israeli chocolates, specially formulated to hold up in hot weather, are clandestinely imported by Saudi Arabia. Business is brisk enough to warrant special packaging by one Israeli manufacturer, so the chocolates do not betray their point of origin.

The Bible lists the most important native crops as wheat, barley, grapes, olives, figs, pomegranates, and dates. Archaeologists believe that the Jordan Valley was the first place where grain was cultivated. Today, Israel imports most of its flour, but its breads are mysteriously wonderful. Grapes remain an important crop, although most varieties grown for the wine industry are originally of French origin. Olives are an important part of the Israeli diet, in biblical times, however, they were used only as the major source of oil for food, fuel, and cosmetics. The process of curing olives for eating was acquired from the ancient Greeks. Figs, pomegranates, and dates are minor cash crops, but the lovely trees on which they grow grace gardens and parks throughout the country.

Israel's major food products were all originally imported from other lands. The almond, frequently mentioned in the Bible, probably came from China in prehistoric times. Other fruits of the prune family—peaches, plums, apricots—came much later. Israel's favorite vegetable, the tomato, one of its favorite starches, corn, and one of its most lucrative exports, avocado, are all native to America. Most ironically, the fruit which symbolizes the native Israeli—the

Sabra—comes from the prickly pear cactus, a native of Mexico! This plant came by some unknown route to the Middle East, where the Arabs use it as a fence, more effective than barbed wire for keeping out intruders. The Israelis identified with its fruit, which is covered by a leathery peel and fierce thorns but is luscious and sweet inside.

Animal husbandry and dairy farming were undoubtedly known to Abraham's ancestors, but the picture is very different in modern Israel. Of the large animals, only sheep are raised in any significant number in Israel. Their numbers are diminishing, unfortunately. If you order shishlik or shishkebab in a restaurant, you should verify that you are getting lamb—many smaller eateries now substitute turkey. Virtually all of Israel's beef comes from Argentina, and it comes frozen. Only the most exclusive restaurants and expensive butchers offer fresh beef.

Poultry, on the other hand, is available in abundance. Chickens were first brought to Israel from India in the time of the Talmud. They quickly caught the fancy of the population—witness the enduring fame of Jewish chicken soup. Rabbis of the Talmudic era considered poultry superior to all other meats, and preferred it for feasts and the Sabbath. Israeli poultry farms are highly mechanized, with kibbutzim leading the way in superyield production of cooking chickens and eggs.

Turkeys are even more important in the Israeli diet. Israeli turkeys are smaller than the common American Thanksgiving bird, but are meaty and flavorful. Ducks and especially geese are a small but important sector of the market. Smoked goose is one of the finest delicacies the country produces. Unfortunately, kosher goose livers are almost impossible to come by, since they are exported for phenomenal sums to be made into nonkosher pâté de foie gras in France. All Israeli hot dogs, salamis, and cold cuts can be assumed to be made of poultry, unless otherwise indicated.

Fish, an important element of Jewish cooking everywhere and in all eras, is also vital to the Israeli diet. The fish native to the Mediterranean and Israel's only major body of fresh water, the Sea of Galilee, have suffered in recent years from ecological assault. The Mediterranean now has a higher salt content because of the Aswan Dam, while industrial pollution and overfishing are problems in Israel, as they are in fishing waters throughout the world. But Israel has invested its technical and land resources in aquaculture, or fish farming. Throughout the country diners can find interesting varieties of kosher fish, best when they are simply prepared, as they are always fresh. Because the country is so small, all kinds of fish are available "locally."

• *Life-style.* The Israeli workday is the child of the nation's pioneer agricultural past. Most businesses open at eight in the morning, with many workers arriving well before to prepare for the clientele. Lunch is at one, and a siesta respecting the afternoon heat of summer is allowed for. Stores open again at 4 P.M. and close for the day at 7. Today many businesses have adopted a faster-paced schedule, allowing only an hour for lunch and closing at five-thirty. But official store hours still influence the kind of meals people eat and when they eat them.

Typically, breakfasts have several courses, including, always, vegetables. They are not like American farm breakfasts, however, in that they never include meat, and rarely fried foods. The effect of the Israeli breakfast is filling but not soporific. There is no such thing as a coffee break in Israel; instead there is a "ten o'clock meal." This frequently includes a small sandwich and fruit. Lunch is the major meal of the day. It is usually a meat meal with appetizer, cooked side dishes, salad, and dessert. Although fewer and fewer Israelis now return home for lunch, this large meal is served by schools, company cafeterias, and restaurants.

Dinner is usually quite late and it is comparatively light. It may be either dairy or meat, omelets and schnitzels (breaded cutlets or hamburgers made from chicken or turkey) being typical fare.

In addition Israelis snack incessantly throughout the day. Vendors of fast food line every major street in the country, while cafes offer entertainment and relaxation as well as rich foods and beverages.

Israelis love to entertain, but their apartments and budgets don't often allow them to host elaborate meals. A common form of entertainment is the after-dinner visit. Before the advent of television in the sixties, the whole country held open house in the evenings. Close friends still drop in unannounced. Cake, cookies, tea, coffee, and fruit are usually served. Israeli visitors often bring sweets, nuts, or a special fruit as a gift on such a visit.

The Israel Defense Forces have had as profound an effect on the nation's eating habits as they have had on virtually every facet of society. Almost every man and over 50 percent of the women serve in the Army. Men serve for three years, women for two, at a time when they are forming the eating habits of their adult lives. The Army has helped homogenize Sephardic and Ashkenazic strains of cooking into what is a distinctly Israeli style. Army food has a good reputation, in general. Quality of cooking is kept high, because officers and enlisted soldiers eat in the same mess hall. The food is suited to the active life of a frontline soldier; it is nutritious and plentiful. One rarely sees overweight men in Israel, since army service continues one month each year until a man retires. The case is far different with women. They tend to be less active than male soldiers, since they do not serve at the front. Moreover, they rarely continue for long in the reserves after their tour of duty is over. Dieting and slimming exercises are as much an obsession with them as with other Western women.

• The last important influence on Israeli cuisine is that of conscious *innovation*. A number of chefs have been trained in European cooking schools. The most successful have opened restaurants with creative menus of considerable sophistication. The poshest eating establishments, and the most expensive, are the restaurants of the deluxe hotels. All of these, except a few in East Jerusalem, are kosher. Many of the chefs in these hotels are not Jewish, oddly enough, although, of course, their work is rabbinically supervised. Often one can find the most original and pleasing dishes coming out of their kitchens, perhaps because they do not see in kashrut a personal burden, but rather, view the restrictions objectively as challenges to be met by their professional talents.

Jewish women of all ethnic backgrounds take extreme pride in their cooking skills. Yet many men cook and suffer no loss of macho pride, especially if they do it well. Newspapers and magazines have extensive food sections and the morning radio program featuring new recipes every day, is one of the most popular in the country. National and international cook-offs have a following as enthusiastic as that of sporting events and get prominent press attention. And amateur chefs throughout the nation go far beyond repeating treasured family recipes.

A GASTRONOMIC TOUR OF ISRAEL

For the kosher diner a trip to Israel is a unique experience. Here there is a freedom of choice unknown anywhere else in the world. While it is true that many restaurants are not kosher, most do abide by the laws of kashrut. Kosher eating places prominently display a certificate of kashrut, which is issued by the Ministry of Religion. Luxury hotel dining rooms and greasy spoons alike lend themselves to exploration. One can shop blithely at a supermarket, choosing baked goods and meats with no consideration but taste. Grocers and butchers must declare clearly if their food is not kosher.

Most travelers will begin their stay at a hotel that offers an Israeli breakfast. This is well worth the price. The standard breakfast consists of fruits and vegetables, a variety of breads and rolls, an assortment of herrings and other fish, yogurts of every flavor and fat content, five or more types of cheese, boiled eggs, several salads, and beverages. Deluxe hotels will have extras like freshly squeezed orange juice and hot dishes to order. But all hotels lay out their breakfasts on an appetizing smorgasbord and include all you can eat for the price.

If you are being accommodated at a youth hostel or rented apartment, you will be making your own breakfast. It's best to rise early, as the Israelis do, and shop at the local *makolet*, or vest-pocket grocery, which can be found in every residential area. You will find numerous rolls and breads, still hot, cheeses that the storekeeper will slice for you, recently delivered yogurts, olives in the barrel, and all the packaged foods you could desire. Be sure to bring your own shopping bag! Then check out the local greengrocer for dewy tomatoes, cucumbers, and fruit.

By midmorning the tourist, like the Israeli, will need a refreshment break. This is a good time to try out a cafe. Always order the fancier items on the menu, such as coffee specialties, cream cakes, and chocolate pastries. Otherwise you will be paying premium prices for instant coffee and pedestrian sweet rolls. Cafes charge for the expected hours you will wile away at their tables, the magazines and newspapers you will read, and the leisurely conversation you will enjoy, as well as for the food. If you want to rest up in a café but are all sugared out, your best bet is to order "toast," which is actually a grilled cheese sandwich.

An alternative spot for midmorning snacks is an ice cream parlor. The most fashionable of these are owned by Argentinian immigrants. They serve a South American version of gelato in many interesting flavors; their prices are expensive, even in American terms, especially in the ritzier parts of Tel Aviv. A delicious specialty in many ice cream parlors is a hot waffle topped with scoops of ice cream.

Tourists are not advised to do as the natives do at lunchtime. Few would want a heavy lunch followed by a long siesta. Most would rather do as mad dogs and Englishmen, dine quickly, and get out to do some sightseeing while the rest of Israel relaxes. The ideal meal on the run is, of course, Israel's national dish, falafel. If you are still hungry after a falafel, you can always have any of a number of snack foods—corn on the cob from a sidewalk caldron is classic.

A bit more leisurely is a meal at a *steakiyah*. These are small restaurants that offer a predictable menu at a reasonable price. Order an appetizer such as hummus, tahina, or an eggplant salad. Follow up with a meat-and-rice-stuffed vegetable—eggplant, cabbage, or grape leaves—or grilled meat—shishkebab, shishlik, hot sausages, or steak. Despite the fact that beef is of poor quality in Israel, you may well enjoy the thin, tough steaks served in these modest establishments. Mostly, you get the savory taste of charcoal! The meat will be accompanied by the ubiquitous *chipsalat,* French fries and diced vegetable salad. The cook will gladly substitute rice for the fries, but if you request another vegetable you will get it in addition to the salad. Israelis just can't conceive of a meal without salad. Any steakiyah worth its salt will have warm pita breads coming as fast as you can eat them.

The one place to avoid at lunchtime is the table d'hôte hotel dining room. These lunches are geared to tourists who are imagined to be middle-aged American Jews with an inexhaustible appetite for Bar Mitzvah food. This kind of lunch is a veritable orgy of chicken soup and chopped liver, with boiled meat accompanied by boiled vegetables. You are safe from canned and frozen vegetables and fruits everywhere in Israel, but one sometimes wishes *these* bland foods were canned. Even a metallic taste might give them some flavor! The hotel dining room is not to be confused with hotel restaurants, which are often superb. Here, too, many customers are tourists, but Israelis also eat there when they can afford to. It is best to splurge at these restaurants in the evening, however, for you should enjoy their carefully prepared dishes at leisure.

Don't forget to drink plenty of liquids throughout the day. Most of the year it is extremely dry in much of Israel, as in the Jerusalem area, while the coastal plain is humid. Either way, the body's fluid supply is severely taxed. If you let yourself get dehydrated you may fall victim to headaches, dizziness, diarrhea, or other vacation spoilers. Many hot-climate customs around the world include the drinking of hot beverages. You may find that coffee and tea are the most refreshing drinks of all. In any case, drink copiously at each meal, snack frequently on fruit, ices, and ice cream, and stick to the shade whenever you can.

The evening meal will be the major one for most tourists. Haute cuisine usually means essentially French food, but in Israel this often has a distinct oriental flair, since many of the chefs trained in France hail from the Maghreb countries. Expect your meal to cost as much as in a similar establishment in the United States.

Ethnic restaurants offer the best value in Israeli dining. Less elegant than the hotel and Continental restaurants, but more serious in their cooking than the steakiyahs and creperies to be found on any corner, restaurants concentrating on the cooking of a single country or region offer real adventure. Two very different examples:

• Leah's Europa, in Jerusalem (Hungarian). The menu here bears the unmistakable mark of a brilliant cook—everything is scrumptious. A simple roast chicken is as delicious as the Hungarian goose. For dessert, the chocolate-and-nut palacinta is not to be missed. Leah's husband presides over the diners like a Hungarian count hosting a weekend for aristocrats.

• Zion Exclusive, in Tel Aviv (Yemenite). The food is not always as good as it might be, but the food is only part of the Zion Exclusive experience. It begins with the taxi ride through a picturesque (but safe) slum called Vineyard of the Yemenites. You wend your way through Zion's, a raunchy steakiyah serving the locals with such specialties as "eggs of male cow." That's right, kosher bull testicles. Beaded curtains and silk fringe usher you into Zion's Exclusive. The Turkish harem decor, intimate carved booths, and low lights make this a great rendezvous for lovers. The menu is just as unusual; lamb baked in clay, candied onions and radishes for dessert (you would never guess their identity) are a few of the offerings.

In most restaurants the European system of tipping prevails. Ten or 15 percent of the bill is added on as a service charge. If the service is exceptionally friendly, you may wish to add an additional 5–10 percent. If the menu does not note a service charge, you should tip as you do in the States.

While posh eateries set their tables with starched linen, more humble establishments usually have very rudimentary napkins. Paper goods are a luxury in Israel and in many restaurants and homes small, tracing-paper napkins are standard. It's a good idea to carry a pack of tissues for various emergencies, as well as to eat neatly.

THE FAT OF THE LAND

Beverages

Alcohol. Israeli wine is good and very reasonably priced. Besides the major Carmel brand, several small wineries produce excellent wines that are not exported. Beer is a popular drink, although its quality is mediocre. Brandy and arak (anise-flavored) are the most popular of the harder liquors; Carmel's are very good. Sweet liqueurs of a wide assortment are good gift items. Other alcoholic beverages are imported, heavily taxed, and, therefore, quite expensive. The finest Scotches are available everywhere, and are considered a status symbol. Alcoholism is still a rarity in Israel—an arrest for drunk and disorderly conduct will make the national news—and there are no laws restricting the sale of alcohol. Strictly drinking establishments such as pubs and bars are rarities.

Citrus drinks. These noncarbonated soft drinks are old favorites in Israel. They contain little actual juice, although they are sold as "orange juice" and "grapefruit juice." The former is very sweet and artificially colored. The latter is mildly sweet, a traditional summer thirst quencher.

Coffee. In coffee as in life, say the Israelis, we have two possibilities: *nes* or *botz.* Those words are slang for instant and Turkish, but their literal meaning is "miracle" and "mud." There is nothing miraculous about Israeli instant coffee; it is quite bad. An excellent gift for American visitors to bring to an Israeli is a jar of premium freeze-dried coffee; there is nothing to compare with it there. Rarely will a percolator or coffeemaker be found in an Israeli home; however, espresso and capuccino can be had at any cafe. Turkish coffee, on the other hand, is a treat to be found everywhere. Because it is a very rich beverage, usually heavily sweetened, it can be a bit much as an accompaniment to a meal. Turkish coffee is never served with milk; it makes a good digestive to a meat meal.

What cafe menus label as "ice coffee" is cold coffee topped with a scoop of vanilla ice cream. Israelis are unfamiliar with the American custom of drinking beverages with ice, but ice is available in cafes and restaurants, if you request it.

Orange juice. In the land where oranges bloom in the desert, you won't find orange juice on the breakfast table. Frozen orange juice and reconstituted o.j. from the supermarket are unknown. Many do squeeze their own oranges, but most Israelis eat whole oranges and grapefruit. You can get fresh-squeezed juice at many larger supermarkets, as well as at juice stands on city streets.

Soda. Coca-Cola is the most popular carbonated soft drink. It is available everywhere except on the West Bank, where Pepsi retains its franchises—the Arab countries have long boycotted Coke for trading with Israel. There are cheaper but inferior local colas, as well. Tempo White is a reasonable knock-off of 7-Up, and sweet orange sodas are also favored. Schweppes, with its distinctive bitter-orange and bitter-lemon flavors, has made deep inroads in a highly lucrative market.

A delicious and uniquely Israeli alternative to cola is so-called black beer. This malt drink is nonalcoholic, but has the slight fizz of beer. Somewhat reminiscent of cola, it is less sweet. Black beer is cheap, refreshing, and probably the only soft drink with nutritional value.

Squash. Concentrated syrups for making soft drinks are the way most Israelis quench their thirsts at a reasonable price. Squashes are available in dozens of flavors, as well as in low-calorie and artificially sweetened forms. Since the squash is mixed with water, the sweetness can be adjusted to individual taste. Raspberry and lemon are favorite flavors.

Tea. For a nation of tea drinkers—many prefer it to coffee and drink it throughout the day—Israel has a sad lack of quality tea. A nondescript bag of pekoe is all that is available at most markets. The Arabs drink a refreshing dark tea, abundantly sweetened and topped with fresh crushed mint leaves. Despite the fact that many Israelis of oriental extraction drank this tea in their native lands, and the fact that mint grows in profusion everywhere—some gardeners regard it as a weed—mint tea is only occasionally served. Another special tea is Russian tea, which is flavored with spices and dried citrus peel.

Water. Tap water is safe to drink throughout Israel. It is not particularly flavorful, perhaps because it is heavily treated in this water-scarce land. In some areas the water is desalinated sea water, but you won't taste the difference. Everywhere in the world tap water contains microorganisms. The types of microorganisms differ in various regions of the world and until one acclimates to a foreign water supply, the intestines may react with diarrhea. More often, tourists' intestinal troubles come from dehydration, heat exhaustion, and/or eating unfamiliar foods.

Blintzes

This old-country favorite has had a big revival in Israel in recent years, with many restaurants specializing in pancakes with a choice of fillings, both savory and sweet. These creperies have more in common with fern bars than with the Lower East Side. Many of these pleasant supper spots offer light, egg-based entrees and waffles, as well as blintzes.

Bread

Israelis eat a lot of bread, and no wonder: it is invariably delicious, as well as fresh and wholesome. Ordinary white bread has heft and body—and flavor. Rolls are light, with flaky, crunchy crusts. Do try some less familiar breads. Israeli rye is heavier, heartier than its American equivalents, more like New York corn rye. Compare the pita bread baked daily in a local bakery with the packaged stuff available Stateside. Don't miss chewy Persian bread, which is round and looks like a quilt. On Fridays there are challahs large and small. People have their favorite bakeries, of course, but you almost can't go wrong buying breads anywhere.

Cakes and Sweets

The Jews are credited with introducing sugar to the Western world. They have developed innumerable cakes and sweets and adopted others from every cuisine. They continue to indulge their sweet tooth in Israel.

The lush cakes of Hungary and Austria form the backbone of the cafe tradition in Israel. Chocolate, whipped cream, egg custards, and chopped nuts mortar sponge cakes and flaky pastries. Second in popularity, but not in richness, are Sephardic confections, such as baklava, which make use of fine, flaky dough, honey, nuts, sesame, and fragrant flower essences. Northern European yeast cakes and pastries, such as babkas, also have their fans.

While bakeries turn out mountains of pastries, many Israeli women wouldn't dream of serving store-bought cake. Since having friends over for cake and coffee is the most usual form of entertaining, a homemade cake is a must for showing off culinary skill. Many homemakers who prepare their main dishes simply, find a creative outlet in making elaborate desserts.

Packaged cookies are, however, the norm. The built-in oven came late to Israel, so that many women made their cakes in stove-top "wonder pots." But cookies need a real oven, and the manufacturers filled that need. Biscuits are a more accurate term for most Israeli cookies, because the plain *petit beurre* type predominates. These are widely available in the United States. They are excellent snacks for traveling, keep well, and are pleasantly but not overwhelmingly sweet.

Besides eating cakes and candies straight, Israelis also love to snack on bread spread with sweet toppings. Halvah, the shredded sesame sweet, is sold in blocks, to be eaten as a spread, as well as in chunks. (It has good food value for a candy but is incredibly caloric!) Another favorite sweet topping for bread is chocolate spread, which is milk chocolate in a buttery consistency.

Condiments

Ketchup. Once laughed at as an American aberration, ketchup has caught on with a lot of Israelis. If you don't see it on the counter, you can ask for it at any steakiyah or burger joint, and at ritzy restaurants as well.

Salad dressings. A freshly diced Israeli salad doesn't need any dressing, but the American custom of pouring bottled dressings on vegetables is catching on in many circles. For those who want to crown the flavor of an Israeli salad, the topping of choice should be olive oil and lemon juice.

Schug (its watered-down version is known as *charif,* that is, "sharp"). An incendiary chili sauce used with Yemenite dishes, such as falafel. You will usually see only a tiny plate of schug at a table set for many. Wise diners will take the hint.

Dairy Products

Israelis eat great amounts of dairy products. Tnuva, the dairy cooperative, is one of the most successful companies in the country. Its distribution is excellent and dairy products are farm-fresh in even the dingiest back-street grocery. Other brands must be at least equal in quality to compete with Tnuva.

Butter and margarine. For some reason, butter is unusually expensive in Israel, so it is considered by most people to be something of a special treat. More commonly you will see margarine in sticks or tubs. Kosher kitchens will usually have both the dairy and nondairy margarines.

Cheese. Cheese is a major source of protein in the Israeli diet, and a large variety is available at every grocery store. The most popular types are sold by weight from large cheeses. These are also available presliced in packages. The European-type cheeses, such as Gouda, Edam, Emmenthaler, Muenster, Provolone, Camembert, Brie, are popular, as are several Mediterranean types, like feta. Cheeses made from both goat's and sheep's milk are available and delicious. Oddly enough, cream cheese is unknown—as are bagels and lox— while a less fatty spread resembling Neufchâtel is so popular it is called, simply, "white cheese." Cottage cheese, once considered an "American" oddity, is now one of the nation's favorites.

Ice cream. The quality of ice cream in Israel ranges from superb to dreadful. Cafe-parlors specialize in certain concoctions, like sundaes and banana splits, or in ice creams of various nations, such as Italian gelati, Argentinian rich creams, or American soft custard. Standard sidewalk cones are reasonable-tasting but their texture may be disappointing, as the butterfat content is low. Chocolate often has a slightly nutty flavor, fruit flavors are quite unusual and tasty, refreshing in the summer. Vanilla is usually a poor choice. Ices are tempting in the heat, but they tend to be oversweet and the artificial flavors are bizarre, so stick with lemon.

Milk. Israelis think of milk as an indispensable addition to instant coffee, and a food for infants. Adults rarely drink it straight, perhaps because many Jews are lactose-intolerant and get an upset stomach from drinking milk. Milk does not come in a waxed-paper container, as it does in most Western countries. Rather, it is sold in small plastic bags—plastic being less precious than paper in this still-being-reforested country. The bag is placed in an open pitcher; a corner is snipped off for pouring. Sterilized milk is often used in the office coffee corner and by those who use milk infrequently, since it does not require refrigeration before opening and maintains its freshness for a long time.

Yogurts and creams. Israeli dairy consumption is largely in the form of yogurt. Sold in individual-serving containers, yogurt comes in various consistencies and flavors. Israelis favor yogurt for breakfast, but eat it with any dairy meal and as a snack. Skimmed leben (nonfat yogurt) has a very thin consistency. It is especially refreshing in hot weather or when eaten with spicy oriental food. Low-fat leben has 3 percent milk fat, and is therefore most similar to American yogurts. Aishel, made with whole milk, 4.5 percent fat, is the most popular consistency in Israel. It is eaten plain or sprinkled with a teaspoon of sugar. Prigurt has the consistency of its American counterpart, and is also flavored. It is made of sheep's milk. Chocolate yogurt makes a nice, light dessert. Sour cream is also sold in plastic cup containers because, it too is eaten as a dish, not just as a topping. It is mainly older Israelis of European origin who favor it; younger Israelis shy away from the calories and cholesterol. Whipped cream is enjoyed as a topping for coffee and hot chocolate and in fancy pastries.

Falafel

The national dish of Israel is, of course, a snack food. Falafel balls consist of deep-fried ground chick-peas and seasonings. Five or six of them are placed in a pita (pocket bread) along with vegetable salad and one or more pickled foods, such as sauerkraut, various peppers, beets, and cucumbers. All is topped by a creamy tahina sauce. A bit of hot sauce is optional. This sauce is so fiery that it is suggested you try a tiny bit on a piece of pita before ladling it on.

Falafel stands can be found in every nook and cranny in Israel, many claiming to be the "king of falafel." Because falafel is pareve, some stands also offer shwarma (leg of lamb on a rotisserie), while others serve ice cream. There are deluxe stands that offer colorful bins full of a staggering variety of fresh and pickled vegetables from which the patron can serve himself.

Yemenite Jews brought the falafel to Israel. It is so universally accepted today as the all-Israeli dish that you will find some Ashkenazic vendors of the delicacy. Scoffers call their product "gefilte fish." The components of the falafel may have originated with the Arabs, but the sandwich—practical, portable, nutritious, and very, very tasty—is quintessentially Israeli.

Fish

Israelis have remained more faithful to gefilte fish than to any other traditional European Jewish dish. However, it is eaten almost exclusively on Friday night. Israel produces excellent canned gefilte fish. Especially good is the stuffed carp—slices of tender carp with a spicy fish stuffing. (In some parts of Europe the term gefilte fish was literally employed, that is, "stuffed fish.") Carp is a good choice in Chinese restaurants, too, because the Chinese, like the Jews, adore this fish but cook it in very different ways.

The Mediterranean bakala (hake) is simply but appealingly cooked, breaded and fried, broiled, or baked in tomato sauce.

A fish unique to Israel is native to the Sea of Galilee. Christians have dubbed it St. Peter's fish; locally it is known as *amnon hagalil,* but by any name it is delicious. Its bones, however, are very fine, so, if possible, order it filleted.

Other popular fish are gray mullet, grouper, bass, red snapper, and sole, which is known as *moshe rabbenu* (our teacher Moses).

Fruit

This is Israel's specialty, one you may miss if you stick too close to restaurants and hotels. A trip to one of Israel's large open markets is fun, especially if you want to meet the "real" people. Thursday afternoon and Friday morning are an event in the major markets such as Jerusalem's Mahane Yehuda, where scores of vendors sell fresh produce to thousands of shrewd shoppers.

American shoppers will at first be chagrined at the comparatively small sizes of fruits and vegetables. Be assured that less is often more where flavor is concerned. Look for good color, heaviness for size, and ripeness when shopping for fruit.

Israel's intensive farming methods include heavy use of fertilizers and pesticides. Some produce is grown in the West Bank or even clandestinely imported from Jordan, where hygienic standards on farms may leave a great deal to be desired. Therefore, always do as the Israelis do: wash all unpeeled fruits and vegetables with dishwashing detergent and a plastic scouring pad (Scotchbrite).

Some Israeli fruits to consider:

Clementines. A relative of the tangerine, it looks like a lime and has something of the lime's fragrance. It is more orangelike in flavor, however.

Custard apples. This tropical fruit is sweet and creamy and eaten with a spoon.

Guava. A sweet tropical fruit much favored by the Arabs. It is also very good in preserves.

Kiwis. These New Zealand fruits have grown very well in Israel. Hairy brown on the outside, they are beautiful inside. Their flavor is unique: sweet, fragrant, slightly acidic.

Loquats. Tiny orange fruits native to China, they should be very ripe when you eat them. The entire fruit is eaten, except for the seeds.

Melons. The Jews have loved melons since, at least, the Egyptian bondage. Many unusual, tasty, and pretty melons can be found in Israel year round. The *Haogen* is very sweet; it looks and tastes like a cross between cantaloupe and honeydew. During the summer watermelon is considered a staple. Israelis have been known to venture into the Gaza Strip under sniper fire for the pleasure of purchasing watermelons from a prize Arab patch. Some oriental communities favor pickled watermelon rind and roasted watermelon seeds, which have a sweet, nutty flavor but take considerable skill to crack and extract.

Oranges. The Jaffa orange is considered by many to be the tastiest eating orange in the world. Because this is one of Israel's leading exports, the pick of the harvest goes abroad, chiefly to Europe. Winter is the season for citrus fruit, and it is then that you are likely to find the best oranges—but they still won't be as large or perfect as the ones that got away. A consolation is that the orange trees in winter are also in flower. They blanket the land in perfume so sweet it is almost edible.

Pomellas. An unusual fruit, which, unlike other citrus, grows in the hottest regions of the country. The pomella looks like an oversize grapefruit, but its flavor is more like that of a very mild orange. Beware unscrupulous sidewalk vendors who try to pass off grapefruit as pomellas. You'll be able to taste the difference with the first bite.

Sabras. The fruit of the prickly pear cactus is the symbol of the native Israeli. It is unavailable at markets but is sold in late summer by sidewalk vendors. These young entrepreneurs do the horrendous work of picking the fruit from the murderously thorny plants. They also peel the fruit with rubber gloves and sell the tender flesh in plastic bags. The fruit is studded with seeds, which should not be eaten. Never attempt to peel a sabra on your own: the tiny hooked thorns are almost impossible to remove from the skin. Sabras are sometimes available in American markets. These fruit come from Mexico or the Southwest. They are neither as sweet nor as juicy as the Israeli variety. For best flavor, lay plastic bags of sabras on ice, or refrigerate.

Jams and Preserves

The Israeli love of fruit extends to its spreadable forms. Jams and preserves usually occupy a full aisle in cramped Israeli supermarkets. The Israelis' admiration for imported goods reaches its most absurd end when citizens buy premium European preserves, for their own products are at least as good and are reasonably priced. One superb preserve: bitter orange marmalade with almonds.

Meat and Poultry

Beef is generally a poor menu choice, unless it is artfully doctored, for example with various stuffings. Veal is frightfully expensive but is treated like the luxury it is. A veal dish is likely to be a chef's masterpiece. Delicate veal sausages are an Israeli specialty. Many traditional veal dishes are made with turkey today.

Most Western Jews are familiar with mutton in only one form: lamb chops.

The Sephardic traditional dishes open up new vistas. Lamb baked in a pastry shell makes an elegant feast, while roadside shishlik and shwarma sandwiches—chunks or flakes of broiled mutton with salad in pita bread—make a delicious lunch or snack.

Israel's excellent turkeys and chickens are the principal meats on the table. Often they take the place of other meats in cutlets, stews, stuffings, and barbecues. Salamis, sausages, and franks are usually made from poultry. They may be less flavorful than their beef equivalents, but they are somewhat more nutritious.

Smoked goose is Israel's most famous meat delicacy. On rare occasions the tourist may find quail or other exotic birds on a hotel menu. For a kosher diner such a meal might be a once-in-a-lifetime occasion.

Nuts and Seeds

These high-protein foods are a nutritious, if annoying Israeli habit. You will hear people cracking seeds everywhere—at bus stops, in taxis, at office desks. Movie theaters have electric signs warning NO CRACKING SEEDS right on top of the NO SMOKING sign. One look at the sign and you begin to crave the addictive little things. Business is so brisk that there are shops that sell only nuts and dried fruits. The bestseller is sunflower seeds, salted and plain, known only as "blacks." Next in popularity are pumpkin seeds, with or without salt, identified as "whites." Peanuts and almonds, with or without their shells, are also loved as a snack. Walnuts are the premier nuts for baking. Many less familiar seeds and nuts are also favored. You will recognize watermelon seeds—they have a sweet and creamy flavor but require some skill to crack. Most favored of all, but fiercely expensive, are pistachio nuts—carefully roasted but never dyed red.

Freshness is the secret of Israel's delicious seeds and nuts. The turnover is high. On Thursdays and Fridays the nuts in the bins are too hot to handle since they are so frequently replenished by supplies fresh from the oven. You may not recognize the taste of a sunflower seed, so different is the flavor of a fresh seed from the packaged seeds occasionally eaten by Americans. Nuts and seeds are a favorite on long Saturday afternoons. Different varieties will be set out separately with an extra bowl for shells and husks.

Olives

There are Israeli versions of the cured olives you may be familiar with, mild American, salty Greek, vinegary Spanish. By far the most popular is the spicy "broken olive." It is tiny, with a thin pit that removes easily because of its characteristic split. Israelis eat olives along with every meal, especially with cheese and with appetizers.

Pickles

Pickled foods are characteristic of Jewish cuisines around the world. In Israel the various communities have adopted one another's pickles with, uh, relish. Oriental pickled beets are especially good, very different from the Russian style of pickled beets. Another specialty, this one from Morocco, is pickled lemons.

Spices and Herbs

Israel is naturally rich in flora that can be used to flavor food. The Bible lists dozens of spices, while almost every spice and herb known today is mentioned in the Talmud. Contemporary Israeli cooks also season their foods liberally. You may find some spices that are rare in the West to be in common use in Israel, for example, juniper berries. The spice that is so characteristic of Arab cooking—it permeates the Arab markets—is sumac (nonpoisonous). Garlic, and onion in all its forms, are lavishly employed.

Vegetables

Canned vegetables are little used in Israel, because superior fresh vegetables are available year round. Nowadays an increasing number of vegetables are to be found frozen. These are usually specialty items.

Corn. Corn on the cob is a much-loved treat. In many cities and towns an elderly man is to be found stirring a giant caldron of corn on the sidewalk. He fishes out the vegetables with tongs and serves them in husks, which serve in lieu of plate and napkin.

Eggplant. Far and away Israel's favorite cooked vegetable, especially loved as an appetizer. Eggplants blend well with meat or with eggs, and with all kinds of cheeses. They are enhanced by sauces spicy or smooth. They can act as the highlight of a meal, as a meat substitute, and are good team players with other vegetables.

Squash. All squashes are popular, especially the summer squashes, green (zucchini) and yellow. They are often included for variety in eggplant dishes, or substitute for eggplants. Squashes absorb much less oil and cook more quickly than eggplant. As a relic of the British Mandate, squash is always listed on menus as "marrows."

FALAFEL   [P]

A food as Israeli as, well, falafel. As with all traditional foods, the amount of each ingredient is approximate, and you will find falafel makers who swear by one recipe and castigate another. For more crunch—and protein—substitute bulgur (cracked wheat) for the bread crumbs. Fresh coriander leaves are the flavoring herb of choice, but if they are unavailable, substitute parsley. There is plenty of hot pepper in this version (falafel itself means "pepper"), but you can halve it or eliminate it, substituting a little dried minced onion.
Serves 4.

1 (15-oz.) can chick-peas	*1 egg*
(garbanzo beans) or 2 cups	*1/4 cup lemon juice*
cooked chick-peas, drained	*1 1/2 teaspoons red pepper flakes*
3 cloves garlic, minced	*1 teaspoon cumin*
1/4 cup coriander leaves, snipped	*1 teaspoon salt*
1 cup fine bread crumbs	*Oil for deep-frying*

Grind and mix all ingredients together in a blender or food processor. Form falafel balls; the traditional size is about 1 1/2 inches in diameter, but you can make them as large as hamburger patties. Fry until golden brown.

Falafel balls on a toothpick are a well-liked hors d'oeuvre, but the standard way to serve them is in the following sandwich: Halve a large pita bread. Carefully open it so that the semicircle of the edge is not broken. Stuff with 4 falafel balls, 1/2 cup of Israeli salad, pickle slices, and sauerkraut. Top with 3 tablespoons tahina sauce and a teaspoon of schug, if desired.

BASIC ISRAELI SALAD   [P]

For Israelis, vegetable salad is a staple of the diet second in importance only to bread. The finely diced, tomato-based dish appears at breakfast, lunch, and dinner, in the homes of the poor and on the tables of the five-star hotels.

Israeli salad is so utterly simple that many tourists who go home and attempt to make it themselves are surprised to find that their own salad doesn't even resemble the ones they enjoyed everywhere in the Holy Land.

One reason is that vegetable varieties are different in the United States. Americans insist on very firm tomatoes, very large cucumbers, and very crisp lettuce. Israelis prefer their tomatoes vine-ripened, their cucumbers very small, with almost invisible seeds, their lettuce deep green. The shelf life of Israeli vegetables is shorter, and they must be handled more gently, but they have deeper, richer flavors than their American cousins.

The flavor of Israeli salad also depends on the interplay of vegetables with a large surface area; ideally the vegetables are cut into neat cubes, each no bigger than a pea. And moisture is provided by the vegetable juices themselves, rather than salad dressings, so that the salad must be prepared immediately before the meal.

To approximate Israeli salad, have for each serving:

2 ripe plum or Italian tomatoes
2 small pickling cucumbers,
   peeled
and/or

2 carefully rinsed and dried
   romaine lettuce leaves from
   the outer layers of the head

Use very sharp knives to cut the vegetables. You may want a serrated blade for the tomatoes. Avoid mashing the vegetables. Never use a mechanical device to do the cutting. The desired tiny cubes will come about with practice. For the first few tries, aim for cubes the size of playing dice, with lettuce leaves cut, not torn, into similar squares.

No dressing is needed, but if you prefer one, add a small amount of olive oil, a squirt of lemon, and a sprinkling of chopped parsley.

HUMMUS   [P]

This most popular appetizer in Israel also makes an excellent, nutritious dip for vegetables.
Makes 3 cups.

1 (15-oz.) can chick-peas
   (garbanzo beans) or 2 cups
   cooked chick-peas, drained
1 cup tahina sauce
1/2 cup lemon juice

2 cloves garlic, minced
1/2 teaspoon salt
1/2 teaspoon cumin
1/4 teaspoon hot pepper sauce

Purée all ingredients in blender or food processor. Refrigerate for several hours. To serve as an appetizer, place a crater of about 2/3 cup hummus on a small plate. Fill the depression with either 1/4 cup tahina or 1/4 cup fine olive oil. Sprinkle with paprika and garnish with sprigs of parsley. Serve with hot pita bread, olives, and pickles.

EGGPLANT SALAD   [P]

A perennial beginning to virtually any Israeli meal—even breakfast. Always accompanied by pita or other dipping bread, olives, and pickles.
Serves 6–8.

1 large eggplant
1 1/2 cups tahina sauce
2 tablespoons snipped parsley

2 tablespoons lemon juice
1 teaspoon garlic salt
1/4 teaspoon hot pepper sauce

Bake the eggplant for 20 minutes at 400°. Pierce twice with a fork, to prevent its exploding. Bake another 20 minutes or until it is very soft. When eggplant is cool enough to handle, peel and trim. Purée in a blender or food processor. Add tahina sauce and blend very well. Stir in parsley, lemon juice, salt, and hot pepper sauce. Best when refrigerated for several hours to blend flavors.

TURKISH EGGPLANT SALAD   [P]

Israelis have adopted eggplant recipes from all over the world, but this one has become a standard of the kitchen repertoire. Prior to World War I, Palestine was part of the Ottoman Empire. The zestful cuisine of Turkey is what Israelis think of as truly "oriental."
Serve as an appetizer, with hot pita bread, spicy olives, and pickled peppers.
Serves 4.

1 large eggplant
Oil for frying
1 large onion, diced
2 large, ripe tomatoes, coarsely
   cubed
2 cloves garlic, minced

2 tablespoons snipped parsley
1/2 teaspoon salt
Freshly ground black pepper
1/4 teaspoon cinnamon
1 small bay leaf

Trim and peel eggplant. Cut into 1-inch slices. Fry in oil until both sides of slices are golden brown (it may be necessary to add oil). Remove eggplant from pan and add onion, sautéing until tender. Return eggplant and all other ingredients to pan. Mash eggplant with a fork. Simmer for 10 minutes, stirring frequently. Remove bay leaf. Serve hot or cold.

HEARTY EGGPLANT [D]

A filling main dish, with an unusual smoky flavor that makes eggs and cottage cheese suddenly exotic.
Serves 4.

1 medium eggplant
4 hard-boiled eggs, chopped
1/2 teaspoon salt

Freshly ground black pepper
2 cups cottage cheese

Roast the eggplant on a hibachi or directly on the burner of a gas stove (this makes a mess, but the burnt peel is an important part of the flavor). Turn frequently. Eggplant is done when a knife or fork pierces it very easily. Trim and skin the eggplant, leaving a few flakes of burnt peel. Mash it very well, and mix in eggs, salt, and pepper. Top with scoops of cottage cheese.

SCHUG (Yemenite Hot Sauce) [P]

A classic for topping falafel, with hummus, or for adding fire to hard-boiled eggs.
Makes about 1 cup.

Juice of 1 lemon
2 tablespoons olive oil
2 tablespoons tomato paste
1/2 cup coriander, snipped
2 cloves garlic, minced

1/2 green pepper, chopped fine
1 tablespoon red pepper flakes
1 teaspoon sugar
1/2 teaspoon salt
1/2 teaspoon cumin

Purée all ingredients together in a blender or food processor. Schug is traditionally thick, but you can thin the sauce by adding, in addition, equal parts lemon juice and olive oil.

ORANGE CHICKEN [M]

A natural marriage of two Israeli favorites, chicken and orange, kissed with spices as varied as the population. Serve with steamed rice.
Serves 4.

1 roasting chicken
2 tablespoons sugar
2 tablespoons lemon juice

2 cups orange juice
1 tablespoon grated orange peel
1/2 teaspoon salt

1/2 teaspoon paprika
1/4 teaspoon ginger
1/4 teaspoon cinnamon

1/8 teaspoon black pepper
2 tablespoons cornstarch
1/4 cup Sabra or orange liqueur

In a 425° oven, roast chicken for 1 hour or until browned. Combine sugar and lemon juice in a saucepan, stirring until sugar melts and begins to caramelize. Add 1 cup of the orange juice, orange peel, salt, paprika, ginger, cinnamon, and pepper. Heat to boiling. Dissolve cornstarch in remaining orange juice. Add and heat, stirring, until sauce thickens. Remove from heat and add Sabra. Pour over chicken.

SHISHKEBAB [M]

Chunks of meat roasted on an open fire must be one of the oldest foods known to humankind, yet each generation discovers it with renewed delight. Shishkebab is a very good food for summer entertaining. It permits the hosts to spend plenty of time with the guests, gives shy newcomers something to do, is perfectly at home on paper plates, and needs no cutlery. You do need skewers for the meat, though. Fancy steel shishkebab skewers are available, or use thin wooden ones, which are disposable. Some form of shishkebab is served in at least half of the meat restaurants in Israel, and it is much favored on outdoor feast days such as Lag Baomer, Maimoona, and Independence Day.
Serves 6–8.

1/2 cup olive oil
1 cup dry wine
1/2 cup honey
1/4 cup lemon juice
3 cloves garlic, minced
2 scallions, sliced
1 teaspoon salt

1 teaspoon each, thyme,
marjoram, and oregano
1/2 teaspoon rosemary
1/4 teaspoon red pepper flakes
3 lbs. lean lamb, beef, or dark
meat of turkey, cut in chunks

Combine first ten ingredients and pour over the lamb, beef, or turkey. Coat the meat well, cover tightly, and refrigerate overnight. Drain immediately before cooking, reserving marinade.
Have ready in bowls:

4 large green peppers, cut into
2-inch squares
1 basket cherry tomatoes

4 onions, quartered, each quarter
separated into 2 chunks
1 lb. medium mushrooms

Let each diner make shishkebabs by skewering meat and vegetables of choice. Place loaded skewers on a barbecue grill or on a rack under broiler. When outside of meat is crisp, turn, brush with marinade. Do not overcook.

Serve with pita or crisp French bread, rice, salads, and corn on the cob.

SHWARMA   [M]

The Israelis turned a universal nomads' food into a fast-food snack, but shwarma is a good meal and a fun barbecue alternative to shishkebab.

Serves 8.

1 leg of lamb
Shishkebab Sauce
8 large pita breads, cut in halves
2-quart bowl of finely diced
  Basic Israeli Salad

Israeli olives
Sliced pickles
Sauerkraut
Schug (optional)

Mount leg of lamb on a rotisserie or place on outdoor grill. Brush with shishkebab sauce. When surface is very well done, chip off quarter-sized flakes of meat with a very sharp knife. Brush meat again and broil until exposed meat is well done. Repeat until all meat is in crispy flakes.

Stuff pita halves with meat, salad, olives, pickles, and sauerkraut. Top with a bit of schug, if desired.

ARMENIAN PRETZELS   [P]

These big sesame rings are to be found at every bus station and kiosk in Israel. In the Old City of Jerusalem they are even sold by Arabs from the backs of donkeys!

Makes a dozen large pretzels.

1 cup warm water
1 tablespoon sugar
1 package dry yeast
1/2 cup margarine, melted
3 eggs, well beaten
1 1/2 teaspoons salt

4 cups flour
1 egg
1 tablespoon water
3/4 cup sesame seeds
2 tablespoons kosher salt

Stir warm water, sugar, and yeast together. Let mixture rest while you mix margarine, eggs, and salt. Combine the two mixtures in a large bowl and add flour. Knead dough, adding more flour, if necessary, to form a soft dough that does not stick to the hands. Oil a bowl and turn dough to grease all sides. Cover with a clean cloth and set aside to rise for an hour, or until double in size. Heat oven to 350°. Grease two cookie sheets. Divide dough into twelve pieces. Roll each piece out in a 14″ rope, then pinch the ends together, forming a circle. (You can also vary the size of the rings and the shapes of the pretzels, making braids, figure eights, etc.)

Beat egg and tablespoon of water together in shallow bowl. Combine sesame seeds and kosher salt in bowl or plate. Dip each pretzel in egg wash, then in sesame mixture. Bake for 10 minutes then remove from oven and drizzle a tablespoon of water over each pretzel. Return for 10 more minutes and repeat. Return for a final 10 minutes in the oven, after which pretzels should be a golden brown. Cool on racks.

CARROT SALAD   [P]

Simple, invigorating carrot salad is known by Israelis as "live carrots," because it is always grated fresh right before the meal. Choose carrots that are thin and straight; they are the sweetest.
Serves 4.

6 carrots, scraped and grated
Juice of 1 lemon
1–3 teaspoons sugar

Toss the grated carrots with the lemon juice. Sprinkle with sugar, the amount depending on how sweet the carrots are. You can doctor the salad with raisins, crushed pineapple, brown sugar, and spices—but there is no need to mask the flavor of first-rate fresh carrots.

LIGHTLY FRIED CAULIFLOWER   [P]

The cauliflower is a much-loved vegetable in Israel. All winter long it serves as both side dish and entree. Usually it is batter-dipped and deep-fried or made into fritters, in which guise it sometimes substitutes for hamburgers. This is a less oily treatment that lets the goodness of the vegetable come through.
Serves 4.

1 medium head cauliflower,
   broken into large florets
3 tablespoons oil

1 cup challah crumbs
1/2 teaspoon salt
1/4 teaspoon paprika

Steam or boil the cauliflower until it is tender but still holds its shape. Heat oil and sauté the challah crumbs until they are light brown. Stir in salt and paprika. Toss cauliflower florets in the pan until all are coated.

ISRAELI APPLE PIE   [P]

Very different from the all-American version in that the pastry is sweeter and the filling less sugary. This pie is customarily baked in a square pan.
Serves 8.

PASTRY DOUGH

1/3 cup vegetable shortening	*1 cup flour*
1/2 cup sugar	*1 teaspoon baking powder*
1 egg	*Pinch salt*
1 1/2 teaspoons vanilla	

FILLING

5 tart apples, peeled, cored, and	*1/2 cup golden raisins*
sliced thin	*1/4 cup chopped almonds*
1/2 cup sugar	*2 tablespoons cornstarch*
2 teaspoons grated orange peel	*1/2 teaspoon cinnamon*
1 teaspoon grated lemon peel	

CRUMB TOPPING

5 tablespoons sugar	*2 tablespoons margarine*
2 tablespoons flour	*1/2 teaspoon cinnamon*

Prepare pastry dough by creaming shortening and sugar. Beat in egg and vanilla. Sift flour, baking powder, and salt together, then mix in well. Roll out the dough and transfer to a floured baking pan, or press the dough directly into the pan.

Mix filling ingredients and spread on dough. Combine topping ingredients and sprinkle on filling. Bake in a 350° oven for 50 minutes.

TURKISH COFFEE   [P]

A perfect way to end a meal, especially a meat meal. Thick, fragrant Turkish coffee, perhaps with a cube of halvah or a diamond-shaped piece of baklava, is the drink of Arabian Nights. A *fenjon*, a small tin pot with a pouring spout and a long handle, is nice for making Turkish coffee, and very inexpensive, but any saucepan will do.

For each serving:

1 heaping teaspoon superfine
    ground Turkish coffee
6 oz. cold water

1 cardamom seed
2 teaspoons sugar

Stir the coffee in water and heat until it froths. Remove from heat and stir. Repeat this procedure three times. Pour into old-fashioned tea glasses. Add cardamom seed and sugar, stirring thoroughly. Wait until grounds settle before drinking.

The Wide World
of Jewish Cuisine

To Americans, traditional Jewish food may mean bagels-and-lox, gefilte fish, and chopped liver. These foods are associated with the Jews because American Jews are overwhelmingly Russian, German, and Polish in ancestry. Yet elsewhere in the world other foods, other flavors are the ones known as "Jewish." Kashrut, of course, is the only true common denominator, but other, more subtle influences, can be found. Among these are:

• Liberal use of onions and garlic. These vegetables grow wild in Israel and were very early found to be unparalleled in the ability to season food. In the Diaspora it was found that these vegetables grew almost everywhere and were easily preserved for long periods. Besides seasoning, onions were used as a cooking vegetable in their own right. The Jews of Yemen even candied them and had them for dessert. The Talmud attributes various restorative and medicinal powers to them. Indeed, garlic has a documented antibiotic effect. Scientific studies indicate that the combined use of onion and garlic has an unusual effect; it counteracts saturated fats in the diet. Populations whose cuisine contains a great deal of onions and garlic have a lesser incidence of heart disease than do similar people with similar—but less pungent—diets.

• An enthusiasm for fish. Often plentiful, kosher fish need not be slaughtered ritually or kashered and can be prepared at either meat or dairy meals. (However, combining fish with meat in the same dish is eschewed—unwary diners might choke on tiny fishbones—and among some Jews, fish and dairy products are not combined either, for the same reason.)

• An appreciation for chicken and other fowl. These meats are enhanced by the kashering process. Also, very common use of eggs, both as the center of a dish (often hard-boiled) and as a thickening agent in cooked foods.

• Certain herbs and spices are used almost universally by Jews. These include parsley, dill, ginger, cinnamon, and—this was distinctive in the early Middle Ages—pepper. The Land of Israel is rich in native grasses and herbs. Trade with the spice-producing nations of the Far East began before King

Solomon's time and dealing in spices continued to be an important occupation for Jews until modern times.

• A fondness for cakes, pastries, and sweets. The Bible mentions cakes way back in Genesis, and sweets are described throughout the Scriptures. Sugar was introduced to Europe by the Jews, who also adopted it wholeheartedly into their own cuisine. Interestingly, many European Jewish cakes and sweet breads are identical with those baked by their Christian neighbors. The main difference is that the Christians call their sweets "Christmas cake" or "Easter bread," indicating the special occasions when they are eaten. The Jews ate these same confections every Sabbath—when they could afford to—while baking even more elaborate sweets for every major and minor holiday of their own. Sephardic Jews also love sweets, preferring small portions of intensely sugary and/or honeyed pastries several times a day, if possible.

• A tendency to eat meat in complicated combinations, including stewed with vegetables; ground, spiced and wrapped in dough; accompanied by strong, zesty sauces and pickled foods, rather than served plain. Also meat is consistently long-cooked in Jewish cuisines around the world. This may be due to the prohibition against consuming blood, a prohibition dealt with by the kashering procedure, and which also results in a certain aversion to meat that is visibly red.

"Now the manna was round as coriander seed, and it resembled crystal. The people casually gathered it and ground it in hand-mills, or crushed it in mortars, or cooked it in pots. And its flavor was that of a cake baked with oil."

(Numbers 11:7–8)

According to the rabbis the manna was a miraculous dish in that it required little effort to gather, was gorgeous to look at, and tasted like any food that one might desire, including those that require extensive preparation. Yet the Children of Israel did not need to make these preparations, the flavor of the raw manna instantly lived up to the richest expectations.

Nevertheless, the Israelites complained, "We remember . . . the cucumbers, the melons, the leeks, the onions, and the garlic. But now our souls are parched; there is nothing but manna to look at." (Numbers 11:5–6)

How is it that the manna, which could taste like any other dish, could not duplicate the flavor of these vegetables? Rabbi Simeon taught: because these foods cause discomfort to nursing mothers and their babies.

Foods become "Jewish" when they meet the needs and excite the interest of a Jewish population. In Israel, certain foods are considered exotically "Jewish-

American." Some of these might surprise Jewish Americans: peanut butter, albacore tuna, and potato chips are among them. American Jews who keep kosher find these foods highly portable and widely available. Immigrants and students in Israel retained their liking for these goodies, brought ample supplies with them, and introduced them to their Israeli friends. Today, they are available all over Israel.

SPINACH AND CHEESE: EAST AND WEST

Common themes of Jewish cooking can result in very different dishes, as demonstrated by these two dishes using many of the same ingredients. The first is a favorite of Syrian Jewry, a community that, since its exodus from Syria, continues to show its flair for sophisticated cuisine in Israel and in the United States. The second, a supper dish of Alsatian Jewry, a community almost as ancient, shows the influence of both France and Germany.

Each dish serves 8.

SYRIAN SPINACH PIE   [D]

1/4 cup butter or margarine
1 large onion, chopped
4 eggs
3 packages frozen chopped
*   spinach, thawed and squeezed*
1/2 lb. farmer cheese (or 1/2 lb.
*   low-fat cottage cheese mixed*
*   with 2 tablespoons flour)*

1/4 cup snipped parsley
2 tablespoons snipped dill, or 2
*   teaspoons dry dill*
1 teaspoon salt
1/4 teaspoon cumin
Freshly ground black pepper
1/2 package phyllo dough leaves
Oil

Sauté onion in butter or margarine until tender. Beat eggs in a large bowl and stir in spinach. Crumble the cheese and stir it in with the spinach. Add onion, parsley, dill, salt, cumin, and pepper. Brush oil on the bottom of a baking pan. Place a leaf of phyllo dough on it, brushing top with oil. Repeat for half the leaves (approximately 8). Spread the spinach mixture. Place remaining phyllo sheets, brushing each one with oil, including top layer. With a sharp knife score the top layers in a diamond pattern, forming 8 diamonds. This will make it easier to cut and serve when pie is baked. Bake at 350° for 30 minutes or until top is golden brown. May be served hot or at room temperature.

ALSATIAN SPINACH SOUFFLÉ   [D]

1/4 cup butter or margarine
1 onion, chopped
3 tablespoons flour
1/2 teaspoon salt
1/2 teaspoon dry dill
1/4 teaspoon nutmeg
Freshly ground black pepper

1 cup milk
1 (6-oz.) package Swiss cheese,
  cut into small pieces
8 eggs, separated
1 package frozen chopped
  spinach, thawed and squeezed

Sauté onion in butter or margarine until tender. Stir in flour, forming a roux. Add salt, dill, nutmeg, and pepper. Slowly add milk, stirring, but not bringing to a boil. Add cheese. While cheese melts, beat egg yolks well. Remove pan from heat, and stir in yolks a little at a time. Stir in spinach. Beat egg whites until stiff. Carefully fold egg whites into spinach mixture. Transfer carefully to greased soufflé dish or casserole. Bake at 350° for 45 minutes or until top feels firm when tapped.

GIVETCH   [P]

Almost every Jewish community has its version of a ratatouillelike vegetable dish. Many can be combined with chunks of meat or beaten eggs to make a filling entree. Givetch is known throughout the Baltic, and in parts of North Africa, differing slightly from place to place. This version is Bulgarian. Serves 8–10.

1 eggplant, peeled and cubed
1/4 cup olive or vegetable oil
2 onions, sliced
3 cloves garlic, minced
2 stalks celery, sliced
1 green pepper, sliced
1 (1-lb.) can tomatoes, with
  liquid
1 small can okra, with liquid
4 small zucchini, sliced
1 large potato, peeled and sliced

1 medium turnip, peeled and
  sliced
1/4 lb. green beans, trimmed
1/4 lb. mushrooms, sliced
1 cup peas or baby Limas
2 tablespoons lemon juice
1/2 teaspoon salt
1/2 teaspoon fennel or basil
1/2 teaspoon oregano
1/2 teaspoon thyme
1 small bay leaf
Freshly ground black pepper

Steam the eggplant until very soft. In a large pot or Dutch oven heat the oil and sauté the onions until just translucent. Add garlic, celery, and pepper, sautéing lightly. Return eggplant to pot. Add remaining ingredients, stirring well. When liquid is bubbly, lower heat, cover, and simmer for 45 minutes. Stir frequently. If liquid dries out, add a cup of water, as needed.

ARTICHOKES ALLA GIUDEA   [P]

The film *The Garden of the Finzi-Continis* portrays the sophistication and tragic end of Italian Jewry. The postwar communities are but a footnote to their millennia-old history, and few Italian Jews retain the elegant, complex cuisine. This recipe, served in many of Italy's finest restaurants, dates back to the Renaissance, when it was one of many dishes "in the style of the Jews" that Italians borrowed from the ghetto.
Serves 4.

1 dozen baby artichokes	*4 cloves garlic, peeled and*
1 lemon	*halved*
Oil for deep frying	*Salt and pepper*

Wash artichokes and trim the tops with scissors. Drizzle with lemon juice. Heat the oil in a large pan and put in garlic and artichokes. Deep-fry the artichokes until golden brown. Drain on paper toweling. Sprinkle with salt and pepper and serve immediately.

ARGENTINE KNISHES   [M]

The Jews of Argentina, while mostly of Ashkenazic descent, have adopted many Spanish-influenced foods. These, known as empanadas, make a delicious first course, or hors d'oeuvres, depending on how big you make the enveloping circles of dough.
Makes 6–8 appetizers or 15 hors d'oeuvres.

2 large onions	*1/2 cup raisins*
2 hard-boiled eggs	*1 teaspoon chili powder*
1/2 cup pimento-stuffed olives	*1/2 teaspoon salt*
3 tablespoons oil	*Freshly ground pepper*
1 lb. ground beef	*Knish Dough*

Run onions, eggs, and olives through grating blade of a food processor, or chop fine. Heat oil and sauté until onions are tender. Add beef and brown. Stir in raisins, chili powder, salt, and pepper.

Roll out dough to 1/4-inch thickness. Cut into 6–8 rectangles, or cut out 15 1/2-inch circles. Fill with meat mixture and pinch closed. Place on greased cookie sheet. Bake at 350° for 30 minutes.

SEPHARDIC STEW   [M]

Throughout the Sephardic world *stifado* or *estofado* appears in various guises, often differing in the types of vegetables that are added, depending on what is locally available.

Serves 6.

2–3 lbs. stewing meat, cubed
3 tablespoons oil
2 large onions, sliced
1 (8-oz.) can tomato sauce
1 tablespoon brown sugar
1/2 cup dry red wine
2 teaspoons chili powder
1 teaspoon salt
1 teaspoon oregano
1/4 teaspoon black pepper
1/4 teaspoon ground cloves
1/4 teaspoon cumin

2 cloves garlic, peeled, sliced in
  half, and impaled on
  toothpicks
1 bay leaf
1 cinnamon stick
2 large tomatoes, diced, with
  their juices
3 zucchini, sliced
3 potatoes, thickly sliced, or
  three ears of corn, cut in
  halves
1 cup green beans or 1 cup peas

In a heavy pot, brown meat in oil. Remove from pot. Sauté onions until tender. Add tomato sauce and lower heat to simmer. Add all seasonings and return meat to sauce. Simmer for 1½ hours. Add vegetables and simmer for 1 hour more. Remove bay leaf, garlic, and cinnamon stick before serving.

THREE DUMPLINGS   [P]

Hungarian cuisine is one of the last undiscovered food thrills. And Hungarian Jews have improved on a great thing, with a cuisine that is just as zesty, but lighter and more delicate than that of the Magyars. It used to be said of any Jewish man who enjoyed eating well, "he seeks a Hungarian bride."

Noodle, potato, and dumpling recipes have many variations in this cuisine. Here is one dough with three very different results.

Each recipe makes 4 servings.

DOUGH

2 boiled potatoes
1 egg

1/2 teaspoon salt
1 cup flour

It is preferable to boil potatoes a day before using. In any case, they should be cold. Peel the potatoes and mash them. Beat in the egg and salt. Knead in flour until soft dough is formed. Knead until smooth.

I Grilled Bread

Divide dough into 8 pieces. Roll them into balls, then flatten and roll out to 1/4-inch thickness. Bake on a grill or griddle until brown. Turn and bake other side. Serve hot with butter.

II Shlishkelech (tiny dumplings)

4 quarts water
1/2 teaspoon salt

3 tablespoons oil
1/2 cup fine dry bread crumbs

Roll dough into ropes the width of your little finger. Cut at 1-inch intervals. Boil water with salt. Add dumplings, avoiding crowding. Boil gently for 12 minutes. Drain and rinse with cold water. Heat oil and sauté bread crumbs in it until golden. Add dumplings and sauté 5 minutes, turning to cover with crumbs.

III Dessert Dumplings

Lekvar (prune butter)
4 quarts water
1/2 teaspoon salt

2 tablespoons sugar, combined
with 1 tablespoon cocoa

Roll dough out to 1/4-inch thickness. Cut into 3-inch squares. Fill each square with 1 teaspoon lekvar. Pinch the ends together and roll into ball. Boil water with salt and drop in dumplings carefully. Boil gently 15 minutes. Drain, rinse in cold water, and roll in sugar and cocoa mixture.

CHICKEN CURRY [M]

Jews have lived in India for more than fifteen hundred years, with the largest community in the city of Cochin. Indian cuisine was easy to adapt to kashrut.
Serves 4–6.

1 chicken
2 tablespoons oil
2 large onions, chopped
3 garlic cloves, minced
2-inch piece of ginger, grated
1 teaspoon salt
2 tablespoons curry powder

1/2 teaspoon ground coriander
1/2 teaspoon ground cardamom
1/2 teaspoon cumin
1/2 teaspoon black pepper
1/4 teaspoon cinnamon
1/4 teaspoon cloves
1/4 teaspoon nutmeg

3 ripe tomatoes, chopped
2 tablespoons snipped fresh
  coriander
1 tablespoon snipped fresh mint

1/2 cup coconut milk or pareve
  cream
4 ounces unsalted cashews

Skin and bone the chicken and cut into bite-size pieces. Heat oil and sauté onions, garlic, and ginger until golden. Stir in salt and spices, cooking for 1 minute. Add tomatoes and herbs, cooking until pulpy. Mix in chicken, cover tightly, and simmer for 45 minutes, stirring occasionally. Blend in coconut milk or pareve cream and cashews and cook 10 minutes longer, uncovered. Serve on a bed of rice.

ETHIOPIAN CHICKEN   [M]

The Beta Yisrael, also known as Falashas, or the Black Jews of Ethiopia, were among the most isolated of all Jewish communities. Despite grinding poverty, they have developed a lyrical holiday cuisine. The Beta Yisrael are called by their neighbors "the people who stink of water," because they observe Jewish ways, including ritual baths and soaking of meat, which are considered a frivolous waste of precious water.
Serves 4.

2 tablespoons oil
1 chicken, cut into serving pieces
2 onions, chopped
2 cloves garlic, minced
1 cup chicken broth

1/2 cup red wine
1 teaspoon salt
1/2 teaspoon cinnamon
1/2 teaspoon ground cloves
1/4 teaspoon ginger

In a Dutch oven or heavy pot, heat oil and brown all sides of the chicken. Remove chicken and sauté onion and garlic until onion is tender. Add broth, wine, salt, cinnamon, cloves, and ginger. Heat to boiling, lower flame, and return chicken to pot. Cover and simmer for 45 minutes.

MOUSSAKA   [M]

Greek Jews cut the eggplant into thin slices and fry each slice. Admittedly, this results in a delicious dish, but the two lower-calorie ways of preparing the eggplant described below will ensure a happy place for it on everyone's menu. Moussaka is also a good change-of-pace dish for Sabbath lunch, as it may be served at room temperature.
Serves 8–10.

2 large eggplants	1 teaspoon cumin
3 tablespoons oil	1/2 teaspoon cinnamon
2 lbs. ground lamb or beef	1/2 teaspoon salt
2 onions, chopped	Freshly ground black pepper
2 cloves garlic, minced	1 cup fine bread crumbs
1 large jar spaghetti sauce	2 tablespoons margarine
1/4 cup snipped parsley	

Prepare the eggplants by either (a) baking at 400° for 20 minutes, piercing twice with a fork, baking another 20 minutes, waiting till eggplants cool, and peeling, or (b) peeling, cutting in 2-inch-thick slices, and steaming until very soft.

In a large saucepan, brown the meat, onions, and garlic in oil. Add spaghetti sauce, parsley, cumin, cinnamon, salt, and pepper, mixing well. Simmer 5 minutes.

Place eggplants in a lightly greased baking pan. Mash them with a fork until they cover the bottom of the pan evenly. Add meat mixture, smoothing with a fork. Sprinkle bread crumbs on top. Dot with margarine. Bake at 350° for 40 minutes. Serve with a green salad.

PERSIAN STUFFED MELON   [M]

Throughout the Middle East—and in the West, as well—Jewish cuisine favors vegetables stuffed with meat mixtures. Stuffed eggplants, peppers, and squashes are all delicious, but stuffed melons are most interesting of all because we in the West rarely treat melons the way Orientals do—as vegetables.

Serves 4.

4 small honeydew or cantaloupe melons	1 cup Minute rice
	1/2 cup raisins
3 tablespoons oil	1/2 cup pine nuts
2 onions, chopped	1/2 cup sweet wine
2 cloves garlic, chopped	2 tablespoons snipped parsley
1 lb. ground beef	1/2 teaspoon cumin
1 (8-oz.) can tomato sauce	1/4 teaspoon salt
1 cup water	Freshly ground pepper

Cut off about 1/4 of the top of each of the melons. Scoop out seeds, drain, and set on baking pan. Heat oil and sauté onions and garlic until tender. Add beef and brown it. Add tomato sauce and water, cooking and stirring until sauce bubbles. Turn off heat, add rice, cover. Wait 5 minutes, then stir in raisins, pine nuts, wine, parsley, cumin, salt, and pepper. Stuff each melon with meat mixture. Cover each melon with its top. Bake at 350° for 1 hour.

BALKAN MEATBALLS   [M]

These spicy tidbits can be made into small balls, impaled on a toothpick, and served with chili sauce. Or, they can be made into hamburgers.

Makes enough hors d'oeuvres for 8, or burgers for 4.

1 lb. ground beef	*1 egg, beaten*
2 tablespoons dried minced	*1/2 teaspoon paprika*
onion	*1/4 teaspoon salt*
3 cloves garlic, minced	*1/4 teaspoon hot pepper sauce*
1/4 cup matzoh meal or oatmeal	*Freshly ground black pepper*
1/4 cup ketchup	

Mix all ingredients. Shape into balls or patties. Broil until well done.

COLONIAL PEAS   [P]

Philadelphia was the heart of the American Jewish community in pre-Revolutionary times. At least one of its members, a Mrs. Glasse, wrote a cookbook. Back in 1751 she referred to kashrut as a quaint folkway, indicating that her community was already highly assimilated. This recipe, a close adaptation, does not resemble either European Jewish pea dishes or later American Jewish recipes. Yet it was known as "Peas the Jews' Way."

Serves 4 as a lunch or supper dish.

1 lb. green split peas	*1/4 teaspoon ground cloves*
2 tablespoons oil	*1/4 teaspoon nutmeg*
1/2 teaspoon salt	*1/4 teaspoon hot pepper sauce*
1/4 teaspoon cinnamon	*4 eggs*

Cook split peas according to package directions until consistency of mashed potatoes. Stir in oil, salt, cinnamon, cloves, nutmeg, and hot pepper sauce. Pour into greased casserole. Break open eggs one at a time, making sure not to break the yolks. Make 4 slight indentations in the peas and place an egg into each. Bake at 400° until eggs set. Serve at once with salt and black pepper to taste.

YEMENITE SOUP   [M]

The Jews of Yemen were isolated from their coreligionists for many hundreds of years. They developed a brilliant culture, highlighted by a spicy, unique cuisine.
Serves 6.

2 tablespoons oil	2 ripe tomatoes, chopped
1 lb. lean beef, cubed	5 cups broth
5 cloves garlic, minced	1/2 teaspoon salt
1/4 cup snipped parsley	Freshly ground pepper
1/4 cup snipped coriander	3 cardamom seeds, whole

Heat oil in a large pot and brown beef. Remove beef from pot. Sauté garlic, parsley, and coriander for 2 minutes. Return beef to pot. Add remaining ingredients. Bring to a boil, then lower heat and simmer 1 hour.

MOROCCAN TRUFFLES   [P]

Makes about 5 dozen confections.

3 cups ground walnuts	3/4 teaspoon ground cloves
2 cups ground almonds	1/2 teaspoon cinnamon
1 1/2 cups sugar	3–4 eggs
1 teaspoon ground ginger	Powdered sugar

Mix together nuts, sugar, and spices. Break 3 eggs into mixture, stirring well. It should be sticky. Add fourth egg if necessary. Cover and refrigerate for 1 hour. Pinch off dough the size of a walnut. Roll in powdered sugar and place in a small candy paper. Repeat for rest of dough. Bake at 350° for 25 minutes.

GREEK RICE PILAF   [P]

Serves 4.

2 tablespoons oil	1 teaspoon sugar
1 large onion, chopped	Freshly ground black pepper
1 cup rice	2 cups boiling broth or water
1 clove garlic, minced	4 large black olives, pitted and
1 (1-lb.) can tomatoes, chopped	chopped
1/4 lb. mushrooms, sliced	1 small can peas, drained
1 teaspoon salt	1/4 cup raisins

Heat oil and sauté onions until tender. Add rice and cook, stirring, for 3 minutes. Stir in garlic, tomatoes, and mushrooms. Add salt, sugar, and pepper, stirring well. Add boiling broth or water, olives, peas, and raisins. Cover tightly, let rest 5 minutes, and serve.

MAMALIGA [D]

Food made from cornmeal mush was served at every meal among the rural Jews of Romania. It could be served straight from the pot, baked into a cornbread and sliced, or as a bland base for any kind of cheese or tomato sauce.
Makes 1 breakfast serving.

1/4 cup yellow cornmeal
1 cup water
1/4 teaspoon salt
Dash pepper

2 tablespoons grated Parmesan cheese
1 tablespoon butter or margarine

Mix cornmeal with a little of the water. Place over medium heat and slowly add rest of water, stirring. Add salt and pepper. Continue stirring until very thick, about 15 minutes. Remove from heat and stir in Parmesan cheese and butter or margarine. Top with more butter and Parmesan cheese, or cream and sugar.

RETES (Hungarian apple strudel) [P]

Retes is the unchallenged queen of the Hungarian Jewish kitchen. Few dishes anywhere have its delicacy of flavor and texture. Fewer still require such dexterity and artistry in composition. To be sure Jews everywhere enjoy some form of apple-filled pastry, but Hungarian cooks look upon those hearty strudels with their thick pastry shells, chunky apple fillings, and raisins as—the saying goes—galoshes at a ball. Non-Jewish Hungarian women take just as much pride in their retes, but its flavor is distinctly different, perhaps because it contains butter instead of oil, mere bread instead of challah, or, perhaps, because it lacks the ineffable flavor of the Jewish celebration on which it is eaten.

There was a time when no Hungarian girl could hope to marry unless her retes dough was stretched as thin and sheer as a tulle wedding veil. This took years of practice. Today machines spew out yards of phyllo dough, an excellent substitute, at the touch of a button. Even proficient Hungarian grandes dames now use phyllo dough for their retes, and certainly novices should feel no shame in using this shortcut, but those who would like to try the real thing should prepare the following dough:

1 egg
1/2 cup warm water
1–2 cups flour

Beat the egg and water together. Stir in flour. Keep adding flour until a soft ball of dough is formed. Knead gently. Roll out the dough as thinly as possible on a flour-dusted tablecloth. Carefully extend both hands under the dough. Claw your fingers so the dough rests on the knuckles. Gently stretch until the dough between your fingers is stretched superthin but does not tear. Work your way back from the center, then go to the opposite side of the table and work your way back from the center again until all of the dough is equally thin. A master retes baker can cover a full-size dining table with this dough.

Even when you use prepared phyllo dough, preparing retes requires craftsmanship and the right equipment and ingredients. You will need:

2 dish towels, soaked, then wrung out
1 goose-feather pastry brush (available at gourmet shops and import stores)
1 package phyllo dough sheets (for best results use a fresh, unopened package, although you will only need a small number of the leaves)
Oil, water, and sugar in containers in which you can dip your fingers
1 shallow baking pan or cookie sheet, well oiled

Two rolls of retes make approximately 24 slices, or 12 servings.

6 small or 4 large apples (choose a variety with some tang, such as Granny Smith, pippin, or McIntosh)
6 leaves phyllo dough
1/2 cup oil
1 cup sugar mixed with 1 tablespoon cinnamon

1/2 cup of fine, dry challah crumbs (if challah is soft, toast it lightly)
1/2 cup ground walnuts
Grated peel of a large lemon
1 egg yolk, beaten
Vanilla Sugar

Peel, core, and grate the apples. Squeeze out juice and roll apples in paper toweling to dry further. Place a damp dish towel horizontally on the working area. Spread a leaf of phyllo dough on it. Cover the unused phyllo dough with the other damp towel. Four inches from the bottom of the leaf, brush a 4-inch band of oil across the dough with a goose-feather brush. Sprinkle the band with sugar mixture and challah crumbs. Place a second leaf of dough on top of the first. Brush on oil directly on top of the other band. Sprinkle with sugar mixture, crumbs, and half the nuts. Place a third leaf on top. Brush with oil, sprinkle with sugar mixture, lemon peel, and apple.

Holding the bottom edge of the towel, not the dough itself, roll the bottommost 4 inches of phyllo leaves onto the filling. Continue rolling the towel until you have a jelly-roll-size loaf. Roll it gently onto the baking pan or cookie sheet. Use a bit of egg yolk to seal the ends of the dough.

Repeat procedure for second roll.

Dip a hand in water and gently pat the top of the retes rolls. With the goose-feather brush dipped in egg yolk, glaze the tops of the loaves. With a sharp knife, score the top layer of the retes so that slicing the baked strudel will not cause excessive flaking.

Bake at 400° for 30 minutes. Lower heat to 300° and bake another 10 minutes or until brown. Dust with vanilla sugar before serving. Retes freezes well.

QUICK BAKLAVA [P]

Baklava is to Sephardic Jews what strudel is to the Ashkenazim. In each case, the heavenly result is deemed worth the great fuss needed to create it. This recipe lets you make a credible baklava—while you take revenge upon that unwieldy phyllo dough.

Makes 20 pieces.

1 package frozen phyllo dough
   leaves
1/2 lb. unsalted margarine,
   melted
1 1/2 cups finely chopped walnuts

1 1/2 cups finely chopped
   pistachios or almonds
1/4 cup sugar
1 teaspoon cinnamon

SYRUP

2 cups sugar
1 1/2 cups water
2 teaspoons grated lemon rind
1/2 teaspoon cinnamon

1/4 teaspoon ground cloves
1/2 cup honey
1 tablespoon lemon juice

Take frozen phyllo dough and shred it with a knife or your hands. Stir in margarine. Place half of dough mixture in greased baking pan. Combine nuts, sugar, and cinnamon and sprinkle on this layer. Layer rest of dough on nut mixture. Bake at 325° for 1 hour.

In a saucepan, bring sugar, water, lemon rind, cinnamon, and cloves to a boil. Lower heat and let simmer 20 minutes. Remove from heat; stir in honey and lemon juice.

As soon as you remove the baklava from the oven, pour the syrup over it. Cover tightly and refrigerate several hours. Before serving, cut the baklava into diamonds by making straight horizontal cuts, then diagonals. Serve at room temperature.

SOME USEFUL TRADITIONS

• Chick-peas may be the oldest Jewish dish. They are common to both Ashkenazim and Sephardim. They are served on both happy and sad occasions. The Yiddish word for them, *arbes,* is derived from the ancient Greek. Sephardim call them *hummus,* from the Arabic. In the Western United States they are sold as garbanzos. Serve them anytime with freshly ground pepper.

• Oriental Jews savor fresh coriander, as do the peoples of all of Asia and Latin America. Use it like parsley. Ground coriander, a spice, is made from the seed of the plant and because it tastes completely different, it is not a substitute for the leaves. It is also known as cilantro and Chinese parsley.

• Paprika is one of the most widely used spices in Jewish cooking around the world. Always add it at the end of the cooking period, as it tends to burn and turn bitter.

• Different vegetable oils lend a distinctly different flavor to a dish. Use very aromatic oils like olive and sesame whenever they are called for in a recipe. Use peanut and corn oils in sweets. Refrigerate to preserve the freshness of rarely used oils. They will cloud but will still taste good. Always look for kashrut certification on all oils and products containing them. Try vegetable-oil sprays for greasing all of your bakeware—it saves calories and effort.

• Always use fine vinegar when it is called for in a recipe. Kosher wine vinegar is available. Also try malt and other salad vinegars. Vinegar and all foods which contain it should have kashrut certification.

The Jewish Vegetarian

The controversy is at least two thousand years old: is the goal of kashrut ultimately vegetarianism? Or is meat a basic right and need of humanity?

The vegetarians, who number among them great rabbis and kabbalists, argue that meat is an unnatural food to begin with. The Bible commentators all agree that Adam had been permitted only vegetables and fruit, as it is written, "And God said, 'Behold I have given you (Adam and Eve) every seed-bearing grass upon the face of the earth and every fruit-bearing tree, these shall be for you to eat. And to every beast of the earth and every bird of the sky and every creeping thing, to everything that has the breath of life in it, I have given the green grass for food.' And it was so." (Genesis 1:29–30) It was only when God saw the corruption of the generation of Noah, when he despaired of mankind's reaching the spiritual heights of which it is capable, did he permit the killing of animals for consumption. "Every moving thing which lives shall be yours for food, just as I have given you the grasses, so do I give you all." (Genesis 9:3)

From that time forward, while meat was permitted within the parameters of kashrut, the desire for meat was termed "lust," a label for near-universal, but not inevitable, weakness with a strongly pejorative connotation (physical desire for one's spouse, for example, is not "lust").

The many restrictive rules of kashrut, say the vegetarians, are comparable to the laws of slavery. At the time the Torah was given to Israel, slavery was universal and it was widely assumed that civilization could not survive without it. Laws giving the slave many rights and the owner many obligations, made people realize that slavery was more trouble than it was worth. Thus restrictive laws accomplished what fiat could not: they abolished slavery. Meticulous observance of kashrut is so difficult, say the vegetarians, that people will realize it is less bother simply to eat no meat—which was God's intention all along.

Moreover, they allege, it is virtually impossible for meat-eaters to completely comply with the law. For example, today almost all chickens are injected with antibiotics and hormones. Because of the size of their bodies, it is difficult to determine exactly where the needle reaches. An animal with a punctured major organ is not kosher, but it is impossible to determine whether a hypodermic needle has punctured a chicken's essential organ. Contemporary rabbis have reluctantly permitted such chickens; to have done otherwise, they reason, would be to so restrict Jews as to tempt many of them to totally abandon kashrut. But this sort of compromise is a concession to weakness, say the vegetarians.

They point to the many laws forbidding cruelty to animals: it is forbidden to injure an animal, forbidden to deny it its natural rights—as in castration—forbidden even to hurt its feelings—e.g., muzzle an ox while it is threshing; gather eggs in the presence of the mother bird. What greater cruelty, they ask, than to kill an animal, even in the least cruel fashion, what greater denial of natural rights than death, what greater betrayal of mercy?

And finally, the vegetarians allege, meat is unhealthful, an agent of disease for primitive and modern people alike. And the Torah has commanded, "Be scrupulous in guarding your health."

But this same argument is used by those who deny vegetarianism. Meat is unparalleled for concentrated nutrients. It is a tonic for the weak and excellent food for pregnant women, they claim.

Furthermore, in Jewish life, meat is eaten in moderation. Throughout Jewish history, most Jews have eaten meat only on the Sabbath. Even the rich, who can afford it more often, are so restricted by the separation rule that they are unlikely to eat meat more than once a day, otherwise, they could not eat dairy products, a much more basic food. What is evil in excess, is often desirable in moderation.

Meat and wine, they say, are the basis of all feasting and rejoicing. When the Temple was destroyed one of the rabbis proposed a complete ban on meat and wine—for how could there be any rejoicing with the heart of Judaism in ruins—but he was overruled by his colleagues' opinion: to deny meat and wine would be to impose too great a burden on the people.

How, they asked, could the rabbis prohibit what the Torah itself permitted, specifying, "Of these you may eat . . ."

Finally, vegetarianism has not proved itself to be a great moral force. Hitler was a vegetarian, as were a number of his close circle. Many Holocaust survivors remember well the scene of men pampering and crooning tenderly to their dogs and cats while slaughtering human beings with unbelievable savagery.

Even so, vegetarianism has had a great appeal for many Jews. Even in prewar Eastern Europe, where meat made up a greater percentage of the Jewish diet than anywhere else at any time, and where few vegetables and fruits were available, many Jewish neighborhoods and most Jewish resorts sported vegetarian restaurants.

In Israel today 4 percent of the population—more people than live in all of the kibbutzim—are vegetarians. This is the highest percentage of any country in the world. Israel was among the first Western nations to make soybean products readily available. These protein and protean foods are a staple for modern vegetarians.

> The rabbi was relating wondrous tales of the World-to-Come. "When the Messiah comes," he told the gape-mouthed pupils, "the flesh of the Leviathan will be the delicacy of the righteous. Then the Creator himself will slaughter the Behemoth. The Leviathan holds the oceans on her tail, while the Behemoth bears all the mountains upon his shoulders, and each is so huge that the flesh of one could sustain the world forever!"
>
> "But," said the bright pupil, "if the Great Fish and the Great Ox could each feed the world, why serve two courses?"
>
> "Well my son, as you know, there are many people who don't care for fish, while others are so pious about kashrut that they never order meat when they eat out."

Vegetarians always like to cite celebrities who share their enthusiasm. Israeli vegetarians are especially proud of the great visionary, Israel's first chief rabbi, the late Rabbi Kook, who became a vegetarian at the age of ten, and wrote eloquently of the mystical and compassionate nature of this way of life. A later chief rabbi, who was also the charismatic chief rabbi of the Defense Forces, Rabbi Shlomo Goren, is a vegetarian, too. And S. Y. Agnon, winner of the Nobel Prize for Literature, was also a confirmed vegetarian who expressed, in his acceptance speech, his gratitude to all the animals who influenced his work.

Today, some Jews are vegetarians by choice, others by default. Unlike their ancestors, most Jews can afford meat, but kosher meat is a luxury for any pocketbook—four dollars per pound of ordinary cuts is not unusual. Outside of the major Jewish centers of population, kosher meat takes some effort to obtain, and then it is almost always frozen. Consequently, some Jews have tried doing without meat and found it a pleasant way of life.

Many more Jews are vegetarians during the week, eating meat only on the Sabbath. And most Jewish vegetarians, unlike the adherents of some religious sects, eat fish, eggs, and milk products. (Jews categorize beef, veal, lamb, goat meat, and poultry as "meat.")

With the recent growth of interest in traditional Judaism, some "returning" Jews and converts have become vegetarians as a temporary or permanent way of fording the difficulties of kashrut.

Vegetarian or not, all kosher cooks can profit by the trends and information that the vegetarian boom has brought. As a rule, vegetarian recipes need no alteration to conform to kashrut. "New" vegetables, fruits, and grains that have been introduced by health-food believers can greatly expand the kosher menu. And, for those who feel deprived, vegetarian meat substitutes can stand in for bacon, cheeseburgers, ham, and other forbidden foods. Nevertheless there are some things to watch out for:

- Be certain that "natural foods" products have kashrut certification. The

The waiter at the most strictly kosher restaurant in town noticed the gentleman perusing the kashrut certificate in the window.

"Have no fear, sir, our kashrut standards couldn't be higher. Why look, there's the chief rabbi dining with the dean of the rabbinical seminary. The most eminent religious dignitaries patronize our establishment."

Still, the customer looked skeptical. The proprietor begged him to come in. "I want you to inspect the kitchen yourself, check the meat, speak to the supervisor. Moses himself could eat here without hesitation."

The would-be customer looked about the spotless, well-organized kitchen, where devout-looking workers went about cooking. Introduced to the supervisor, he engaged the venerable scholar in a Talmudic discussion. The supervisor responded brilliantly, showing himself to be more than well versed in the minutiae of his profession. Satisfied at last, the gentleman was seated.

With a flourish, the waiter handed him a menu. Brushing it away, the patron gave his order:

"Two hard-boiled eggs, please. And tell them to leave the shells on."

goals of naturists and kashrut observers are not always identical. The packager who cringes from using vegetable-derived glycerides may think nothing of substituting some "natural" lard.

• Products containing grapes or cheese are not kosher according to Orthodox standards, unless they are specifically prepared for a kosher market.

• True vegetarians should take pains to prepare special foods for the Sabbath and festivals. Since the types of food used for entrees are likely to be limited, good candidates for "honored" dishes would be those that require elegant preparation or presentation, expensive nuts, or out-of-season fruits.

CABBAGE SOUP [P]

Hearty and interesting for winter.
Serves 4–6.

1 package Israeli vegetable soup mix
5 cups water
1/2 head of cabbage, shredded

2 tart apples, peeled, cored, and shredded
2 tablespoons fresh dill, snipped

Dissolve soup mix in water and bring to a boil. Add cabbage, apples, and dill. Reduce heat to simmer, cover, and cook 15 minutes. Garnish with sprigs of dill.

BAKED SOUP   [D]

A filling, fragrant soup to serve with good fresh bread.
Serves 6–8.

1/4 lb. mushrooms	*1 cup dry white wine*
1/2 package tofu	*5 cloves garlic, minced*
4 ripe tomatoes	*1/4 cup snipped parsley*
4 zucchini	*2 cubes vegetable bouillon*
2 onions	*1 small bay leaf*
1 green pepper	*1 (8-oz.) bar Cheddar cheese,*
1 red pepper	* shredded*
1 (15-oz.) can chick-peas	*1 cup sour cream*
1 (15-oz.) can small green peas	*Grated Parmesan cheese*
2 cups water	

Run the mushrooms, tofu, tomatoes, zucchini, onions, and peppers through the grating blade of a food processor. Pour into ovenproof pot. Add chick-peas, green peas, water, wine, and seasonings. Cover and bake at 400° for 1 hour. Stir in Cheddar cheese until melted, then stir in sour cream. Sprinkle each bowl of soup with Parmesan cheese.

VEGETARIAN STROGANOFF   [D]

A hearty main dish in a creamy sauce.
Serves 6.

12 oz. egg noodles	*1/2 teaspoon basil*
1 1/2 lb. broccoli	*1/2 teaspoon salt*
1/4 cup butter or margarine	*Freshly grated black pepper*
1 onion, chopped	*1 cup grated Jack cheese*
1/2 lb. mushrooms, sliced	*1 cup grated Muenster cheese*
2 cups crumbled tofu	*1/2 cup fine bread crumbs*
1 cup sour cream	

Cook noodles and steam broccoli. Meanwhile, sauté onions and mushrooms in butter or margarine. Stir in tofu, sour cream, basil, salt, pepper, and Jack cheese. Heat until cheese melts. Drain noodles and separate broccoli into small florets. In a greased casserole or baking pan combine creamed mixture, noodles, and broccoli. Top with combined Muenster cheese and bread crumbs. Bake in 400° oven for 15 minutes. Serve with salad.

STIR-FRIED VEGETABLES   [P]

Chinese cooking lends itself easily to vegetarian dishes. This basic recipe for a vegetarian main dish can also be an excellent way to use leftover chicken, turkey, or beef. Just substitute the meat for part of the vegetables.
Serves 4–6.

*3 tablespoons oil (preferably
  sesame oil)*
1/2 cup almonds
3 cloves garlic, minced
*6 cups assorted vegetables, cut
  into bite-sized pieces (see
  suggestions below)*
1/4 cup soy sauce

1/4 cup sake or dry white wine
1/4 cup cold water
1 teaspoon sugar
1/2 teaspoon ground ginger
1 tablespoon cornstarch
3 cups steamed rice
1 cup Chinese noodles

In a wok, heat the oil to just below smoking. Fry the almonds and garlic and remove with a slotted spoon. Fry the vegetables quickly by turning them constantly on the surface of the wok. Start with the hardest vegetables, cooking for a few minutes only, quickly add the next softest, and so on. Mushrooms, bean sprouts, and tofu are usually the last additions, and they need only a minute or so of contact with the heat. Return almonds to wok. Combine soy sauce, wine, water, sugar, ginger, and cornstarch very well and pour into wok. Keep stirring and turning vegetables until the sauce thickens and clears and coats the vegetables. Serve at once over rice and sprinkle with Chinese noodles.

SUGGESTED VEGETABLES:

Carrots, sliced
Celery, cut diagonally
Broccoli, cut in florets
Cauliflower, cut in florets
Zucchini, sliced
*Eggplant, peeled, quartered, and
  sliced*
Scallions, cut in 1" pieces
*Tofu, 2" cubes, marinated 10
  minutes in soy sauce*
*Cabbage or bok choy, coarsely
  shredded*

*Snow peas, whole pods with
  stems trimmed*
*Green beans, fresh, whole, with
  stems trimmed*
Bean sprouts
Bamboo shoots
Water chestnuts
Baby corn
*Mushrooms, whole small ones,
  or thickly sliced larger ones*

SPAGHETTI DINNER   [D]

A perfect meal for working parents: easy to prepare, nutritious, economical —and kids love it.
Serves 4.

3 quarts water
1/2 tsp. salt
8 oz. thin spaghetti
2/3 cup soy granules
2/3 cup boiling water
1 (15-oz.) can tomato sauce
1/4 tsp. oregano

1/4 tsp. basil
1/4 tsp. garlic powder
2 tablespoons snipped parsley
8 oz. mozzarella cheese, sliced
  thin or coarsely grated
1/4 cup grated Parmesan cheese

Cook spaghetti in boiling, salted water in an uncovered pot. The pasta will be done in about 8 minutes, but check by fishing out a noodle and tasting it. Spaghetti should be firm but have no starchy taste. While spaghetti cooks, reconstitute soy granules in boiling water. Heat tomato sauce in a saucepan. When it bubbles, add the soy granules and the herbs and garlic powder. Let sauce simmer for a few minutes, adding up to a canful of water to reach desired consistency. Remove from heat and stir in parsley.

Layer spaghetti, mozzarella, and sauce on each plate. Sprinkle with Parmesan cheese. Serve with steamed broccoli and a tossed salad.

CHALLAH QUICHE   [D]

Using leftover challah can save you the trouble of making a pie crust for a quiche.
Serves 4.

4 slices challah
2 tablespoons butter or
  margarine
1 onion, sliced and broken into
  rings
1 clove garlic, minced
1 cup sliced carrots
1 cup sliced zucchini
1 cup green beans
1 cup broccoli florets

1 cup cauliflower florets
4 eggs
1/2 cup cottage cheese
1 tablespoon snipped parsley
1/2 teaspoon thyme
1/2 teaspoon chervil
1/2 teaspoon salt
4 oz. Swiss cheese, grated
1/2 cup sliced mushrooms

Preheat oven to 350°. Grease a deep-dish pie pan or square baking pan. Toast the challah slices and arrange them to cover the bottom of the pan. In a skillet, melt butter or margarine and sauté onions and garlic till tender. Add vegetables and toss to coat with butter or margarine. Cover and cook for 5 minutes. Spread vegetables on challah. In a bowl, beat eggs and mix in cottage cheese and seasonings. Pour over vegetables. Mix Swiss cheese and mushrooms and sprinkle over the quiche. Bake until set, approximately 30–35 minutes.

EGG CURRY [D]

Spicy Indian cuisine presents a piquant addition to the vegetarian menu. Some parts of India have a native vegetarian tradition, so the feel of the cuisine is not one of "substitution."
Serves 4.

2 tablespoons butter or margarine
1 onion, chopped
1 green pepper, chopped
2 cloves garlic, minced
1 tablespoon curry powder
1/2 teaspoon salt
1/4 teaspoon hot pepper sauce
1 1/2 cups vegetable broth
1 carrot
1 zucchini
1 cup fresh or frozen green beans

1 cup cauliflower florets
1/4 lb. mushrooms
1 apple, peeled, cored, and diced
2 sprigs fresh coriander leaves, snipped (if unavailable, use flat parsley)
1 tablespoon flour
2 hard-boiled eggs, chopped
2 cups plain yogurt
4 cups cooked brown rice
1/2 cup peanuts
1 cucumber, peeled, seeded, and diced

Sauté onions, pepper, and garlic in butter or margarine. Stir in curry powder, salt, and hot pepper sauce. Add broth and heat to boiling. Dice the vegetables and add to pan. Stir in apple and coriander leaves. Cover and cook 20–30 minutes, stirring occasionally. When vegetables are tender, stir in flour until sauce thickens. Add eggs, mixing well. Remove from heat and stir in 1/2 cup yogurt.

Serve the curry on a bed of brown rice. Sprinkle with peanuts. Accompany with a cooling side dish of cucumber stirred into the remaining yogurt.

SPICY EGGPLANT [P]

Serves 4.

1 large eggplant
1/4 cup sesame oil
1 large onion, coarsely diced
1 tablespoon lemon juice
1 teaspoon salt
1 teaspoon curry powder

1 teaspoon chili powder
1 teaspoon dry mustard
1/2 teaspoon cumin
1/4 teaspoon ginger powder
1/4 cup coconut milk or nondairy
  creamer

Bake eggplant at 400° for 30 minutes. Peel, quarter, and slice. Fry the eggplant in oil in a nonstick pan for 10 minutes. Add onion and continue cooking until onion is translucent. Add seasonings and continue cooking and stirring for 5 minutes. Add creamer and heat through but do not boil. May be served hot or at room temperature.

POPEYE PIE [D]

This casserole is a favorite with kids and an easy dish to prepare, in multiple, for a crowd.
Serves 4.

4 eggs, well beaten
1 cup milk
1 tablespoon Worcestershire
  sauce
1/4 cup butter or margarine,
  melted
2 teaspoons dried, minced onion

1 1/2 teaspoons salt
4 oz. Cheddar cheese, shredded
2 (10-oz.) packages frozen
  chopped spinach, completely
  thawed
3 cups cooked rice

Preheat oven to 350°. Grease a deep-dish pie plate or square baking pan. Combine all ingredients in order given. Pour into pan. Bake 40 minutes.

I'm Popeye the Sailor Mensch
After I eat I bensch (recite the Grace)
I scoot to the finish because I am Yiddish
I'm Popeye the Sailor Mensch
Rub-a-dub dub
Thanks for the grub
Yeah God!
                    –Schoolyard ditty from a Brooklyn yeshiva

---

CREAMY POTATOES   [D]

A tempting side dish for a simple omelet-and-salad supper.
Serves 4.

4 large potatoes
2 tablespoons butter or
   margarine
3 tablespoons flour
2 tablespoons dried minced
   onions
1/2 teaspoon salt

Freshly ground pepper
1 cup sour cream or plain yogurt
1/2 cup milk
1 (8-oz.) stick Cheddar cheese,
   grated
1 cup bread crumbs

Peel and slice potatoes. Cover with water and bring to a gentle boil. Cover
and cook for about 15 minutes until tender, then drain. In a flameproof casserole or iron skillet, on low heat, melt butter or margarine. Stir in flour until
smooth. Add dried onions, salt, and pepper. Stir in sour cream or yogurt, milk,
and half the cheese. Stir constantly until cheese melts, making sure that sauce
does not boil or stick to pan. Stir in potatoes. Top with mixture of remaining
cheese and bread crumbs. Place under broiler until topping browns.

MOCK CHOPPED LIVER   [P]

*If someone tells you that such-and-such is as good as an egg, you may
be certain that an egg is better.*–The Talmud.

Even so, there are some ersatz foods that are delicious in their own right.
People who are not enamored of liver might actually prefer this recipe.
Serves 6–8.

2 cups lentils
1/4 cup oil
1 large onion, chopped
1/2 medium eggplant, peeled,
   sliced in thirds
8 hard-boiled eggs

1 cup chopped walnuts
2 tablespoons peanut butter
1 tablespoon dry minced onion
1 teaspoon salt
Freshly ground pepper

Cook lentils in boiling water for 45 minutes. Heat oil and sauté onions.
When barely translucent, add eggplant slices. Pour all ingredients into a food
processor. Pulse on and off until the pâté is slightly grainy in texture. Refrigerate
for several hours before serving.

VEGETABLE LOAF WITH GRAVY   [P]

A substantial entree to please even die-hard meat lovers.
Serves 6–8.

1 cup textured soy granules
1 cup hot vegetable broth
1/4 cup oil
1 large onion, chopped
2 stalks celery, chopped
1/4 lb. mushrooms, chopped
2 cloves garlic, minced
1 cup uncooked oatmeal
3/4 cup ground walnuts

1 (8-oz.) can tomato sauce
3 eggs, beaten
2 tablespoons snipped parsley
1/2 teaspoon basil
1/2 teaspoon oregano
1/2 teaspoon salt
Freshly ground pepper

Cover soy granules with broth and let it reconstitute while other ingredients are being prepared. Heat oil and sauté onions and celery until onions are tender. Add mushrooms and garlic, sautéing 1 minute more. Combine all ingredients and pour into loaf pan. Bake at 350° for 45 minutes. Serve hot or cold.

GRAVY

Makes 2–3 cups.

1 lb. mushrooms
2 tablespoons margarine
2 teaspoons pareve bouillon
3/4 cup cold water

2 tablespoons cornstarch
1/2 teaspoon salt
Freshly ground pepper

If using button mushrooms, leave whole; slice larger mushrooms. Melt margarine and add mushrooms. Cover and simmer 5 minutes. Stir in bouillon. Dissolve cornstarch in water and add to mushrooms. Add salt and pepper. Cook, stirring, until gravy thickens.

INDONESIAN RICE TABLE   [D or P]

More than just a dish, *rijstafel* (the Dutch adopted it during their colonial period) is a whole cuisine, depending on what foods you add to it. Although it is ordinarily made with chicken, its symphony of flavors plays well with tofu, too. For a pareve dish, substitute coconut milk for the regular milk.
Serves 6–8.

3 tablespoons butter or
  margarine
1 onion, chopped
2 cloves garlic, minced
2 tablespoons fresh ginger,
  grated
2 tablespoons peanut butter
1 teaspoon cumin
1/2 teaspoon curry powder
1/2 teaspoon ground coriander
1/2 teaspoon salt

1/2 teaspoon red pepper flakes
1 quart milk
2 tablespoons cornstarch
2 cups shredded coconut
2 cups diced tofu
2 cups button mushrooms
1 cup cashew nuts
8 bananas, sliced lengthwise
1/4 cup brown sugar
6 cups cooked rice
2 hard-boiled eggs, chopped

Heat 1 tablespoon of the butter or margarine and sauté onion until tender. Add garlic and ginger, sautéing another minute. Stir in peanut butter and seasonings. Dissolve cornstarch in some cold milk. Add to pot, then slowly add rest of milk. Heat to just below boiling. Stir in coconut, tofu, mushrooms, and cashews. Cook, stirring constantly, for 10 minutes. Melt remaining butter or margarine in a frying pan and fry bananas until golden. Sprinkle with brown sugar. Arrange rice on a large platter. Surround with fried bananas and garnish with chopped eggs.

TEMPURA [P]

This is a seductive dish. The hardest thing about tempura is ending the meal.

Serves 4.

8 cups of vegetables, from
  among the following:
Eggplants, peeled and cut in
  wedges
Onions, cut in wedges
Zucchini, cut in thick slices
Cauliflower florets

Broccoli florets
Mushrooms, medium, whole
Tofu, thick slices
Green peppers, thick slices
Carrots, sliced lengthwise and
  cut in half
Sweet potatoes, thickly sliced

BATTER

1 cup ice water
2 egg yolks, well beaten
1/4 teaspoon baking soda

1/4 teaspoon salt
1 cup flour
1/3 cup cornstarch

SAUCE

1 cup vegetable broth
1/4 cup soy sauce
1/4 cup dry wine
1 tablespoon grated daikon
(white radish)

1 tablespoon grated ginger
1 scallion, cut in thin strips

Mix sauce ingredients together and garnish with scallion strips. Have ready oil for deep-frying. Mix batter ingredients briefly; batter should be lumpy. Set batter bowl in a larger bowl containing ice. Dip vegetables in batter and fry, uncrowded, until golden. Serve on a bed of brown rice. Let diners dip each piece of vegetable into sauce.

LAND OF MILK AND HONEY

According to one *midrash* (original interpretation of holy writ), the reason that Israel is called the Land of Milk and Honey is that these two are the only foods obtained without killing a living thing. When the Messiah comes, all of nature will rejoice in love, peace, and eternal life. Nothing, not even a plant, will have to die in order to feed another. Miraculously, all righteous creatures will feast on sumptuous heavenly delicacies to their hearts' content.

Adapting
the Cuisines
of the World

You are blessed, Lord our God, King of the universe, who nourishes the entire world in his goodness; graciously, generously, compassionately. He gives bread to all flesh, for his kindness is endless. And in his great goodness he has never failed us, nor will he ever fail us in providing food. His Name is great, for he is the God who feeds and supports everyone, and is good to everyone, and prepares sustenance for all he has created. You are blessed, Lord-who-nourishes-all.

–from the Grace After Meals.

The explosion in food information has brought the world's menus to every household. And every supermarket now carries items once considered exotic. The kosher cook can greatly expand his or her repertoire by taking advantage of these trends. Although some cuisines are based on foods forbidden by kashrut, ingenuity and discrimination can bring foods from virtually every culture into the Jewish home.

This chapter presents a few ideas for adapting foods that may have seemed alien to the observer of kashrut.

Some tips for "converting" foods:

• Choose foods that have exotic vegetable, fruit, and grain ingredients, because these are all kosher.

• Invest in spices peculiar to a particular cuisine. These will add the flavor of a culture at little cost and with minimal effort.

• Choose complex recipes to adapt, as the substitution of a kosher ingredient or two for nonkosher ones will be less discernible among all the other ingredients that are common to the two dishes.

• Choose recipes in which the nonkosher ingredient provides texture and flavor rather than bulk. It is pointless, for example, to try to imitate a baked ham or boiled lobster with kosher ingredients. On the other hand, bacon omelets or seafood salads made with kosher substitutes can be tasty dishes.

• Consider cuisines in which there is a strong vegetarian tradition, such as those of India and China. Some of the most impoverished nations have of necessity devised delicious dishes from humble ingredients that often include little or no meat.

- Gain easy introduction to a new cuisine by first trying the desserts.
- Shop at ethnic markets for interesting nonprocessed ingredients.
- To substitute for bacon, use kosher beef fries or artificial bacon-flavored soy chips. The latter are pareve and can be used in dairy dishes. However, they are very strongly flavored, so use only about a fourth of the amount of the bacon called for in a recipe.
- To substitute for smoked pork, especially in Italian and Mexican recipes, use pastrami or salami.
- To substitute for salted pork, use corned beef.
- To substitute for boiled ham, use cooked tongue.
- To substitute for pork in casseroles and stews, use kosher sausages, hot dogs, turkey, or tofu.
- To substitute for shrimp, use any nonoily white fish, or cauliflower.
- To substitute for crab, lobster, or scallops, use fish or chicken (but not both in the same dish).
- To substitute for oysters, clams, mussels, and snails, use mushrooms or fried eggplant.
- To substitute for meat in a dairy recipe, use textured soy granules (for ground meat) or soy chunks (for stews).
- To substitute for cheese in a meat recipe—where the food is to be cooked—purée egg yolk, tofu, oil, and salt.
- To substitute for milk in a meat or pareve recipe, use nondairy creamer and water. Be sure such creamers are certified kosher. Many so-called nondairy creamers actually have milk or nonkosher ingredients.
- Other pareve substitutes for milk: coconut milk, soy milk, almond milk, pareve baby formula.
- To substitute for cream, use creamer of the same amount.
- When cream is being used to thicken, substitute 1 tablespoon cornstarch per cup of any cold liquid. Dissolve it well and add to the dish to cook for several minutes (cream is usually added when the dish is removed from the heat).
- Another nondairy thickener for soups and sauces is cooked, puréed vegetables, which also intensify the flavor of the dish.
- To substitute for 1 cup buttermilk use 1/2 cup creamer, 1/2 cup minus 2 tablespoons water, and 2 tablespoons lemon juice.
- To substitute for sour cream, add 2 tablespoons cornstarch to the above.
- In cakes, water substitutes well, in many cases, for milk. Use slightly less water than the milk called for, and add 2 tablespoons margarine per cup.
- In frying, oil may be substituted for butter or lard. However, in baking, use margarine (preferably unsalted) for butter and solid vegetable shortening for lard.

> Rabbi ben Azariah taught, "One should not say 'I have no desire to eat pork,' but rather, 'I would like to eat it, but what can I do, seeing that my Father in Heaven has commanded against it.' "
>
> –The Talmud

AFRICA

A number of African cuisines offer exciting taste sensations, and the major meat is chicken.

AFRICAN PEANUT SAUCE   [P]

A sauce to give character to leftover turkey, hard-boiled eggs, or fried tofu squares.

2 tablespoons oil	1 can coconut milk
1 large onion, chopped	1 tablespoon lemon juice
3 cloves garlic, minced	1 tablespoon soy sauce
1 (12-oz.) jar crunchy peanut	1 tablespoon sugar
butter	1 teaspoon red pepper flakes
1 (8-oz.) can tomato sauce	1/2 teaspoon ground coriander

Sauté onions and garlic in oil until tender. Add remaining ingredients, blending well, until heated through.

AMERICAN CREOLE

The food of New Orleans is one of the most distinct of American regional cuisines, influenced by French, Spanish, African, and native American styles of cooking. Alas, it is completely alien to the Jewish kitchen, as it relies heavily on pork, shellfish, and even blood sausages. The Jewish community in New Orleans has labored heroically to translate Creole dishes into the kosher idiom. Jambalaya, a word derived from the Spanish for ham, is here created with beef sausage, while chicken is substituted for the traditional shrimp. Filé powder, much used in Creole cooking, is ground sassafras leaves, a thickener as well as a flavoring agent.

JAMBALAYA   [M]

Serves 8.

1 tablespoon oil
1 lb. Italian-style sausages or
   salami, sliced
1 large onion, chopped
1 green pepper, chopped
1 clove garlic, minced
1 tablespoon filé powder
Contents of 1 (1-lb.) can
   tomatoes, chopped, with liquid

3 cups water
3 cups cooked chicken, cubed
2 cups rice
2 tablespoons Worcestershire
   sauce
1 teaspoon salt
1/2 teaspoon thyme
1/2 teaspoon hot pepper sauce
Snipped parsley

Heat oil and fry sausage until it begins to brown. Add onion, pepper, and garlic. Stir in filé powder until sauce is thickened. Add tomatoes, water, and chicken. Heat to boiling. Add rice and seasonings. Cover and cook 20 minutes or until the liquid is all absorbed. Sprinkle parsley on each serving.

AUSTRIA

Heavy Middle European cookery is not the trend these days. Austria, however, has some of the most luscious desserts in the world, some reflecting the influence of long-ago Turkish occupation. Not all are superrich.

AUSTRIAN TOAST   [D]

A fancy, easy Sunday breakfast, made with Saturday's challah leftovers. Makes 1 serving.

2 slices egg challah
2 tablespoons sweet white wine

2 tablespoons butter
Jam

Sprinkle challah with wine. Melt butter in frying pan and sauté both sides of challah until golden brown. Spread with jam.

BRAZIL

BLACK BEANS AND RICE   [P]

The people and food of Brazil are of diverse background. Black beans, with their distinctive flavor, are much used. In combination with rice they make a complete and inexpensive protein. If you add 2–3 pounds of cubed beef to this recipe, you will get a very interesting Sabbath Cholent. Or serve as is for supper with a loaf of good bread and a crisp salad.
Serves 8–10.

1 lb. black beans
2 tablespoons oil
2 onions, chopped
4 cloves garlic, minced
2 cups cooked rice
2 tablespoons bouillon powder
2 tablespoons vinegar

1 tablespoon bacon-flavored soy
   chips
1 teaspoon salt
1 teaspoon cumin
1 teaspoon oregano
1/4 teaspoon hot pepper sauce

Wash and sort beans. Soak overnight in cold water. Remove half the beans to a blender or food processor with some water. Purée and return to pot. Add enough water to cover, plus 1 quart. Bring to a boil. Meanwhile heat oil and sauté onions and garlic until tender. Pour them into the soup pot. Add remaining ingredients, stirring well. Simmer 1 hour.

CHINA

The Jews' admiration for Chinese cooking needs no explication here!

CHINESE BEEF WITH ASPARAGUS   [M]

A quick and pleasing dinner entree.
Serves 4.

2 tablespoons oil
1 lb. steak, sliced into thin
   2-inch strips
1 lb. asparagus, sliced into
   2-inch strips
2 onions, sliced thin, separated
   into rings

1/4 cup water
1 teaspoon cornstarch
3 tablespoons soy sauce
1/2 teaspoon sugar

In a wok or large skillet, stir-fry steak, asparagus, and onions until meat is brown. Lower heat, add water, cover and cook while preparing sauce. Mix cornstarch, soy sauce, and sugar until cornstarch is dissolved. Pour in sauce and continue to stir-fry until sauce thickens and coats the meat and vegetables.

HIDDEN TREASURES CHICKEN   [M]

Here's a delicious dinner you can put together quickly from leftovers and cans. If you have fresh or frozen vegetables on hand—such as broccoli, cabbage, snow peas, mushrooms—so much the better. Just add up to 3 cups of sliced vegetables instead of, or in addition to, the canned ones.
Serves 4.

3 tablespoons oil	*1 can water chestnuts, sliced*
1 onion, sliced	*1 can baby corn*
1 clove garlic, minced	*1 tablespoon cornstarch*
1/2 cup almonds, walnuts, or cashews	*1/4 cup water*
	1/4 cup soy sauce
2 cups cooked chicken in bite-size pieces	*1/2 teaspoon ginger*
	Pinch each of cinnamon, cloves, fennel, and thyme
1 stalk celery, sliced	
1 can bamboo shoots	

Heat the oil to high temperature in wok or large frying pan. Quickly stir-fry onions, garlic, and nuts until onions are translucent. Add chicken and vegetables and stir-fry until they are well-heated through. Mix rest of ingredients thoroughly in a cup. Stir in wok until sauce begins to thicken and clear. Keep stirring the dish until all the vegetables, nuts, and chicken chunks are coated with sauce. Serve immediately.

FRANCE

For a serious food lover French cuisine is the most enticing of all. For kosher cooks its greatest difficulty lies in the liberal use the French make of butter and cream in meat dishes. In many cases these ingredients are not just thickeners and emulsifiers but important taste enhancers that require the freshest and best quality dairy products. Of course there are many classic recipes that do not combine meat and dairy. Wine sauces gild many delicious meats, while fish can form the basis of an elegant French meal.

An important recent trend in French cooking is *cuisine minceur*, an attempt at eliminating many of the rich butter and cream sauces, introducing more vegetables and fruit, and simplifying some techniques. This is a good place for the kosher cook to get started on French cooking, especially as this leaner cooking uses far less pork than traditional French cooking.

Sometimes, French cooking is so complex with flavors that substituting even an important ingredient will cause little harm, as in the following dish.

FILET MIGNON WITH HERB SPREAD   [M]

Serves 4.

1 (4-oz.) stick margarine, at
    room temperature
1/4 cup finely minced fresh
    herbs: parsley, watercress, dill,
    garlic, chives, or shallots (at
    least 3 kinds)

1/2 teaspoon dried chervil
1/2 teaspoon dried tarragon
1/2 teaspoon grated lemon rind
4 filet mignons or other premium
    steaks
Meat tenderizer

Mash together margarine, fresh and dried herbs, and lemon rind. On a sheet of waxed paper or plastic wrap, form into a thick sausage shape. Place in freezer. Tenderize the meat and broil, grill, or pan-fry it. Do not overcook. Remove herb spread from freezer and place two slices on each steak. Serve with green beans and rice, on which the herb spread is also delicious.

GREECE

A blend of European and Middle Eastern styles, Greek food is of special interest and adaptability.

GREEK FISH KEBABS   [P]

This makes low-calorie barbecue fare. Each diner can thread a skewer with ingredients to taste.
Serves 6.

2 lbs. firm-fleshed fish fillets
1/2 cup dry white wine
1/4 cup olive oil
2 tablespoons lemon juice
2 scallions, minced
2 cloves garlic, minced
1/2 teaspoon oregano

1/2 teaspoon salt
Freshly ground black pepper
12 medium mushrooms
12 cherry tomatoes
2 green peppers, cut into squares
2 onions, cut into sections

Cut fish into 2 dozen cubes. Combine wine, olive oil, lemon juice, scallions, garlic, oregano, salt, and pepper. Marinate fish in this for several hours. Thread fish cubes and vegetables on skewers and barbecue or broil for 5 minutes. Brush with marinade, turn, and cook another 5 minutes. Serve with rice.

HAWAII

HAWAIIAN CHICKEN   [M]

Pork is the original and native meat of Hawaii, and the aboriginal Hawaiian cuisine is difficult to translate into a kosher idiom. However, Hawaii has become an oriental melting pot and this dish reflects Indian, Chinese, and Polynesian influences.

Serves 4.

1 bag oven-fried chicken mix
2 tablespoons curry powder
1 chicken, cut up into 8 pieces
2 cans papaya nectar
1/4 cup chopped crystallized
  ginger

1 tablespoon brown sugar
1 tablespoon cornstarch
3 tablespoons lemon juice
5 cups cooked rice
2 papayas, peeled and sliced thin
1/2 cup shredded coconut

Add curry powder to breading mix and combine well. Coat chicken pieces, arrange in a single layer in a baking pan and bake at 400° for 1 hour. Prepare sauce by cooking 1 can of nectar, ginger, and sugar to boiling. Lower flame and add second can of nectar with cornstarch dissolved in it and lemon juice. When sauce thickens, remove from heat. Arrange chicken pieces on rice-covered serving platter. Place papaya slices on chicken pieces and cover with sauce. Sprinkle coconut on top.

ITALY

Few countries have cuisines with a wider appeal. Moreover, the traditional proximity of Jewish and Italian neighborhoods in the Northeastern cities of the United States has resulted in intimate acquaintance with each others' cuisine. Italian food frequently includes combinations of meat and cheese. When the cheese amounts to no more than a few tablespoons of Parmesan, it can often be eliminated. When the cheese is prominent, it is best to make the dish dairy, substituting textured soy protein for the meat.

LASAGNA BOTH WAYS　[M or D]

Lasagna is a triumph of the Southern Italian kitchen, a happy interplay of textures and flavors. But it presents the kosher cook with a dilemma: true lasagna combines meat and cheese. Here are two kosher versions to try, one meat with a cheese substitute, the other dairy with a meat substitute. Serve either with a fresh salad. Each lasagna serves 6 to 8, and either is very good when reheated.

FOR EITHER DISH:

*1 package lasagna noodles,
boiled until tender. (All pastas
should be certified kosher, as
some brands are made with
animal-derived glycerides.)
2 tablespoons oil
1 medium onion, chopped
3 cloves garlic, finely minced*

*3 (8-oz.) cans tomato sauce
1/2 teaspoon freshly ground
pepper
1/4 cup snipped parsley
1/4 cup snipped fresh basil or 1
tablespoon dried basil
1/2 teaspoon oregano
Pinch rosemary*

Sauté onions and garlic in oil until onions are tender. Add tomato sauce, pepper, and herbs. Lower heat and simmer while preparing the rest of the dish.

FOR MEAT LASAGNA

*4 Italian sausages, diced
1 lb. ground beef
1 (15-oz.) package tofu*

*4 egg yolks
1/4 cup oil
1 teaspoon salt*

Over medium heat, cook the sausages, which will release some of their own fat. Stir in the ground beef and cook until it is all browned. In blender or processor purée the tofu, egg yolks, oil, and salt.

Place half the noodles on the bottom of a greased baking pan or casserole. Top with half the meat mixture. Pour on half of the tomato sauce. Spread with half of the tofu purée. Repeat with the remainder of the noodles and of each mixture. Bake in 350° oven for 40 minutes.

FOR DAIRY LASAGNA:

*3/4 cup soy protein granules
3/4 cup boiling water
1 (10-oz.) package frozen
chopped spinach, thawed
2 cups (8-oz.) mozzarella cheese,
shredded*

*1 cup (4-oz.) Gouda cheese,
shredded
1 lb. low-fat, small-curd cottage
cheese
3 tablespoons grated Parmesan
cheese*

Soak soy granules in salted boiling water for 10 minutes. Mix with chopped spinach. Combine mozzarella, Gouda, and cottage cheeses.

Place half the lasagna noodles on the bottom of a greased baking pan or casserole. Top with half the soy-spinach mixture. Pour on half the tomato sauce. Layer with half the cheese mixture. Repeat with remaining noodles and each mixture. Sprinkle with Parmesan cheese. Bake in 350° oven for 40 minutes.

PASTA PRIMAVERA [D]

Italian pasta is not necessarily eaten with tomato sauce. This dish incorporates a variety of vegetables into a filling and nutritious sauce.
Serves 4.

8 oz. macaroni, shells, or other small pasta
1/4 cup butter or margarine
3 scallions, sliced into small pieces
1 zucchini, shredded
1 carrot, shredded
1 cup cauliflower, broken into small florets
1 cup broccoli, broken into small florets

1/2 cup sliced mushrooms
1 clove garlic, minced
2 tablespoons flour
1 cup milk
1/4 teaspoon salt
1/4 teaspoon pepper
1/4 teaspoon basil
4 oz. mozzarella or Muenster cheese, sliced
Parmesan cheese

Cook pasta according to package directions. Melt butter or margarine and cook the vegetables briefly. Sprinkle on the flour and blend well. Add milk gradually, stirring constantly while sauce thickens. Stir in salt, pepper, and basil. Stir in cheese slices until they melt. Serve sauce on pasta. Sprinkle with Parmesan cheese.

The word "scallion" comes to English by way of Latin. The Romans imported their best spring onions from Judaea, shipping them through the seaport of Ascalon (modern Israel's Ashkelon).

JAMAICA

There are many unique spices in this zesty cuisine, as well as exotic fruits.

CARIBBEAN ICE CREAM   [P]

A refreshing hot-weather dessert.
Serves 6.

2 cups coconut milk
1 cup sugar
2 fresh limes

1/2 cup crystallized ginger,
    chopped

Combine coconut milk and sugar and freeze for 1 hour. Stir in the grated rind and juice of the limes and the ginger. Freeze for at least 2 more hours.

JAPAN

Japanese cooking opens new vistas to the kosher cook. Much of it is light, healthful, and delicately seasoned. Like Chinese cuisine, it rarely uses dairy products, so many meat recipes can be used as is. While favoring many nonkosher seafoods, the Japanese also make very original use of kosher fish.

JAPANESE STEAK   [M]

True to the Japanese sense of form, this is a beautiful, as well as flavorful, treatment of that old favorite.
Serves 4.

4 boneless rib steaks
1/4 cup soy sauce
1/4 cup margarine
1 lb. bean sprouts
1/4 cup lemon juice

1 teaspoon sugar
Freshly ground black pepper
1 (8-oz.) can mandarin oranges,
    drained

Brush steaks with soy sauce and broil to desired doneness. Melt margarine in frying pan and sauté bean sprouts until golden. Add lemon juice, sugar, and pepper, and any soy sauce left over from the steaks. Stir until well blended. Stir in mandarin oranges just until heated. Ladle sauce onto steaks. Serve with rice.

MEXICO

Mexican food appeals to those who like filling but not heavy food. However, it uses a great deal of pork, and lard is the predominant fat. In addition, many dishes combine cheese or sour cream with meat. But adaptations are possible—and tasty.

MEXICAN FISH   [P]

This toothsome alternative to fried fish is easy to prepare.
Serves 4.

1 (7-oz.) bag of corn or tortilla
* chips*
1 egg, beaten with a tablespoon
* of water*

1 lb. fish fillets, rinsed and dried
1 (1-lb.) can stewed tomatoes
1–3 teaspoons chili powder

Preheat oven to 450°. Crush chips in a food processor. Coat fish in egg, then press into crushed chips. Place the fish in a single layer in a lightly greased nonstick baking pan. Bake 10 minutes. Meanwhile, pour the stewed tomatoes with their juice into a small pan. While heating, crush the tomatoes with a fork. Add chili powder and simmer for 10 minutes. Pour sauce over fish or serve the sauce on the side.

> When moving to a new location, always check out the varieties of fish locally available. To be kosher they must have both fins and scales. Do not depend on names; see for yourself. Turbot, for example, is the popular name for several types of fish from both Atlantic and Pacific. Some are kosher, others are not.

THE SOUTH PACIFIC

The kosher cook is at first attracted to the cooking of the South Pacific, which, for most of us, is the epitome of exotic locales. Yet he or she can grow quickly disappointed, since so many of the dishes are based on pork, nonkosher seafood, and hard-to-obtain fruits.

Nevertheless many of the Polynesian specialties can be achieved in a modified kosher form. They offer a refreshingly different culinary point of view.

BALINESE CHICKEN SOUP WITH GARNISHES   [M]

This soup serves 4–6 as a first course (perhaps of a luau), or, if all of the chicken meat is used and the garnishes doubled, an entire meal in itself.

2 tablespoons oil	*1 (3-lb.) chicken*
1 onion, chopped	*3 teaspoons instant beef bouillon*
2 cloves garlic, finely minced	*1 teaspoon coriander*
6 macadamia nuts, ground	*1/2 teaspoon turmeric*

In a large pot sauté the onions, garlic, and nuts in oil until the onion is tender. Add the chicken and enough water to cover. Bring to a boil. Add bouillon, coriander, and turmeric. Lower heat and cook for about 1 1/2 hours or until chicken is very tender. Remove chicken from soup. Skin and bone the chicken breast. Shred the white meat and return it to the pot. Cook for another 15 minutes. Arrange the following garnishes in colorful heaps on one or more platters. Encourage the diners to try each of the garnishes in his soup.

1 (5-oz.) bag potato chips	*1/2 cup chopped watercress or*
1 cup Chinese noodles	*parsley*
1 cup bean sprouts	*3 pickled hot red peppers, seeded*
1 cup finely shredded cabbage	*and cut into strips*
3 hard-boiled eggs, thinly sliced	*2 limes, sliced*

SCANDINAVIA

While it is true that the Scandinavians favor pork as their meat, they are so inventive with so many different types of foods that the adventurous will do well to experiment here. Surprisingly for the climate, there are numerous light dishes on the Scandinavian menu—even oriental influences. The Scandinavians treat many foods familiar to Jews—lox, herring, sour cream, cheese, winter vegetables, fruit soups, coffee cakes—in refreshingly different ways.

SWEET COLE SLAW

Serves 6–8.

1/4 cup grape jam
1/4 cup lemon juice
1 small head red cabbage, shredded

Mix the grape jam and lemon juice together very well. Toss with shredded cabbage.

THE DEEP SOUTH

The cooking of the American South is a lot like traditional Jewish cooking in that both are remembered with nostalgia but neither is quite suitable as daily fare for today's health-conscious diet planners. Much of Southern cooking is based on ham and bacon, usually in a preserved form. Cooking fat is usually lard. The major seafoods are catfish, crawfish, crabs, and shrimp—none kosher. But the South can broaden kosher cuisine by introducing novel ways with grains and legumes, as in this traditional side dish.

Serves 6–8.

HOPPIN' JOHN

2 cups black-eyed peas
1 tablespoon bacon-flavored soy
   chips

1 teaspoon salt
1 cup rice

Soak black-eyed peas in water overnight or simmer for 2 hours. Add water, if necessary, to make at least 2 cups of liquid. Stir in soy chips and salt. Bring to boil. Lower heat and stir in rice. Cover and cook 20 minutes or until liquid is absorbed.

> The Talmud recommends a fish called *shibuta,* whose flesh resembles the pig's in flavor. But for two thousand years no one has been able to identify it.

SPAIN

Since the expulsion of the Jews from Spain in 1492 until modern times, few Jews had ventured into Spain. The brilliant cuisine of the Spanish Jews has its roots in the Moorish Age. Christian Spaniards developed a style of cooking based almost entirely on pork. Even so, Spanish food has a sunny, Mediterranean cast that fits right in with the new Jewish cuisine.

SPANISH DIP AND CANAPÉS   [M]

Makes approximately 2 cups.

1/4 lb. pastrami, chopped fine
1 (6-oz.) can chopped black
   olives
1 red bell pepper, seeded and
   chopped fine

2 cloves garlic, minced
1/2 cup mayonnaise

Mix all ingredients together thoroughly. Serve with Melba toast and raw vegetables.

Canapés: thin slice of corned beef wrapped around a pitted date, fastened with a toothpick; large, pitted green and black olives, stuffed with whole almonds.

VIETNAM

VIETNAMESE CORN-CHICKEN SOUP   [M]

Vietnamese cooking uses liberal amounts of fish sauce, the fermented product of various seafoods, including nonkosher fish. Worcestershire sauce is also a salty flavoring containing (kosher) fish. The combination of meat or fowl with fish is forbidden by ancient law for safety reasons. However, according to most contemporary rabbis, the amount of fish in this versatile condiment is so small that it may be used with meat dishes.
Serves 6.

6 cups cold water
2 chicken legs and thighs
1 (15-oz.) can creamed corn
1 tablespoon chicken bouillon
   powder
1 tablespoon dry white wine

2 teaspoons Worcestershire sauce
1 teaspoon vinegar
1 teaspoon garlic salt
1 egg, beaten
Freshly ground black pepper

Place chicken in the water and bring to a boil. Cover and cook over medium heat for 30 minutes. Remove chicken from pot. Skin and bone the chicken and shred the meat. Return the meat to the pot. Add corn and seasonings. Bring to a boil, then simmer, stirring, for 5 minutes. Add egg and separate it into filaments by stirring the soup with a fork. Sprinkle each serving with pepper.

BEERMEAT [M]

Fair warning! Questions of kashrut aside, bear and other large game have a powerful flavor that is not to everyone's taste. This dish, from a recipe for wild game, is also very strongly flavored.
Serves 6.

3 lbs. chuck roast, sliced 1/2 inch
  thick
2 tablespoons oil
2 large onions, sliced
2 cloves garlic, minced
1 (8-oz.) can tomato sauce
1 cup water

2 tablespoons sugar
1 tablespoon bouillon powder
1/2 teaspoon salt
1/2 teaspoon thyme
1/2 teaspoon chervil
Freshly ground black pepper
1 (12-oz.) can beer

Brown beef in oil. Remove from pan. Sauté onions until tender. Add garlic and sauté 2 minutes more. Add tomato sauce and water, bringing to a boil, then lower heat to simmer. Add seasonings, stirring well. Remove from heat and add beer. Return meat to pan and refrigerate immediately. Marinate overnight or longer, turning meat occasionally. Simmer meat for an hour before serving, or remove meat slices from marinade and broil for 3 minutes on each side.

LOW-CALORIE BLT [D]

A visually appealing lunch for a dieter.
Makes 1 serving.

1/2 cup low-fat cottage cheese
1 scallion, chopped, or 1
  tablespoon snipped fresh
  chives
1 tablespoon snipped parsley
1 teaspoon bacon-flavored soy
  chips

1/4 teaspoon oregano
Salt and pepper to taste
Lettuce
1 small tomato, sliced
Melba toast

Mix cottage cheese with scallion, parsley, soy chips, oregano, salt, and pepper. Arrange on a bed of lettuce and surround with tomato slices and Melba toast.

OYSTERS ROCKEFELLER   [P]

Oyster mushrooms, which some claim resemble the real thing, are a delight in themselves. With this stuffing they are as opulent as their title suggests. Serves 4.

1/4 cup margarine
1/4 cup chopped spinach
1/2 small onion, chopped
1/2 stalk celery, chopped
2 tablespoons snipped parsley
1/2 teaspoon bacon-flavored soy chips

1/4 cup fine dry bread crumbs
Dash salt
Dash hot pepper sauce
24 oyster mushrooms
Anisette or arak

Melt margarine and sauté spinach, onions, celery, parsley, and soy chips for 5 minutes. Purée in blender or food processor. Stir in bread crumbs, salt, and pepper sauce. Place mushrooms caps down on a baking pan. Top each mushroom with a teaspoon of filling. Sprinkle liqueur over all. Broil for 5 minutes, or until top begins to brown. Serve immediately.

"PORK" FRIED RICE   [M]

When leftover cold cuts find no takers, toss them into this hearty side dish. Serves 4.

3 tablespoons oil (preferably sesame)
4 scallions, chopped
4 cups cooked rice
1/4 head cabbage (preferably bok choy)
1/2 lb. pastrami or corned beef, shredded

1 tablespoon grated fresh ginger
1/2 teaspoon beef bouillon powder
1/2 teaspoon sugar
2 tablespoons soy sauce
3 eggs, well beaten

Heat oil in a wok or large frying pan. Stir-fry the scallions for 1 minute. Add rice and stir-fry for 3 minutes. Add cabbage and stir-fry 3 minutes more. Add meat and seasonings, frying until heated through. Make a hole in middle and add the eggs. When they have set, mix them through the rice. Serve immediately.

"PROSCIUTTO" HORS D'OEUVRE   [M]

Easily prepared the day before a party. Also makes an attractive appetizer. Makes about 2 dozen small servings.

2 small honeydew melons
1/2 cup of light rum or 80-proof vodka
1/4 lb. thinly sliced corned beef

Slice the melons into thin sections and peel. Pour rum or vodka over the slices and cover tightly. Marinate in the refrigerator for several hours or overnight. Wrap each slice of melon with a slice of corned beef and secure with a fancy toothpick.

FRENCH "RABBIT"   [M]

An *haute* French recipe that makes an elegant party dish of turkey. Serves 4.

2 turkey legs with thighs
1 cup dry red wine
2 tablespoons vinegar
1 teaspoon thyme
1/2 teaspoon garlic powder
1/2 teaspoon salt

Freshly ground pepper
1/4 cup oil
1 (5-oz.) package dried apricots
1 cup chicken soup, fresh or
*   canned*

Bone the turkey legs and cut the meat into bite-size pieces. Make a marinade of the wine, vinegar, thyme, and garlic powder. Stir the turkey in the marinade, cover tightly, and refrigerate overnight.

Remove turkey from marinade, reserving the liquid. Dry the meat and season with salt and pepper. Heat oil in a pan and brown the turkey in it. Add reserved marinade, apricots, and chicken soup. Cover and simmer for 30 minutes. Serve with noodles.

"SHRIMP" COCKTAIL   [P]

As with many dishes, it's all in the sauce. These cocktails are so spicy the only thing one notices about the underlying food is its texture—close enough to shrimp.
Serves 4.

1 tomato, diced
2 scallions, minced
1 small clove garlic, minced
3 tablespoons snipped parsley
3 tablespoons lemon juice
1 tablespoon ketchup

1 tablespoon horseradish
1/4 teaspoon chili powder
1/4 teaspoon hot pepper sauce
3 drops Worcestershire sauce
1 head cauliflower

Put all ingredients except cauliflower in a jar and shake well. Refrigerate for at least 1 hour. Break the cauliflower into small florets and place in ice cream dishes or parfait glasses. Pour sauce over cauliflower.

> Israeli aquaculturists recently began cultivating giant prawns from Southeast Asian waters. These giant shrimp have thrived in Israel; they grow to a size—and fetch a price—greater than those of any other prawns in the world. The entire catch of the nonkosher seafood is exported to the European gourmet market.

Cooking for the Sabbath

"He who labors before the Sabbath shall feast upon the Sabbath." This Hebrew proverb represents a weekly realized fact of Jewish life, as well as a veiled reference to the duties of this world, and the pleasures of the world to come. The Sabbath meals require forethought and preparation; not by happenstance does the family table become the holy altar, the spirit and heart, of the Sabbath experience.

The Fourth Commandment is couched in two different terms, "Remember the Sabbath day to make it holy," and "Honor the Sabbath day to keep it holy." Why the change in language? The Sages taught that one is for the positive acts of observing the Sabbath, making it special, the second, for refraining from those activities that desecrate the Sabbath, jar its spirit, and prevent the individual from knowing its holiness.

Where food is concerned, one "remembers" the Sabbath by preparing for it the most desirable and delightful dishes one can afford. One "honors" the Sabbath by refraining from cooking and other acts of food preparation, including: turning any source of flame or heat on, off, higher, or lower; beginning or terminating the use of any electrical appliance; using a mortar, mill, or similar mechanical tool for food preparation; kneading or preparing dough; picking out undesirable parts of foods to be presented at the table.

The positive and negative aspects of Sabbath observance thus present a challenge: how to prepare the most pleasing of dishes long before they are consumed. Historically, this challenge has been met with brilliant élan. The most distinctively Jewish dishes have been invented to meet the special needs of the Sabbath.

If hot foods are desired, the kitchen must be made to accommodate the Sabbath laws. One or two stove burners can be left on a low flame with a *blech* (Yiddish for tin) on the gas or electric burners. This is a plain metal sheet, which fulfills the requirement prohibiting leaving food on a direct flame. A round asbestos pad also serves this purpose. To keep foods warm throughout the Sabbath it is also possible to leave an oven on a very low setting (no direct flame or heating element touches the pots). An electric hot pot is useful for keeping water available for making tea and coffee, as boiling water is prohibited. Other convenience appliances come in handy, as long as they maintain the heat of cooked foods. They may not be used to cook raw foods, or continue the cooking process in a significant way.

Food served on the Sabbath should be edible before the Sabbath. It need not be fully cooked, however. For example, if a cholent stew is prepared, the meat should be browned before the Sabbath. It need not be cooked as well done as the diners like it. Potatoes must be cooked for a few minutes before the Sabbath, as raw potatoes are usually considered inedible. In warming overnight, the stew will, of course, result in supertender meat and melting potatoes.

The commandment to remember the Sabbath is incumbent on everyone, male and female, and it is customary among traditional Jews to have the men of the household contribute in some way to preparing the food. Where cooking is the province of the women, men often do some of the shopping or cleanup. The Talmud tells of one rabbi who was credited with fulfilling the commandment "Remember the Sabbath" every day. On Sunday he would shop for the finest provisions to be had and would save them for the Sabbath. He would go shopping every succeeding day, and if he found a better food, he would save that one for the Sabbath and eat the food he bought previously.

Traditional foods for the Sabbath incorporate that which is "best." These usually mean fish, meat, poultry, white bread, fancy fruits, and sweets. All of these were luxuries for most Jews prior to modern times.

The typical menu for the Sabbath (regional differences were slight) might include:

Friday night dinner. This is served after evening synagogue services, the time varying with sundown. In the winter this meal might be eaten as early as 5 P.M., in the summer, as late as 9:30. The meal must begin with blessing the wine, ritual hand-washing, and blessing the challah, a fine bread. The first course was customarily fish, either gefilte, in aspic, or in some other cold form. Legendary chicken soup came next, usually with some form of dumpling or crouton. The chicken itself was the main course—it was considered the most digestible meat to eat late in the evening—accompanied by cooked vegetable side dishes. A compote and/or cake served as dessert.

Sabbath breakfast. Not considered a meal, often skipped altogether. For those who require some food before synagogue services, pastry with tea or coffee is served.

Kiddush. The repast immediately after morning services must include wine or liquor and some other refreshment. Often this is served in the synagogue itself. The food might include a small snack of pastries or a quasi-meal with a hot and cold buffet. However, bread is not served.

Sabbath dinner. This meal is the largest and most leisurely. It begins with challah. The first course is usually a cold fish, pâté, or cold soup. The main course often has several hot dishes, including cholent (a distinctive stew), stuffed derma (a flour sausage), kugel (a starchy casserole), and baked or stewed meats. In summer the latter is replaced by cold meats. Salads like cole slaw and potato salad intersperse the hot foods. An elaborate dessert follows.

Snacks. The afternoon is a time of leisure and neighborhood visiting. Hot and cold drinks, fresh fruit, nuts, and cakes are nibbled.

Seuda Shlishit, "The Third Feast." The early evening meal on Saturday is a simple one and always cold. Fish, such as pickled herring and smoked whitefish, egg salad, and vegetable salads compose the meal. It is often dispensed with in winter, when the Sabbath ends early.

Melave Malka, "Accompanying the Bride." (The Sabbath Queen is the mystical bride of Israel.) A post-Sabbath meal, Saturday night, honors the Sabbath in its going. This meal is rarely eaten by the family, but is a good excuse for all kinds of parties and social get-togethers. No Sabbath restrictions apply to cooking after the Sabbath, consequently, the meal can take the form of anything from dips-and-chips to catered affair. It is most usual in winter, when the Sabbath ends early.

Some new trends in Sabbath cooking:

• Fresh vegetable salads (which may be made on the Sabbath) accompany each major meal.

• Chicken soup is being replaced by other soups, with the chicken prepared in ways other than boiling for the Friday night meal.

• The main Saturday meal features only one meat course, which may be the cholent or a cold chicken or turkey dish.

• Grain dishes, such as tabouleh, and marinated vegetables are replacing some of the starchy side dishes.

• Compote desserts are being replaced by fresh fruit and pareve frozen desserts.

While arrangements are usually made to keep foods eaten on Saturday hot overnight, it is often inconvenient and wasteful to leave a burner or oven going all day for a food to be eaten at the Friday night meal. The main course will usually retain some warmth if it is heated right before the Sabbath. Soup, however, might be distressingly tepid by the time the prayers and amenities are completed. Energy-conscious cooks are bringing back a method of heat preservation much appreciated in the colder parts of Europe. The soup is heated to boiling just before the Sabbath begins. The pot is wrapped in a large towel, placed at the foot-end of a bed, and covered with quilts. The soup will stay warm—and the bed will feel toasty.

If you have a waterbed, do not try this method! Instead wrap the pot in several blankets. The soup will stay piping hot for two or more hours.

CHALLAH [P]

Special bread for the Sabbath is a sacred obligation. In most places where Jews have lived the custom was to eat dark, grainy bread during the week and light, soft, sweet bread on the Sabbath. Egg is often used, so much so that many commercial bakers call it "egg bread." However, Jews from some parts of Europe use no eggs and only a little sugar. The effect is that of a large, fluffy French bread. Saffron is sometimes used to flavor and color the challah, and because it is the most expensive of spices, to show honor to the Sabbath.

The following is a traditional sweet egg recipe.

Makes 4 loaves.

2 packages yeast
1 1/2 cups warm water
5 tablespoons sugar
4 eggs
1/2 cup oil
1/4 cup honey

2 teaspoons salt
7–8 cups flour
1 egg yolk, beaten with 1
tablespoon water
Poppy or sesame seeds

Dissolve yeast in the warm water, to which 1 tablespoon of the sugar has been added. Wait 5 minutes for yeast to activate. Mix in remaining sugar. Beat in eggs one at a time. Beat in oil and honey. Stir in salt. Stir in flour 1 cup at a time until mixture is a sticky dough. Turn out on a floured board and add more flour, kneading until a soft, smooth dough is formed, at least 10 minutes. Place in a greased bowl, cover with a dish towel, and let rise until double in bulk, about 1 1/2 hours. Punch down dough and knead gently for 5 minutes. Pinch off a piece of dough the size of a Ping-Pong ball for the ritual challah. Burn or discard in a paper napkin. Divide dough in four parts. Braid each piece or twist it into a round shape. Set on a lightly greased baking sheet. Cover lightly and let rise again, about 1 hour. Brush with egg-yolk wash and sprinkle with poppy or sesame seeds. Place in a cold oven. Set temperature to 350° and bake for 1 hour and 10 minutes.

For challah success:
- Use fresh yeast. Try the new quick yeasts.
- Bread flour is preferable to all-purpose flour.
- Have water at 110°, about the temperature of a baby's bath.
- Knead adequately.
- Let rise in warm area. In cold weather use the oven with a bowl of boiling water placed in it, or the top of a clothes drier, or the top of a refrigerator.
- Provide adequate moisture. In very dry weather wet the dish towel in warm water and wring out.

TWO CHALLAHS, NO WAITING   [P]

The fastest possible recipe, when there is no time for yeast dough to rise.

2 eggs
1/3 cup sugar
1/3 cup margarine, melted
1 1/2 cups water
5 cups flour
2 tablespoons baking powder

1/2 teaspoon salt
1/2 cup raisins (optional)
*1 egg yolk, beaten with 1
  tablespoon water*
Poppy or sesame seeds

Beat eggs, sugar, margarine, and water together with mixer or egg beater. Sift together dry ingredients. Add to moist ingredients a cup at a time, stirring well after each. Add raisins, if desired. Remove a piece of dough the size of a Ping-Pong ball for the ritual "challah." Burn it or discard in a paper napkin. Divide the dough in two. Braid, or fashion round challahs. Place on a greased baking pan. Brush with egg-yolk wash and sprinkle with poppy or sesame seeds. Bake at 350° for 1 hour.

YEMENITE CHALLAH   [P]

A true Sabbath bread, kept hot until the Sabbath midmorning meal, when it is eaten with Yemenite Eggs or jam.
Makes 1 large loaf.

1 cup warm water
1 package yeast
3 tablespoons sugar

2–3 cups flour
*1/2 cup salted margarine, at
  room temperature*

Combine water, yeast, and sugar. Wait 5 minutes for yeast to begin action. Gradually add flour until a firm dough is formed. Knead well. Place in a greased bowl, cover with a dish towel, and let rise until doubled, about 1 1/2 hours. Pinch off ritual challah—a piece the size of a walnut—and burn it or discard in a paper napkin. Pinch off egg-sized pieces of dough. Roll out each piece until paper-thin. Spread margarine on top, fold in half, and roll up tightly. Grease a large heavy pot and place the rolls of dough in it in a tight-fitting arrangement. Cover with cloth and let rise 1 hour. Brush with margarine and cover with a tight-fitting pot lid. Bake at 325° for 1 hour. Leave overnight on a *blech* or in a warm oven.

GARLIC CROUTONS   [P]

It is traditional to have some sort of dumpling or noodle in the soup—whether matzoh balls, wontonlike kreplach, feathery *mandlen,* soup nuts, egg noodles, or farfel. If you are in a hurry, no soup addition is faster than this one, which also includes another Friday-night tradition, garlic.
Serves 4.

2 matzohs
1 plump clove garlic

Split the clove of garlic lengthwise and rub over both sides of each matzoh. Break matzohs into bite-size pieces and drop into hot soup.

YEMENITE EGGS   [P]

A treat for Sabbath. Can be served as an appetizer, or with the Cholent. Serve each egg with a lemon wedge.
Serves 6.

6 eggs
1/4 cup olive oil
Skin of 1 onion

2 tablespoons coffee grounds
1 teaspoon salt
1/2 teaspoon pepper

Put all ingredients in a heavy pot. Add water to cover. Bring to boil, then simmer for 10 minutes. Cover pot and place on a *blech* or in a warm oven overnight.

BREAKFAST CAKE   [P]

Nutritious and not too sweet, this cake is just right for Saturday morning, when tradition and common sense both dictate a light breakfast.

11/2 cups whole wheat flour
1/2 cup oats
2 teaspoons baking powder
1/4 teaspoon baking soda
1/2 teaspoon salt
1/2 teaspoon cinnamon
1/3 cup margarine

3/4 cup brown sugar, packed
   firmly
2 eggs
1 teaspoon vanilla
1 teaspoon almond extract
2 firm fruits, apples, pears, or
   peaches, peeled and shredded

Preheat oven to 350°. In a large bowl, mix flour, oats, baking powder, baking soda, salt, and cinnamon. Melt margarine and sugar, stirring. Remove from heat and beat in eggs and extracts. Stir in shredded fruit. Pour mixture into the dry ingredients and mix only until moistened. Pour batter into greased baking pan. Bake 35 minutes or until wooden toothpick tests clean.

EGG SALAD   [P]

This tastes especially good on matzoh and makes a fine appetizer or week-day lunch.
Serves 6–8.

6 hard-boiled eggs	1/2 teaspoon salt
2 potatoes, boiled and peeled	1/4 teaspoon pepper
1 sweet red onion, chopped fine	Mayonnaise or oil
1 pickle, chopped fine	

Mash the eggs and potatoes together with a fork. Stir in onion, pickle, salt, and pepper. Add just enough mayonnaise or oil to make the salad spreadable.

Cold soup is a classic Sabbath first course in summer (year-round in warmer climates). It is most refreshing in itself and a perfect foil if hot Cholent is to follow. In Europe this was invariably fruit soup, which included sour cherries, apples, quince, and whatever else was available in season. The possibilities are wider today.

BLUEBERRY SOUP   [P]

A deliciously clear taste, and beautiful to look at.
Serves 4.

1 basket fresh blueberries	1/3 cup sugar
(2 cups)	2 tablespoons cornstarch
1 quart water	1 teaspoon grated lemon peel

Wash the blueberries and bring them to a boil with the water and sugar. Lower heat and simmer 10 minutes. Dissolve cornstarch in a little water and add to soup. Stir and simmer 5 minutes more. Remove from heat, stir in lemon peel. Chill overnight.

"Prepare the feast of perfect faith, the joy of the holy King/Prepare
the feast of the King, the feast of the field of sacred apples/ . . .
God's Presence rests upon the people/She takes pleasure in delicacies and sweets." (From a table hymn by Rabbi Isaac Luria, six-
teenth-century kabbalist of Safed, Israel.)

ALMOND-GRAPE SOUP   [P]

A cinch to prepare; elegant to serve.
Serves 4.

1½ cups blanched almonds
1 cup seedless green grapes
2 cups water
1 cup Sauterne

2 tablespoons oil
1/2 teaspoon salt
1/4 teaspoon garlic powder

Place chopping blade in food processor and grind the almonds until very
fine. Add grapes and purée. Add remaining ingredients, mixing well. Refrigerate
overnight.

"On Friday we arrange all manner of delicacies/While it is yet day we
prepare stuffed fowl/We provide a variety of delights, and scented
wines/To pamper ourselves with delicacies at all three meals/To indulge in luxuries,/Swans, quails, and fish." (From a table hymn by
the composer Menahem, 1545.)

GAZPACHO   [P]

Wonderful, with enough substance to balance a summer meal where the
entree is cold sliced meat.
Serves 6–8.

3 cups vegetable broth
4 cups tomato juice
1/4 cup lemon juice
2 ripe tomatoes
2 green peppers
2 cucumbers, peeled

1 large sweet red onion
1/2 cup snipped parsley
3 cloves garlic
1 teaspoon salt
1/4 teaspoon hot pepper sauce

Combine broth and juices in a tureen. Dice tomatoes, peppers, cucumbers, and onion, or shred in a food processor. Add to liquid. Stir in parsley. Peel garlic cloves, halve each and impale on toothpicks. Stir in with salt and red pepper flakes. Refrigerate overnight. Just before serving, remove toothpicks with garlic, and stir well. Place an ice cube in each bowl of soup.

"If you observe the Sabbath, God will protect you/Like the apple of his eye/Your son and daughter also will he protect/Declare the Sabbath pleasure, and you will be granted Divine pleasure/Today is the Sabbath of God.

"Eat rich foods and delicacies/And sample exquisite morsels/Soft-shelled nuts and pomegranates/Eat and be satisfied and bless the Lord/Today is the Sabbath of God." (Medieval table hymn.)

CREAM OF CAULIFLOWER OR BROCCOLI SOUP   [P]

Serve this at room temperature, with croutons. On other occasions you can serve it hot, as well.
Serves 6.

2 lbs. fresh or frozen cauliflower *or broccoli*	*1/4 cup flour* *4 cups vegetable broth*
1/4 cup margarine	*1/2 teaspoon salt*
1 onion, chopped	*Freshly ground pepper*
1 stalk celery, chopped	*Paprika*
1 carrot, shredded	*Shredded lettuce*

Steam the cauliflower or broccoli until tender. Heat the margarine and sauté onion, celery, and carrot. Stir in flour, making a smooth paste. Add broth a cup at a time, stirring until smooth. Add cauliflower or broccoli, salt, and pepper. When soup boils, lower heat, cover, and simmer for 20 minutes. Purée in a food processor or blender. Garnish each bowl with a dusting of paprika and some shredded lettuce.

SESAME-TOMATO DIP   [P]

Since the main course of the Sabbath meal is often substantial, and accompanied by serious side dishes, you may choose simpler appetizers to precede them, perhaps in the style of hors d'oeuvres. This dip, based on a Mexican sauce, may be served hot, cold, or at room temperature. Accompany the dip with corn chips and raw vegetables, including sticks of radishlike jicama.
Serves 4–6.

1/4 cup sesame seeds
1 tablespoon oil
1/2 onion, chopped
2 cloves garlic, finely minced
2 cups tomato juice
1/4 cup snipped parsley
1 cube vegetable broth

1/2 teaspoon salt
1 teaspoon paprika
1 teaspoon cumin
1/2 teaspoon oregano
1/4 teaspoon hot pepper sauce
1/4 teaspoon cinnamon
Pinch cloves

In an ungreased saucepan, over medium heat, toast the sesame seeds. They will pop wildly. Chop the seeds in a blender or processor. Add oil to saucepan, sauté onion and garlic until tender. Return crushed seeds to saucepan and add all other ingredients. Heat to boiling. Reduce heat and simmer, stirring occasionally, for 5 minutes.

STEAMED ARTICHOKES   [P]

The artichoke was a symbol of good luck to the Jews of Renaissance Italy. It appears as an artistic motif on marriage contracts and other decorated religious objects. To Jews in other communities, the artichoke was unknown, and at first sighting—usually in New York's ethnic markets—threateningly thorny and prohibitively expensive.

Artichokes, once you have gotten used to them, can be addictive. They are considerably more fussy to prepare than, say, a stalk of celery. But your efforts of preparation will be rewarded when you serve and eat this delicious, elegant vegetable.

Very small artichokes have their fans; they can sometimes be eaten whole. However, most people prefer the larger sizes that are such fun to disassemble leaf by leaf. Choose vegetables with leaves that are tightly closed.

Hold the artichoke by the stem and rinse under running water. Rinse again —sand and bugs fit snugly into the leaves—by submerging in a large bowl of water.

With scissors, snip the thorny top of each leaf. Then, with a sharp knife, cut off the top of the artichoke where the leaves are too small and tightly packed to trim individually. Cut off the very bottom of the stalk. Peel off the small leaves that grow on the stalk below the head of the artichoke.

Place artichokes in a steamer (any direction). Be sure that there is plenty of water as artichokes need a long time to cook. Large artichokes require 45–60 minutes of vigorous steaming. If the cover does not fit tightly, you may need to add boiling water during the steaming.

If you have no steamer you can cook artichokes by standing them on their stems in an inch or two of boiling water. Cover and continue to boil gently for 45–60 minutes. In this case you can add lemon juice and olive oil to the water for flavor, but some of the vegetable's natural flavor and nutrients will be lost in the cooking process.

Test for doneness by peeling off one of the bottom leaves. It should come off easily. Scrape the inside of the leaf with your upper or lower teeth. If the artichoke is cooked, there will be some tasty "meat" even on the bottom leaves. Artichokes taste good, and somewhat different, whether served hot, at room temperature, or cold. Cold artichokes are best with dressings and dips.

A medium artichoke makes an ample appetizer; the jumbo size serves two. In the latter case cut the artichoke down the center, or serve on a single plate between two people and observe how this vegetable attained its reputation as an aphrodisiac!

Artichokes are finger food, but you should place a teaspoon or serrated grapefruit spoon at each place for removing the choke.

The kibbutz tradition of the *kolboynik* will be appreciated when artichokes are served. The kolboynik is a receptacle for organic refuse placed among several settings. It often seems that the artichoke is larger after it is eaten than before.

To eat an artichoke peel off a leaf, dip the tender end in sauce, and scrape its interior with your upper or lower front teeth. Discard the rest of the leaf. As you work your way to the top of the artichoke, the leaves become progressively more tender. Toward the top the leaves are entirely edible. When all the leaves have been removed, the stem, heart, and choke will be visible. Scrape the fuzzy choke out with a spoon and discard it. The heart and stem are the rewards for your hard work!

Virtually any sauce or dip complements artichokes. You can serve a variety of the following:

Lemon juice and/or olive oil　　　*Bottled salad dressings*
Melted butter or margarine　　　*Horseradish sauce*
Mayonnaise　　　　　　　　　　*Chili sauce*
Yogurt-based dressings

The preferred beverage with artichokes is plain cold water, which will taste exceptionally sweet.

MARINATED ARTICHOKE HEARTS　[P]

These artichokes glorify any salad in which they are tossed. Or serve the artichoke hearts as an appetizer with lettuce and tomato wedges and reserve any leftover marinade for salad dressing.

1 package frozen artichoke hearts　　　*1 small sweet red onion, minced*
1 cup fine olive oil　　　　　　　　　*　fine*
1/2 cup salad vinegar　　　　　　　　*2 cloves garlic, minced fine*

1 teaspoon oregano   *1/2 teaspoon dry mustard*
1/2 teaspoon salt   *Freshly ground black pepper*

Prepare artichoke hearts according to package directions and place in a jar. Mix remaining ingredients and pour over artichokes. Cover tightly and marinate in refrigerator for at least 24 hours.

GUACAMOLE

This is a wonderful dip, if made with the right ingredients. Choose Hass avocados, the ones with black, nubby skins. They should be fully ripe, i.e., soft but not mushy when you squeeze them. When avocados are too ripe their flesh becomes discolored. Cut away any black or gray parts as these have an unpleasant smoky flavor that will permeate the dip.

Tomatoes must also be fully ripe. Dice them with a sharp knife, discarding the seeds and juice.

Makes 2 cups or appetizer for 6.

2 avocados   *minced (if unavailable,*
3 tablespoons lemon juice   *substitute 1 teaspoon chili*
2 tomatoes, diced   *powder)*
2 tablespoons finely minced red   *2 tablespoons mayonnaise*
* onion*   *1/2 teaspoon salt*
1 canned chili pepper, finely   *1/4 teaspoon cumin*

Mash avocados and immediately sprinkle with lemon juice to prevent discoloration. Mix in remaining ingredients. If preparing ahead of time, preserve the dip's lovely color by inserting the pit and covering with plastic wrap right on the surface.

Serve with corn chips and sliced vegetables.

CHOLENT   [M]

Of all the dishes in the cuisine, the most supremely Jewish is cholent. The quintessential Sabbath stew reflects its people's customs, laws, and history in a way that no other food does. It is cholent that makes the rich, leisurely, beautiful Saturday afternoon meal "like the offering upon the altar." It is cholent that turns the prohibition against cooking on the Sabbath into a blessing. It is cholent that warms the family and guests in the glow of hospitality and love made tangible. It is cholent that has remained recognizable for at least twenty-five hundred years and is to be found in every Jewish community in the world. Cholent: butt of a thousand jokes, recipient of millions of appreciative sighs.

The word cholent is derived from the Old French for "hot." By the early Middle Ages, when significant numbers of Jews had migrated to France, the dish that was so named was already ancient. In Hebrew the name is hamin, which also means hot, and in various oriental communities words meaning "warm" or "hot" are invariably used to describe this food. Indeed, the one and only indispensable ingredient is heat.

Moses and the generation that received the Law may well have contemplated the paradox: only a hot, cooked dish could adequately honor the Sabbath, yet cooking itself is forbidden on the day to be honored. The solution, in that time, or surely soon after, was leaving a covered pot of precooked foods that do not disintegrate or spoil in prolonged heating to simmer from before the Sabbath until the time of the main Sabbath meal. Legumes, grains, meat, hard vegetables, and spices may have been used from the very earliest Sabbaths.

Certainly by the time of the Talmud, cholent, called simply "the Sabbath dish," had become so famous, that many non-Jews were familiar with it and the special place it held in Jewish cuisine. Later, wherever the Jews settled, they adopted some local elements into their cholents, retained some others. Many other nations had long-simmering stews of their own, but never were they to be wholly confused with cholent, a dish that remains uniquely tied with Judaism. (One rarely finds cholent in "kosher-style" restaurants or cookbooks, and no wonder. Cholent without the Sabbath and its customs is gravel in the mouth and cement in the stomach.)

The emperor Hadrian had tasted the special stew of the Judaeans and was much impressed. He ordered his imperial chefs to prepare the dish for him. The chefs watched Jewish cooks prepare it and copied the recipe meticulously. Yet when they prepared it for the emperor, it did not meet with his approval.

"Why does this food taste different when your cooks prepare it?" asked the Caesar of Rabbi Judah the Prince.

"We have a special spice, known only to our people, that is used in this dish."

"Tell me the name of the spice," demanded the emperor.

"It is the Holy Sabbath," the sage replied.

Cholent, the central dish of the Sabbath meal, was prepared well in advance. Beans were a common ingredient and had to be soaked in cold water on Thursday night to be usable by Friday. The rest of the ingredients were added on Friday morning. (The Sabbath begins eighteen minutes before sundown on Friday. In some northern regions, during winter, the Sabbath begins at 2:30 Friday afternoon, or even earlier.)

Until recent decades, the indoor oven was an exotic luxury in many Jewish communities. Indeed, the family cooking stove was a high-tech item until about one hundred years ago. In many places the need for continuous heat throughout the Sabbath was met by the professional baker. It was he who accommodated the cholent pots of many families in his huge community oven. The cholent pot was delivered to the bakery on Friday morning and picked up on Saturday on the way back from synagogue services. The cholent pot was made of heavy-duty material, such as earthenware, cast iron, or bronze. Standard issue for a girl's trousseau, it was meant to take a lifetime of weekly use, and was sometimes engraved with the family name and decorations.

As the stove became popular in the nineteenth century, the communal baking of cholent disappeared. The housewife could make her cholent, then place it on a tin sheet above the fire to warm until the fire in the stove died out. Small, top-of-the-stove ovens were ideal for cholent. They were widely used in Israel until recently, when American-style ovens have become popular. Contemporary cooks usually place their cholents in a tightly covered pot in the oven and leave it on a very low setting—the exact temperature can be tricky, depending on the individual oven—throughout the Sabbath. This method results in excellent flavor, but it is energy-inefficient. It can be intolerable in warm weather.

The electric slow cooker is an appliance that seems to have been created with cholent in mind. It produces the right amount of heat, uses little energy, and is easy to clean. In very hot weather it can even be left to bubble away on a terrace or patio. (My mother, with over half a century of cholent-cooking experience behind her, swears she has never made such tasty cholent as she has since she acquired a slow cooker.)

In past times, the cholent was invariably preceded and accompanied by other meats and starchy dishes. The new Jewish cuisine leaves cholent to be savored without calorie guilt or dyspeptic misgivings. With a light appetizer, accompanied by a soufflélike kugel and salads, followed by a light dessert, cholent can be filling and rich-tasting without being overwhelming.

The following recipes are deliberately shy on salt. Many of the ingredients in a cholent can be salty—sausage, bouillon, the meat itself—so that no salt at all need be added. In other cases, less salt will be used, and enjoyed more, if added at the table to individual taste.

The traditional cholent invariably contained a lot of fat, once the symbol of graciousness and plenty. The most marbled cuts of meat were considered desirable and usually additional chicken fat or olive oil were tossed into the pot. Health-conscious cooks have found that cholent does not suffer from using lean cuts of meat and skipping additional fats altogether.

The making of a cholent

Ingredients and cooking methods are highly individualized. The variables mean that no two cholents, even from the same cook, using the same recipe, will ever be the same.

Said the skeptic to the rabbi, "How can you believe that the dead will be brought to life in the time of the Messiah? There exists not even a hint of proof that resurrection is possible."

"On the contrary, my son, you have proved it yourself!"

"How so, Rabbi?"

"On the Sabbath do you not eat cholent?"

"Of course."

"And afterward, do you take a nap?"

"After cholent, one must!"

"And after your nap . . ."

"I get up."

"Aha! Proof that the dead can rise!"

Beans

Because beans maintain their character, and are even enhanced, through long hours of cooking, they are an important part of the cholent. Small beans have the most delicate flavor—and take the longest to cook. Pea and navy beans are the standards. Pink, small red, and pinto beans have similar flavors. Large beans, such as kidney and Great Northern, add a distinct beany taste and lend an interesting texture. Sephardic Jews favor chick-peas, yellow split peas, favas, Limas, and lentils. To rehydrate beans, which must be done before they are cooked with the other ingredients, soak in cold water overnight. Or cover beans with cold water, bring to a boil, and simmer for 1½ or more hours. Or, bring to a boil, cover, and let stand 2½ or more hours. Always wash beans well before soaking and cover with at least twice as much water as there are beans.

Potatoes

Russian Jews use potatoes instead of beans, others add potatoes in with the beans and other ingredients. Potatoes absorb flavors very well, and are an excellent remedy in case too much seasoning has been used. If potatoes are fresh, there is no need to peel them. Just wash well, cut into any size cubes, and boil briefly in the cholent pot or a separate pan, before setting the cholent out for the long simmer. Where the potatoes are not the main ingredient, they can be placed whole, like baking potatoes, into the cholent. Once again, they should be cooked for about 10 minutes, because they must be edible before the Sabbath.

Barley

Barley adds its own flavor and also acts as a binder for the cholent's juices. Prepare it like, or together with, the beans. Sephardic Jews use rice instead of barley. Steam the rice for about 15 minutes, or, for a special flavor, fry the uncooked rice in olive oil. Cracked wheat or wheat germ are also good alternatives.

Meat

Although meat is not absolutely necessary in a cholent, it is usually considered the most important part of the dish, fulfilling the dictum "there is no feast without meat and wine." In times past the fattiest cuts were selected for the best cholents. Today, most cooks trim the meat of excess fat. Flanken, short ribs, or brisket are often used, but any cut of beef, even the toughest, will do well in a cholent, and will be meltingly tender after long simmering.

Sephardim use lamb rather than beef, and, once again, the traditionalists prefer plenty of fat, while modern cooks go for the lean. Chicken is used as the primary meat by the Jews of Iraq, Afghanistan, and other oriental communities. Other Sephardim and Ashkenazim add chicken pieces in addition to the other meat.

All kinds of sausages find their way into the pot, with very hot ones mellowing out overnight but adding zest to the entire stew.

Bones are another good flavoring agent. Kosher butchers sell marrow bones especially good for cholent. Avoid putting the smaller chicken bones into cholent, as they sometimes disintegrate and splinter.

Vegetables

Of necessity the vegetables that go into a cholent must be very firm so that they do not dissolve entirely. Onions are often used in both Ashkenazic and Sephardic cholents, as are large chunks of carrots. Other vegetables, such as celery, turnips, squash, and parsnips, are used as flavoring agents only, because they do not maintain their integrity in the cholent. Syrian Jews bake their cholent in a hollowed-out pumpkin.

Spices

The flavoring agents used most frequently in both East and West are black pepper and garlic. In the Ashkenazic cholent paprika, bay leaf, and/or ginger are sometimes added. The Sephardim use a broader palette of spices and herbs:

cinnamon, cardamom, mint leaves, red peppers, saffron, rosemary, turmeric, coriander, even rose petals.

The more delicate herbs tend to get lost in the well-blended flavor of the cholent, but there is no harm in adding them.

Bouillon powders and cubes work well for the cook in a hurry.

Eggs

In some Sephardic communities eggs are *de rigeur* in the hamin. Unshelled eggs are placed directly into the cholent. By lunchtime the eggs are brown and flavorful right through to the yolk, and the shell itself is edible.

Fruit

A few pieces of tough fruits such as quince, prunes, or apricots, give cholent an extra dimension without changing its basic nature.

Dumplings

Almost every Jewish ethnic group has a type of dumpling that is cooked on top of, not in, the cholent. They can be matzoh balls, pieces of kugel, stuffed derma, or meatballs. They are carefully placed on top of the completed cholent shortly before the Sabbath. The dumplings are steamed, and their flavor is fortified, by the cholent.

> "The cholent takes after the guests," goes an old Yiddish saw. A good cholent intimates that the guests are righteous, a poorly flavored one casts a shadow on their honor, as well as the cook's. Therefore, it is always wise for the guests to praise the cholent.

Cholent is always made in quantity, assuming that every Jewish home will practice hospitality during the Sabbath, inviting friends and strangers to share the afternoon meal. Occasionally, there are likely to be leftovers. While cholent cooked for a weekday just doesn't taste like the real thing, leftover cholent is a Sunday treat. Assuming that the cholent has been refrigerated—once it has been removed, it may not be returned to the heat on the Sabbath—it can be reheated either by replacing it in an oven or slow cooker or placing it in a saucepan with a nonstick surface and heating on a low flame. A quick way to reheat: stir-frying in a wok.

BASIC CHOLENT   [M]

Serves 8.

1 cup small beans
1/2 cup large beans
1/2 cup pearl barley
3 lbs. beef, in 2-inch cubes
3 bouillon cubes

12 medium potatoes, peeled and
quartered
2 sausages, skinned and
quartered

In a large, heavy pot, rinse beans and barley, discarding floating beans. Add cold water to cover, then another quart of water. Rehydrate by soaking overnight or cooking for 2 hours. Bring to second boil. Add beef and bouillon cubes. When beef has lost all trace of red, add potatoes and sausages. Cover and cook on high heat 20 minutes. Stir all ingredients, adjusting amount of liquid, which should be an inch below the surface of the stew. Add an inch or more hot water if the cholent is to be placed in the oven. Cover tightly and place in oven at 225°, on a *blech,* or in a slow cooker. Let simmer (do not stir) for approximately 24 hours.

TEX-MEX CHOLENT   [M]

Sabbath chili!
Serves 6.

1 lb. pinto or pink beans
1 quart water
2 tablespoons oil
2 lbs. lean beef, cubed
1 (8-oz.) can tomato sauce
3 cloves garlic, minced
1 small onion, chopped
1 chili pepper, chopped

1 tablespoon flour
1 tablespoon chili powder
1 tablespoon cumin
1 tablespoon vinegar
1 1/2 teaspoons salt
1 teaspoon oregano
1 teaspoon bacon-flavored soy
chips

Cook beans in water for 2 hours. Brown beef in oil. Combine beans with liquid, meat, and remaining ingredients in slow cooker, or place tightly covered pot in oven or on a *blech.* Simmer for approximately 24 hours. Serve with saltine crackers or tortilla chips, and accompany with ice-cold beer.

MOROCCAN CHAMIN　[M]

Exotically seasoned, this cholent is excellent in hot weather.
Serves 8.

2 lb. lamb or 1 lb. beef plus 1
　lb. chicken
2 tablespoons olive oil
2 quarts water
3/4 cup lentils
1/2 cup fine egg noodles
1 can chick-peas
2 onions, chopped
2 stalks celery, with leaves,
　chopped

1 can tomatoes
1/4 cup parsley, snipped
11/2 teaspoons turmeric
1 teaspoon salt
1 teaspoon black pepper
1 teaspoon cinnamon
1/2 teaspoon ginger
1/2 teaspoon saffron

Cut the meat into bite-size pieces and brown in the oil. Add water and
lentils. Bring to a boil, cover, and cook 30 minutes. Add noodles, cook 10
minutes more. Add rest of ingredients and simmer in oven at 225°, slow cooker,
or on a *blech,* for about 24 hours. Serve with lemon wedges.

BOSTON CHOLENT　[M]

The famed New England pot of Boston baked beans has a history with
more than a few similarities to that of the Jewish cholent. The Puritan Sabbath
lasted from sundown, Saturday, to sundown, Sunday. While Puritan housewives
were not forbidden to cook on their Sabbath, they were busy with other tasks
and needed to provide a festive meal on both Saturday night and Sunday afternoon. On Saturday morning the goodwife would prepare her bean-and-pork
dish. The community baker would pick up the pot before noon and place it in
the town oven. He delivered it that evening, and after the family was served, the
pot would go back into a fireplace warmed by a few embers, there to simmer
until the Sunday meal.

This is a fine cholent to prepare in an emergency, when there is little time
to cook before the Sabbath.
Serves 4–6.

4 (1-lb.) cans vegetarian baked
　beans in tomato sauce
1 package frankfurters, skinned
　and cut in quarters

1/2 package onion soup mix
1/2 cup molasses
1 tablespoon dry mustard
1 teaspoon vinegar

Combine all ingredients. Add water, if necessary, to almost cover the beans. Bake in a slow cooker or 225° oven, or on a *blech*, for about 24 hours.

KUGEL

Virtually every Jewish community in the world has at least two types of kugel (other names are used among Sephardim, while Israelis call it pashtida) that are commonly made for the Sabbath. Stiffer than a pudding, moister than a bread, this casserole can be sweet or savory, hot or cold, and contain virtually any ingredient. Most kugels are improved by overnight heating on a *blech* or in a warm oven—but keep the heat very low to prevent burning and cover to prevent drying out. Some kinds of kugel can be left to steam on top of the cholent. Most Ashkenazic kugels are based on noodles, rice, or potatoes. Many Sephardic kugels are pielike—for example, layers of seasoned dough alternate with layers of potato and onion mixture. Kugels can be either side dishes or desserts—or both.

BEST RICE KUGEL   [P]

Serves 6–8.

1 cup sugar
1/4 cup oil
1 teaspoon grated lemon peel
1/2 teaspoon cinnamon
1/2 teaspoon vanilla
3 eggs

3 cups cooked rice
1/2 cup raisins
1/3 cup crushed pineapple, with juice
4 walnuts, shelled and chopped

Beat together sugar, oil, lemon peel, cinnamon, and vanilla. Beat in eggs, 1 at a time. Stir in rice, combining thoroughly. Stir in raisins, pineapple, and walnuts. Bake at 350° for 1 hour or until top is golden.

BULGUR AND WALNUT KUGEL   [P]

A Sephardic favorite that is very good served cold.
Serves 8–12.

2 cups bulgur (cracked wheat)
5 cups water
1 cup sugar
2 eggs, well beaten

1/4 cup honey
2 cups ground walnuts
1 tablespoon cinnamon
1/2 teaspoon salt

Bring bulgur and water to boil. Reduce heat and simmer, stirring frequently, for 30 minutes. Add sugar, eggs, honey, walnuts, cinnamon, and salt. Pour into greased baking pan. Bake at 300° for 40 minutes.

JERUSALEM KUGEL [P]

Sweet and peppery, this unusual kugel, with overtones of both Sephardic and Ashkenazic cooking styles, is unique to the Holy City.
Serves 8.

1 lb. thinnest spaghetti	*6 eggs, beaten*
1 cup oil	*3 teaspoons black pepper*
1 cup sugar	*1 teaspoon salt*

Cook spaghetti al dente. Drain and dry very carefully with towel. In a large saucepan cook oil and sugar until sugar begins to caramelize. Add spaghetti immediately and carefully. Mix in eggs, pepper, and salt. Bake at 350° for 1 1/2 hours.

ROMANIAN KUGEL BALLS [P]

Serves 6–8.

1 cup cornmeal	*1/2 teaspoon paprika*
1 cup flour	*Freshly ground black pepper*
2 tablespoons sugar	*1/2 cup oil*
1 1/2 teaspoons salt	*1/2 cup boiling water*

Stir all ingredients together. Drop heaping tablespoons of mixture into cholent covered with bubbling-hot liquid.

FARINA KUGEL [P]

Iraqi sweet kugel that is excellent as a companion to chicken dishes.
Serves 8.

1/2 cup farina	*1/2 teaspoon salt*
2 cups water	*1 teaspoon grated lemon rind*
1 tablespoon margarine	*5 egg yolks, beaten*
1/2 cup sugar	*5 egg whites*

Cook farina and water until boiling. Lower heat, add margarine, sugar, and salt and cook for 5 minutes. Remove from heat and let cool while you beat the egg whites until stiff. Mix lemon rind and egg yolks into farina mixture. Fold in egg whites. Bake at 350° for 20 minutes.

STOVETOP POTATO KUGEL [P]

Crunchy and delicious, for Friday night.
Serves 4.

1/4 cup margarine
1 small onion, chopped
2 potatoes, unpeeled, grated and drained

1 egg, beaten
1/3 cup matzoh meal
1/2 teaspoon salt

In a large skillet, melt margarine and sauté onions until tender. Remove with slotted spoon and mix together with remaining ingredients. Pour into skillet, pressing down. Cover and cook on low flame until bottom is well browned. Flip over and brown other side with cover removed.

ORANGE-RICE KUGEL [P]

For an extra-light kugel, you can separate the eggs and beat the whites until soft peaks form. Mix yolks and other ingredients, then fold the whites in carefully.
Serves 8–10.

3 cups cooked rice
1 cup pareve creamer
1 cup orange juice
1/4 cup orange-flavored liqueur
4 eggs
1/2 cup sugar

2 tablespoons flour
1/2 teaspoon salt
1 teaspoon grated orange rind
1/4 teaspoon nutmeg
1 large navel orange, chopped
3/4 cup raisins

Preheat oven to 400°. Mix all ingredients and pour into lightly greased casserole or soufflé dish. Bake 45–50 minutes.

Passover:
The Taste
of Freedom

The eight days of Passover (seven in Israel) form a remarkable dietary event. At this time the taste, artistry, and even nutritive value of food take second place to its symbolism. The foods eaten, and not eaten, on Passover raise profound questions about the purpose of the Jewish nation, and its destiny.

THE SEDER

The Seder is a banquet held on the first night of Passover (outside of Israel, also on the second night). It is derived from the ceremonial eating of the Paschal lamb, as described in the Bible. This was the primary symbol of redemption from Egyptian bondage. The Paschal sacrifice practiced in the days of the Temple consisted of a lamb or young goat slaughtered at the Temple. After certain parts of the animal were removed for burning as sacrifice, the remainder was roasted and shared by a number of families. The Bible specifies a number of laws in connection with the Paschal lamb, some of which are reflected in the contemporary Seder.

The sacrifice was a national event. Everyone participated in the ritual at the specified time, because it symbolized the freedom of the entire people. Today, the Seder remains a symbol of national unity and virtually every Jew who considers himself a Jew celebrates this event.

The sacrifice had to be roasted; it could not be boiled or prepared in any other way. Roast lamb was a food of nomads, of people free to go where they chose. Among Ashkenazic Jews lamb is never served at the Seder, and many also decline to roast any meat or fowl. This is to symbolize the conviction that no ceremony can truly replace that of the Paschal sacrifice. Among Sephardim roast lamb is specifically served, a symbol of the sacrifice that was and is to be. The lamb was accompanied by unleavened bread and bitter herbs. The matzoh symbolized the haste with which the Jews had to leave Egypt; the herbs represented the bitterness of oppression. Today these two foods are the primary symbols of Passover.

It was forbidden to leave over any of the meat of the lamb. Once again, a symbol of haste. To assure complete consumption, it was customary for several families to share a single sacrifice. Each individual had a modest portion of food. Today it is customary to celebrate the Seder with one's entire family and, if possible, other friends as well. It is right to eat well at this meal, but not to gorge.

Jews who were ritually impure and non-Jews were prohibited from sharing in the Paschal lamb. With the destruction of the Temple, the dissolution of the holiness cult and ritual purity, the Paschal sacrifice ceased to be. This was the shell of the concept of Passover. The spiritual core of the celebration, on the other hand, continues, for many, to be more meaningful than ever. Consequently, it has become customary to invite Jews who have been alienated from their religion and non-Jews to share in the Seder, which is a concise introduction and explanation of the Jewish faith.

It was forbidden to break the bones of the Paschal lamb, or to eat the marrow. The reasons were manifold: to show that no creature of God should be destroyed to "the last bone," even when being used for a holy purpose; to show that the lamb was being eaten for religious reasons, not to satiate base hunger; to show exquisite table manners, as befits the "royal" participants of the meal, as each diner is designated a "king" or "queen."

The Seder ceremony puts the actual meal in the middle, showing that it is not the most important aspect of the rite. It is unfortunate that in many deracinated Jewish homes the Seder has degenerated to being no more than an opportunity to indulge in excessive amounts of fancy food. Wherever the Seder is conducted properly, a fine and ample meal is served, but not one that is a show of egotism or gluttony.

In keeping with the idea of nobility, it is customary to sit at the table in a reclining position, with pillows on the chair, in the manner of the Greek aristocracy.

The Paschal lamb was to be eaten in the home. Today, the Seder is a principal reminder that Judaism is centered in the home. One shares this meal with a family, one's own, if possible, or with those who share love and belief, ties that are stronger than blood.

Besides a full-course meal, a number of ritual foods are incorporated in the Seder. Foremost among these is matzoh, unleavened bread, signifying the haste of the Exodus, when the dough for bread could not be left to rise. Matzoh is obligatory at the Seder, but the fact that no other bread, roll, or wafer can be eaten throughout the holiday, makes matzoh a staple for eight days. It is customary to eat no matzoh for a month before Passover.

Shmura (guarded) matzoh is a marvelous unleavened bread made especially for the Seders. Complying with the strictest rules for making matzoh, it has a haunting flavor, leaving little doubt that this was exactly the food eaten by the Israelites four thousand years ago. In large Jewish population centers it is available at special bakeries and supermarkets. Elsewhere it must be ordered well before Passover through an Orthodox rabbi. Hand-made shmura matzoh sells for about eight dollars per pound. Machine-made shmura, with a somewhat less distinctive taste and appearance, is also available. "Whole wheat" matzohs, egg matzohs, and chocolate-covered matzohs are inappropriate for use at the Seder. Matzoh is also available ground into course matzoh meal, excellent year-round for use as a full-flavored breading. Matzohs ground to powderlike consistency constitute Passover cake meal.

THE MAKING OF SHMURA MATZOH

Shmura matzoh is a bread for which the ultimate precautions against leavening have been taken. The "guarding" for which shmura matzoh is named begins in the field of wheat. The wheat is harvested while still slightly green, because a fully ripened sheaf can begin to ferment when dampened by dew or rain. The grain is specially milled and stored. Water is drawn from a natural spring or brook in brand-new earthenware vessels. It is specially filtered and stored overnight at a consistent low temperature (warm water causes dough to rise).

The matzoh bakery is specially constructed for Passover. Workers are assigned to constantly clean all surfaces touched by flour or dough. From the time that the first drop of water reaches a batch of flour to the time when a completely baked matzoh is taken from the oven, no more than eighteen minutes may elapse. The dough is rapidly rolled thin and pricked. The matzoh oven is monitored for maintaining a specific high temperature, because dough put into too cool an oven will begin to rise. After each batch, all the working surfaces, bowls, and utensils are cleaned so that no dough from a previous batch will cling to the new one.

Matzoh bakeries have facilities for individuals to come in and bake their own matzoh under a supervisor. This is considered a pious deed. Under no circumstances are matzohs baked in the home oven.

Wine is essential to the Seder ritual. A robust red wine is customary for at least the first of the required four cups.

Bitter herbs can be any pungent vegetable. Ashkenazim traditionally use horseradish, freshly grated or chopped (prepared horseradish should not be used; since it is mixed with other ingredients, it lacks essential purity). Any bitter lettuce, carefully washed to remove insects, may be used, as may radishes.

Charoset is a pastelike mixture meant to resemble the mortar of the buildings that the Israelites were forced to build in Egyptian slavery.

Karpas is a vegetable eaten before the meal begins. Its main purpose is to act as a foil for salt water, representing the tears shed in slavery. Parsley, watercress, celery, or radish all serve nicely, as long as the chosen vegetable is not the same one used for "bitter herbs." Many Europeans use a freshly boiled potato for this purpose, which is delicious. However, care must be taken not to overindulge, as this ritual is not part of the meal. Half a small potato is the maximum serving.

The first course of the meal is traditionally a *hard-boiled egg*, served with more salt water. The egg is a Jewish symbol of mortality, round as the cycle of life. It is meant to turn one's mind to contemplation, even as the festive meal begins.

PREPARING FOR PASSOVER

No special foods are prescribed for Passover; its cookery is notable for what is excluded. The Bible says that leaven is not to be eaten on this holiday—and it says it seven times. In addition to consumption, leaven may not be enjoyed in any way, profited from, possessed, or even looked at during Passover. Leaven owned by a Jew during Passover may not be used by any Jew even after Passover. Obviously, the level of strictness inherent in this prohibition goes far beyond that of any of the standard laws of kashrut. It is customary, therefore, for observant Jews to be supercareful about their food during Passover.

The following preparations must be completed by 9 A.M. of the morning before Passover:

• All leavened foods cleared out of eyesight.

• All food preparation surfaces thoroughly cleaned and covered with aluminum foil, wooden boards, or other coverings.

• Food that cannot be eaten before Passover is stored away and sold, via a rabbi, to a non-Jew. (The contract stipulates a return to ownership immediately after Passover.)

• All crumbs are cleaned away. This includes crumbs in coat pockets, on car floors, in office desks, in gym lockers, etc.

• A ceremonial inspection is held the night before Passover. The bread crumbs gathered are burned the next morning.

• Special dinnerware, flatware, glassware, dishwashing equipment, and all utensils are bought for Passover. Two sets of each are needed, for meat and dairy. (All of these can be used after Passover for year-round use, but, if so, may not be used again for Passover.) It is customary to use double tablecloths on all tables. Disposable items, such as foil pans, paper plates, plastic forks and knives, are perfectly acceptable.

The prohibition against leaven includes the following:

- All breads, cakes, cookies, wafers, crackers, and other items made with grain flour. Also, the flour itself, except matzoh cake meal and potato flour or starch.
- All foods and drinks made with grain alcohol, including most liquors, beer, vanilla, and other extracts.
- All foods made with legume products, seeds, and grainlike foods, including corn, beans, peanuts, peas, sesame, and rice. Most Sephardim, however, eat some of these, especially rice, but not others, like corn. This is an especially important point in modern times, as corn sweeteners and soybean oil have become the primary sweetening and emulsifying agents in processed foods.
- Any food made with utensils or on machinery used for "leavened" food.
- Practically speaking, only a few foods, such as fresh fruits and vegetables, and pure juices, may be used; most others may not, unless they have special Passover kashrut certification. The regular laws of kashrut also apply during Passover.

Some Jews practice special restrictions above and beyond those called for by law. Customary restrictions include eating only in one's own home, no matter how sterling the reputation of a friend or a restaurant; eating no foods made with matzoh meal—including matzoh balls; eating no dairy products (frequently adulterated at a previous time); eating only those fruits and vegetables that can be peeled.

Because of the limitations of the foods permitted on Passover, this holiday's cuisine can be heavy. Too often the lack of regular starches is made up with an excessive use of potatoes, matzoh meal, and eggs. Few convenience foods are available at this season, while a large variety of kosher-for-Passover sweets can be found. When families get together after long absences, especially when they are gathered around a table, the temptation to snack can be overwhelming.

To cut down on Passover calories:

- Plan dairy meals. At this time of year the freshest dairy products are to be found. After all, foods labeled kosher-for-Passover cannot have a long shelf life.
- Prepare only lean meats, poultry, and fish, no matter what fatty meats are "traditional."
- With the cost of Passover foods so high, it makes economic, as well as health and culinary sense to buy a variety of good vegetables and fruits, even hothouse varieties, to expand the menu.
- Provide hard-shelled nuts for snacking; they take a rather long time to crack and pick clean. They go well with fresh fruits, too.

CHAROSET [P]

Charoset is the symbol of slavery on the Passover plate. It is meant to remind the diners of the mortar with which the Israelites were forced to construct buildings in Egypt. The only required ingredient is red wine, in commemoration of the blood that was shed in slavery. The charoset is eaten in a prescribed manner: a small amount is wadded together with an equal amount of bitter herbs and eaten together in one bite.

The following should provide enough charoset for ten Seder participants. Adjust the ingredients to taste and to insure that the consistency is that of a paste.

2 apples, peeled, cored, shredded
2 tablespoons sweet red wine
*1/3 cup ground nuts (do not use
  peanuts on Passover)*

*1/4 teaspoon cinnamon or 1/8
  teaspoon ginger*

If you like charoset enough to eat in more than ritual quantities, try adding any of the following ingredients to taste.

Apricots, dried, chopped
Almonds, ground
Brandy
Chestnut purée
Dates, chopped
Figs, chopped
Ginger root, grated
Hazelnuts, ground

Honey
Orange peel, grated
Pears, shredded
Pine nuts, chopped
Poppy seeds
Raisins
Walnuts, ground

MATZOH BREI SUPPER [D]

A treat on Passover and throughout the year. This versatile dish can be served at any meal, even as a hearty breakfast. For lunch and supper accompany with steamed vegetables and a fresh salad.

Makes 1 serving.

2 matzohs
Water or milk
1 tablespoon butter or oil
*1/2 onion, sliced and broken into
  rings*

1 large egg, well beaten
1/4 teaspoon salt
2 slices Swiss cheese

Break the matzohs into bite-size pieces in a bowl and cover with water or milk. While matzohs soften, heat butter or oil and sauté the onion rings until golden. Pour excess liquid from the matzohs and stir in egg and salt. Pour this mixture onto the onions. Fry until browned. Flip matzoh brei over and cover with cheese slices. Cover pan while second side browns. Serve immediately.

MARZIPAN FISH   [P]

Marzipan, a candy made of almonds or coconut, is a Passover specialty. It appears here in a most unusual form. This fish makes a definite change of pace from meat, dairy, and gefilte fish holiday entrees.
Serves 6–8.

2 tablespoons oil
3 onions, chopped
2 cloves garlic, minced
1/4 cup marzipan
1/4 cup jam or jelly
2 tablespoons margarine

2 tablespoons lemon juice
1/2 cup chopped almonds
1/2 teaspoon cinnamon
1/2 cup hot water
2 whole fish, about 2 lbs. each
  (trout, carp, or bass)

Heat oil and sauté onions and garlic until tender. In a bowl, mash together marzipan, jam, margarine, and lemon juice. Add chopped almonds and cinnamon. Pour onion mixture into baking pan and add hot water. Lay fish, cavities up, on the onions. Stuff each fish with marzipan mixture. Bake at 375° for 40 minutes or until fish flakes easily.

PASSOVER PIZZA   [D]

Pizza, that perennial workhorse, can be topped with olives, mushrooms, onions, and/or peppers, in addition to, and at the same time as, the cheese.
Makes 8 slices.

3 cups crushed matzoh
3 cups hot water
4 large eggs, well beaten
1/2 teaspoon salt

2 (8-oz.) cans tomato sauce
1 (8-oz.) bar mozzarella cheese,
  shredded
2 oz. grated Parmesan cheese

Cover the matzoh with hot water. Let soak 10 minutes. Drain and mix with eggs and salt. Press into greased pizza pan. Bake at 375° for 30 minutes. Spread on tomato sauce. Sprinkle with cheeses. Continue baking for 15 minutes.

VEGETABLE KUGEL [P]

You can vary the type and proportion of vegetables for a variety of flavors. Serves 6–8.

3 zucchini
2 bunches broccoli, stalks only
   (use florets in salads or
   steamed)
2 carrots, scraped
1 potato, peeled

1 large onion, peeled
3 eggs
1/2 cup oil
1 1/2 teaspoons salt
Freshly ground black pepper

Grate zucchini, broccoli stalks, carrots, potato, and onion. Beat together eggs, oil, salt, and pepper. Pour into greased baking pan. Bake at 350° for 1 1/4 hours.

SWEET POTATO PIE [P]

The bright orange of sweet potatoes makes this an attractive side dish as well as a good one. Serve with oven-fried chicken and a green vegetable and no one will miss the standard dinner starches!
Serves 8.

CRUST

1 cup matzoh meal
1/4 cup melted margarine

2 tablespoons sugar
1/4 teaspoon cinnamon

FILLING

1 1/2 cups cooked, mashed sweet
   potatoes
1/3 cup sugar
1/2 teaspoon salt
1/4 teaspoon cinnamon

2 eggs, well beaten
1/2 cup water
1/4 cup melted margarine
8 pecan halves

Mix crust ingredients well and press into an 8" pie pan. Thoroughly mix filling ingredients, except pecan halves, and pour into crust. Press pecan halves in a circle on top of the pie. Bake at 400° for 45 minutes.

PASSOVER PANCAKES [P]

These are good at any meal. For breakfast top with cinnamon and sugar. At other meals, they are best as a side dish. Top with plain yogurt when serving with dairy meals; applesauce, when serving with meat meals.
Serves 4.

2 potatoes	*1/2 teaspoon salt*
2 eggs, separated	*Oil for frying*

Boil potatoes until tender. Let cool, peel and mash. Mix well with egg yolk and salt. Beat egg whites until very foamy but not stiff. Fold into potato mixture. Fry until golden. Turn once and brown other side. Drain on paper toweling.

PASSOVER GÂTEAU AHARÓN [P]

Passover is a time for feasting, and there is no need for desserts to be a monotony of sponge cakes and macaroons. This version of the French Gâteau St. Honoré is decidedly different in flavor and texture, and pretty enough to adorn the most elegant Seder table.
Serves 10 or more.

1 plain round Passover cake, 10"	*4 egg yolks*
diameter, no more than 2"	*1/2 cup sugar*
high	*1/4 cup orange juice*
1 cup sugar	*Grated peel of 1 orange*
1/4 cup water	*1 tablespoon Sabra liqueur*
2 tablespoons honey	
2 packages Passover soup nuts	
(look like little cream puffs)	

Place cake in center of serving platter. Heat 1 cup sugar, water, and honey to boiling, stirring constantly. Continue cooking until a golden brown syrup is formed. Spoon some syrup in a band around the top edge of the cake. Dip each soup nut in syrup and glue into a tight circle on the top edge of the cake, forming a crown. If syrup begins to harden, reheat slightly. Drizzle leftover syrup over the soup nuts. Beat egg yolks very well. Add 1/2 cup sugar and orange juice, beating constantly. Place egg mixture on low heat and stir constantly until it is a thick custard. Remove from heat and add orange peel and Sabra. Pour into center of the crown. Refrigerate until serving.

Celebrating
with Food

Special foods characterize all Jewish celebrations, whether they are holidays or occasions that mark personal milestones. Some of us wouldn't dream of Rosh Hashanah without a whole carp or a Bar Mitzvah without chopped liver molds. Others would like to try something just as festive but a bit more adventurous.

ROSH HASHANAH (Jewish New Year)

To symbolize the hope that the year will bring good luck, prosperity, fertility, sweetness, and freedom from sin and sadness, Rosh Hashanah incorporates a variety of foods. Honey and apples, glazed carrots the color of gold coins, avoidance of sour foods and nuts (whose Hebrew name equals that of "sin" in Jewish numerology) are just some of the traditions. Another is eating fish, a token of wisdom, fortune, and fertility. At the major evening meal the diners recite upon the fish, "May it be God's will that we be as the head and not as the tail."

Not everyone relishes the head of a carp, and some don't care for traditional poached fish. The following is a vivid, showy alternative.

SALMON SOUFFLÉ   [P]

Serves 4–6.

1 can salmon, drained
3 egg yolks
1 tablespoon lemon juice
1 tablespoon fresh dill, snipped
1/4 teaspoon salt
Freshly ground black pepper

1/4 cup margarine
3 tablespoons flour
3/4 cup water
3 egg whites, stiffly beaten
5 brightly colored feathers

In a processor or blender, purée salmon, egg yolks, lemon juice, dill, salt, and pepper. Melt margarine over medium heat and stir in flour. Add water, stirring until mixture bubbles and thickens. Mix with salmon purée. Fold in egg whites. Carefully pour into a greased mold that is the shape of a fish, but avoid getting batter into the tail part. Bake at 350° for 45 minutes or until toothpick inserted in center comes out dry. Let the soufflé cool for 15 minutes, then insert the mold into hot water for 1 minute. Invert onto a serving platter. Arrange feathers to form a tail for the fish.

A HUNGARIAN FEAST FOR SUCCOTH   [M]

According to the greatest of all biblical commentators, Rashi, one is under divine commandment to eat magnificently during this eight-day holiday. Succoth provides a true showcase for the avid cook. Dishes may be freshly prepared for every meal, as they may not on the Sabbath. In contrast to Passover, there are no limitations to the types of food one may use, and there are few obligatory or universally customary dishes to cramp one's style.

The Succoth meals are eaten in a booth outdoors. The interior of the booth is gaily decorated and pine boughs or palm fronds serve as a roof. In short, the dining ambiance could not be more delightful. Succoth comes in autumn and in most areas where Jews live today, there is likely to be just a hint of crisp weather to sharpen the appetite.

The following, from the great classic cuisine of the Hungarian Jews is certain to please. This meal is not exactly light, yet neither is it as heavy as the traditional holiday cooking of other parts of Europe. A Succoth dinner is to be eaten at leisure, perhaps for the better part of the afternoon. The greatest difficulty in serving this meal is in tactfully reminding the diners not to fill up on the first courses—the dishes to come are just as good, if not better!

ROYAL VEAL ROAST   [M]

For a Succoth feast, you might begin with stuffed cabbage or pepper. Next, a salad of fresh cucumber slices dressed with sugar, vinegar, and snipped dill. Accompany the veal with Shlishkelech. Serve Retes for dessert.

Ask the butcher to give you the veal saddle—second rib and back. This will serve six. He should French-cut the roast so that it will hold together but lend itself to carving at the table.

1 veal rib roast
2 tablespoons oil
1 small onion, chopped
Contents of 1 large can stewed
   tomatoes, chopped (reserve
   liquid)

1/4 lb. mushrooms, sliced
1/2 teaspoon salt
Freshly ground pepper
1 tablespoon cornstarch

Do not rinse the meat; wipe it with a damp towel. Rub oil over the roast and place it on a rack in a Dutch oven. Cover and bake at 325° for 2 hours. Uncover and roast 30 minutes more. Transfer the veal drippings to a saucepan. Heat to simmer and add onion, tomatoes, and mushrooms. Season with salt and pepper. Dissolve cornstarch in tomato liquid and add to sauce. Simmer 5 minutes. Pour over roast.

Each of the seven days of Succoth has a patron; Abraham, Isaac, Jacob, Moses, Aaron, Joseph, and David. A charming custom is that boys and men who bear these names "sponsor" the designated day. They bring some special snack to the synagogue Succah (booth) to be shared by all. These Hungarian snaps suit the purpose well. They are also known among some Polish Jews as *flitlech*.

CSÖRÖGE (vanilla-scented Snaps)

Yield: 1 dozen snaps

1 egg
2 tablespoons water
1 cup flour

Oil for deep frying
2 tablespoons Vanilla Sugar (see
   below)

Beat egg and water together well. Add flour 1/4 cup at a time until a soft dough is formed. Knead gently for 5 minutes. On a floured board roll out the dough until it is a paper-thin rectangle. With a sharp knife (an X-acto, available at stationery and art supply stores, is ideal) cut horizontally into two-inch strips. Cut diagonally at three-inch intervals. Each snap will be a parallelogram. In the center of each snap, cut a small T. Heat oil and add a few snaps at a time. Remove carefully when golden brown and drain on paper toweling. Just before serving, arrange the snaps on a platter and shake on the vanilla sugar through a fine strainer.

VANILLA SUGAR

Slice a vanilla bean lengthwise and break each half into four pieces. Place in a small jar with a tight-fitting cap. Fill the jar almost to the top with confectioners' sugar. Close jar and shake to distribute vanilla bean pieces. The longer the jar is left closed (up to a year or more) the more fragrant the sugar becomes. After using the sugar, replace the vanilla pieces in the jar and add more sugar.

SIMCHAT TORAH (REJOICING IN THE LAW)

Immediately following Succoth, Simchat Torah is a one-day holiday of singing, dancing, and drinking. It celebrates the completion of the reading of the Five Books of Moses, and the beginning of the Book of Genesis once again. Jews rejoice in having the privilege of studying the Written Law (Bible) and the Oral Law (Talmud).

RABBI YOCHANAN'S DELIGHT [D]

The Talmud declared Rabbi Yochanan the most handsome of men, likening his beauty to the grains of the pomegranate in a cup of silver, surrounded by a wreath of red roses. This dessert is beautiful and fragrant, as well as delectable. Serves 8.

1 cup sugar	*1/4 cup rose water*
3/4 cup water	*1 quart vanilla ice cream*
Pinch salt	*Kernels of 2 large pomegranates*

In a saucepan heat sugar, water, and salt until sugar melts and begins to turn golden. Remove from heat, cool slightly, and stir in rose water. Scoop ice cream into dessert bowls or crystal water goblets. Pour on syrup and sprinkle with pomegranate kernels.

CHANUKAH

SOOFGANIOT (Chanukah Doughnuts) [P]

Soofganiot, like latkes, are a fried food, and therefore worthy of being served on Chanukah. (Fried foods commemorate the miracle of the temple oil.) In Israel, soofganiot are the more popular of the two dishes, perhaps because they are readily available at every ice cream parlor and falafel stand, fresh and hot. Americans have to make their own, since most Jewish bakeries have not yet caught on to this new trend.
Makes about 18 doughnuts.

2 packages yeast
3 tablespoons sugar
1/4 cup warm water
3 egg yolks
3/4 cup pareve creamer
1/4 cup vegetable shortening,
   melted

1 teaspoon brandy
1 teaspoon vanilla
1 teaspoon grated lemon peel
3 1/2 cups flour (approximately)
Raspberry, grape, or other jelly
Oil for deep frying
Powdered sugar

Stir yeast and a bit of the sugar into warm water. When yeast bubbles up, stir in remaining ingredients. Add sufficient flour to form a soft dough. Turn out on a floured board and knead until smooth. Cover with a towel and let rise until doubled, about 1 hour. Punch down and roll the dough out to 1/4-inch thickness. Cut circles out with a cup, place a teaspoon of jelly on half the circles, cover with remaining circles of dough, and pinch together. Let rise again for 1/2 hour. Heat oil and fry doughnuts rapidly, turning each once. Drain on paper toweling. Sprinkle with powdered sugar immediately before serving. Soofganiot are best when hot.

COTTAGE CHEESE LATKES   [D]

The traditional food for Chanukah is potato pancakes, known as *latkes* or *chremslach*. Although they are undoubtedly delicious, those who stand by tradition can easily overdose by the third day. These latkes remain in the spirit of the holiday but are somewhat more virtuous, especially if you use whole wheat flour. Serves 4.

1 cup flour
1 tablespoon sugar
1 teaspoon baking powder
1 teaspoon salt

4 eggs, beaten
2 cups cottage cheese
Oil for frying

Mix dry ingredients well, then stir in eggs and cottage cheese. Drop heaping tablespoonfuls on hot griddle or skillet. Serve immediately with applesauce, sour cream, and/or fruit preserves.

TU B'SHVAT

ETHROG CAKE   [P]

The ethrog is one of the four species of plants used in the beautiful Succoth ceremony, the blessing of the lulav. (The others are a palm shoot, myrtle branches, and willow fronds.) The Bible calls the ethrog "the fruit of the beautiful tree." *Citron medica* looks like a large lemon, but the two are not botanically related.

While citrons are used commercially as candied peel and perfume ingredients, they are not available anywhere as fresh fruit. They must be ordered through Jewish bookstores a month or so before the Succoth holiday. The religious qualifications for an ethrog are strict, and there is great competition for the best of the crop. An ethrog will cost from twenty-five dollars to one hundred dollars or more.

After the holiday, the ethrog is traditionally made into a compote or jelly. The extreme bitterness of the fruit, however, makes massive amounts of sugar necessary if it is to be palatable.

In modern times many have given up on the possibility of eating the fruit. The ethrog does make a heavenly sachet or, studded with cloves, a lovely pomander that retains its fragrance for almost a year.

This recipe uses the ethrog in a popular form, a delightfully scented cake. Exotic fruits are traditional for Tu b'Shvat, the Jewish Arbor Day.

1 ethrog	*1½ cups sugar*
Juice of a lime	*3 eggs*
1 tablespoon lemon juice	*1 cup plus 1 tablespoon orange*
2¾ cups cake flour	*juice*
3 teaspoons baking powder	*1 cup confectioners' sugar*
¼ teaspoon salt	*1 teaspoon vanilla*
¾ cup margarine	

Preheat oven to 375°. Spray a tube pan with vegetable oil spray. Grate the ethrog peel and add the juice of the lime, the lemon juice, and whatever juice you can squeeze from the ethrog. (Be sure to strain the ethrog juice through cheesecloth, as it is very membranous and has dozens of seeds.) Reserve 1 tablespoon of the citrus mixture for the glaze.

Sift flour, baking powder, and salt together. Cream the margarine with the sugar. Add citrus mixture and blend. Add eggs and beat well. Alternate adding half of the flour mixture with the cup of orange juice, beating well after each addition. Bake the cake for 45 minutes.

Blend together remaining tablespoon of citrus mixture, confectioners' sugar, tablespoon of orange juice, and vanilla. Remove cake from pan and, while it is still warm, drizzle glaze on top.

PURIM

The merry holiday celebrating the victory of Queen Esther and her people has many delightful food customs, including *hamentashen* (tiny filled pastries) and gift baskets of dainty edibles exchanged by friends. In addition, it is commendable to drink intoxicants on this day. A royal dinner is served on Purim afternoon. The following would make a suitable entree.

COQ AU VIN [M]

Serves 4.

2 tablespoons oil
1 chicken, cut into serving pieces
4 slices salami, diced
1 cup pearl onions
1 clove garlic, minced
1 carrot, scraped and sliced
2 tablespoons flour
2 tablespoons brandy
2 tablespoons snipped parsley

2 teaspoons tomato paste
1/2 bay leaf
1/2 teaspoon salt
1/2 teaspoon chervil
1/2 teaspoon thyme
Freshly grated black pepper
1 1/2 cups dry red wine
1/2 lb. mushrooms, sliced

Heat the oil in a large pot and brown the chicken pieces on all sides. Remove chicken from pot and add salami, onions, garlic, and carrot. Stir until lightly browned. Stir in flour until thickened. Add remaining ingredients, stirring well. Heat to boiling. Return chicken pieces to pot. Lower heat to simmer and cover tightly. Cook for 1 hour. Place chicken in a casserole or a shallow bowl and pour sauce on top. Serve immediately—and include a small ladle for the sauce.

ISRAEL INDEPENDENCE DAY

What better way to celebrate than with a brunch patterned after the fabled Israeli hotel breakfast? Decorate a buffet table in blue and white and cover it with a wide variety of dishes, including:

Deviled eggs
Smoked and marinated fish

Several eggplant salads
Carrot salad

Israeli vegetable salad
Yogurt
Olives and pickles
Fresh breads and rolls

Hard and soft cheeses
Fruit juices
Israeli champagne

Fruit salad is nice at brunch, but skip the apples, pears, and grapes that bore everybody and compose one from more exotic fruits, such as:

Fresh pineapple
Kiwi
Strawberries
Guavas
Mangoes

Papayas
Canned lichees
Bananas
Grapefruit

Toss with canned Bing cherries and their syrup and sprinkle with shredded coconut.

LAG BAOMER

Lag Baomer is a minor holiday celebrating the Talmudists of the Second Temple period—in particular, those who delved in the Kabbalistic mysteries. It is celebrated with picnics and bonfires and games of archery, symbols of defiance of Roman rule. Hot dogs are simple fun fare on this occasion, especially spiked on branches and roasted in an open fire. The following will dress them up.

FANCY RELISH FOR HOT DOGS   [P]

Enough for a dozen frankfurters.

1/3 cup spicy mustard
3 medium pickles, chopped
3 tablespoons chopped sweet
   onion

2 cloves garlic, minced
3 tablespoons capers
3 tablespoons oil
1 tablespoon vinegar

Place all ingredients into food processor with cutting blade in place. Press the pulse button five times. Do not overprocess. Or, chop each of the vegetables finely by hand and stir vigorously with a fork until blended.

JERUSALEM DAY

Since the reunification of the city in 1967, Jerusalem Day has been cele-brated each year to mark the special place the City of David has in the hearts of the Jewish people. What better way to observe it than serving this glorious cake in its honor.

CITY OF GOLD CAKE　[P]

In ancient times the noblewomen of Israel wore a tiara fashioned to resem-ble the skyline of Jerusalem. It was called "the city of gold." This cake, too, is meant to resemble that skyline, gilded by the sun, reflecting its special glory. And it is marbled to simulate the pink-gold stone peculiar to Jerusalem.
Serves 12.

1 cup margarine, at room	*2 tablespoons vanilla*
temperature	*3½ cups flour*
⅔ cup solid shortening	*6 drops red food coloring*
2 cups sugar	*2 tablespoons honey*
5 eggs	*Gold candy flakes*
⅔ cup water	

Cream margarine, shortening, and sugar together until light. Beat in eggs. Add water and vanilla, beating well. Beat in flour, a little at a time. Pour batter into a well-greased bundt pan. Drop food coloring at even intervals on the top. With a fork, rake through the food coloring drops, forming whorls of pink through the cake. Leave cake in a warm place for 20 minutes. Bake at 350° for 1½ hours. Let cool for 10 minutes, then invert the pan. Spread a layer of honey on the top of the cake. Sprinkle gold candy flakes on top and press gently to adhere.

SHAVUOT (Feast of Weeks, Pentecost)

This early summer holiday features dairy foods, as a rule. The reasons are many. For example, since it commemorates God's giving the Torah at Mount Sinai, the dairy foods recall the time when the Israelites became aware of—but had not yet mastered—the complex laws of kashrut that deal with meat. Hence dairy foods were eaten to be on the safe side. A lovely rabbinic simile: God nurtures Israel on the Torah as a mother nurses her beloved infant with milk.

SCARLET SILK SOUP [D]

In ancient Israel the farmers would note the first fruit of each crop as it budded by tying it with a scarlet ribbon. At Shavuot they would bring these fruits as an offering to the Temple. This soup is a bit of a break from the Shavuot standards, blintzes and cheesecake.

Serves 4–6.

1 (1-lb.) can tomatoes, with
  liquid
1 lb. carrots, scraped and sliced
2 tablespoons butter or
  margarine
2 tablespoons flour

1 cup vegetable broth
1 teaspoon dried dill
1/2 teaspoon salt
1/4 teaspoon hot pepper sauce
2 cups whole milk

Heat tomatoes and carrots to a boil. Lower heat, cover tightly, and cook until carrots are soft, about 20 minutes. Melt butter or margarine and stir in flour. Add vegetable broth, stirring constantly until sauce thickens. Purée tomatoes and carrots in a blender or food processor. Add to sauce. Stir in dill, salt, and hot pepper sauce, bringing all to a second boil. Stir in milk until heated but not boiling. Serve hot or cold.

THE NINTH OF AV

Just as there are customs for happy occasions, there are also food customs for times of mourning. The Ninth of Av is the anniversary of the destruction of the Temple and of the sovereign nation of Judaea. It is marked each year by a daylong fast. Unlike the fast of Yom Kippur, this fast contains no element of joy.

Before nightfall, when the fast begins, a simple meal is eaten, with only the immediate family present. Only one cooked food is consumed at this time. It should not contain meat. A hard-boiled egg daubed with ashes is a symbol of mourning. Bland and unsalted food is the rule, as the midsummer fast usually coincides with hot weather, and one wishes to protect against dehydration. Quantities of bread and beverages such as iced tea are the best preparation for the fast.

The breaking of the fast is also low-key, since, according to rabbinic teaching, the fire in the Temple continued well into the tenth of Av. A simple dairy meal, such as scrambled eggs, is customary.

THE SABBATH OF CONSOLATION
THE FIFTEENTH OF AV

Following the period of national mourning that culminates in the Ninth of Av is a time of consolation. In the synagogue, the prophets' visions of a messianic idyll are read, and women wear white dresses. That same week brings the Fifteenth of Av, a Jewish Valentine's Day. In ancient times the maidens would come out to dance before the young men and matches would be made. It was the custom for rich girls to lend their poor sisters dresses for this event. Dressed similarly in pure white, the young women sang while they danced, "Seek not wealth and honor, but a virtuous wife."

Today the Sabbath of Consolation and the Fifteenth of Av have combined in a modern rite, the singles weekend. A party at this time might include the following spread as a centerpiece. Its pure white color and the fresh berries of the season make it particularly appropriate, as does the shape of the mold.

COEUR À LA CRÈME   [D]

Makes about a quart.

2 (8-oz.) packages cream cheese,
    at room temperature
2 tablespoons milk

1 cup sour cream
1 basket fresh berries, rinsed and
    drained

Whip the cream cheese and milk in a food processor or blender. Add the sour cream and blend until smooth. Pour into a heart-shaped mold. Refrigerate at least 2 hours. Arrange berries around the edge of the dish. Serve with fresh fruit salad and crackers.

JEWISH MILESTONES

Life's most important events are celebrated with food—that's almost an imperative. A beautiful meal or tempting buffet helps one share a personal joy with one's entire community.

After the *birth of a boy,* it is the custom to visit his parents on the Friday night before his circumcision. Sweet liqueurs, cookies, and chick-peas are traditionally served.

The *circumcision* itself is always performed during daylight, so, if weather permits, an outdoor setting is ideal for the meal that follows. When a circumcision is held on a work day (it must be done on the eighth day after birth) a bagel-and-lox-type brunch, with buffet salads and spreads, is appropriate and easy at breakfast or lunchtime—when most guests can attend.

The *redemption of the firstborn son* takes place a month after birth. For the ceremony, in which the boy's father redeems him from a cohen (priest), ten adult males must be in attendance. Practically speaking, this means dinner for at least twenty people. A dairy or cold meat buffet will be suitable for the guests in most homes. At this time it is customary to put out bowls of sugar cubes and garlic, symbolizing a sweet and healthy life for the child.

The *birth of a girl* is usually celebrated with an elaborate kiddush given at the synagogue, usually on the Sabbath after her birth. It is also possible to celebrate this event at any time with a *seuda* (feast) featuring either a buffet or sit-down meal.

Incidentally, it is contrary to Jewish custom to throw a baby shower before the birth of a baby. This is to save the parents grief in case the pregnancy ends in a stillbirth. It is heartbreaking to think of bereaved parents sorting through tiny clothing.

A child's *third birthday* is a special one on the Jewish calendar. At this age he or she is considered capable of understanding some of the teachings of Judaism. At the child's birthday party an item symbolizing one of the commandments is given to him or her. A boy might be given tzitzit (a ritual garment); a girl might be given a candlestick, which she will light and bless on the following Sabbath eve. Kids and grownups will attend this party, so serve foods which bridge the generations, such as pizza and ice cream.

Bar Mitzvah and *Bat Mitzvah* celebrations have taken a turn for the modest in recent years. A gaudy display of parental largesse is no longer the primary function of these events, in fact, many young people are insisting on a meaningful Jewish experience at this time. For example, some youngsters are "sharing" their party with another child in the Soviet Union. Guests are handed stamped envelopes addressed to Soviet officials and asked to write on behalf of the emigration of the Bar/Bat Mitzvah partner.

Bar Mitzvah boys usually read from the Torah at synagogue services, and sometimes deliver an address. A Sabbath kiddush and/or a party (not on the Sabbath) follows. Bat Mitzvah girls go through a similar round, except that in Orthodox synagogues they do not read from the Torah. Some Orthodox communities have instituted the practice of a Friday night dinner and Sabbath address by the Bat Mitzvah girl.

Interestingly, the Bar Mitzvah "ceremonies" go back less than a hundred years; Bat Mitzvah is an even more recent institution. Prior to that time children gradually undertook adult religious responsibilities. By the time they were twelve (girls) or thirteen (boys), they were considered completely responsible for all ritual obligations.

For many boys, a Bar Mitzvah at the Western Wall in Jerusalem is the ultimate in celebration. But those who can't make the trip might enjoy a buffet centerpiece that is a model of the Wall made from sugar tablets "mortared" with syrup. Sprigs of fresh mint serve as the Wall's characteristic moss. And it can all be used to sweeten the guests' tea afterward.

Centuries ago the *engagement* of a Jewish couple resulted in almost as much festivity as the wedding. Today engagements are once again becoming more elaborate. Because so many young adults live away from their parents—sometimes thousands of miles away—there are often two sets of relatives and friends in two far-apart locations. A compromise is to have a big engagement party for those who cannot attend the wedding. If more than forty people are to attend such an affair, and if the couple or their parents can afford it, a catered buffet or dinner is sensible.

Prewedding showers, stag parties, and rehearsal dinners are not Jewish customs. However, on the Sabbath before a wedding the groom is called up to the Torah. When he goes to accept this honor, the congregation pelts him with candies, for good luck. The children in the synagogue soon pick up this literal windfall. After services his family sponsors a kiddush for the entire congregation. In some communities, the bride has a party that afternoon, at home, for her women friends. Fancy pastries are served.

The logistics of kashrut supervision, as well as those of serving a large number of people, mean that almost all *weddings* are catered today. A caveat for brides and grooms: the typical pareve wedding cake is a bland thing indeed. Devoid of butter and milk, a white cake is not likely to be very good. Since most weddings feature meat, consider richly flavored cakes—chocolate, carrot, walnut—even if they aren't white. Go for rich fillings, too, such as rum, almond, hazelnut, and more chocolate. White and pastel frosting will provide an adequately bridal look.

For six nights *following the wedding,* traditional couples are fêted by their families and friends. Each evening a full-course dinner is given. Since this type of festivity requires a minimum of ten adult males, these parties will have at least twenty in attendance. The bride and groom sit at the head of the table, no matter how distinguished the guests. They do not sponsor any of the Seven Blessings themselves, nor do they help serve or clean up in any way. It is traditional to have a stranger as one of the guests at each of these dinner parties (or at least someone who has not attended the wedding).

Few food customs attend Jewish *mourning* rites. A pre- or postfuneral buffet or wake is distinctly forbidden. During the seven days of mourning (shiva) the spouse, children, siblings, and parents only are required to desist from meat and wine. It is customary for the spouse or friend of a mourner to prepare light meals for him or her. A simple meal should be waiting for the mourners after the funeral, and they should be reminded to eat periodically because grief may cause them to neglect their health. Coffee, tea, cold drinks, and fruit may be kept on hand to refresh those who come to pay consolation calls and stay for a long period at the request of the mourner, but cakes and other festive foods should not be served.

The Table
Is Set:
The Jewish Way
of Dining

WINE

Few chapters in food history are as fascinating as the long and variegated relationship of the Jews with wine and liquor. The enigmas continue in modern life: of all ethnic groups in the United States, Jews have by far the lowest rate of alcoholism—and the lowest rate of abstention from alcohol.

It all began in the Garden of Eden, perhaps, when Adam and Eve ate from the Tree of Knowledge, which many rabbinic commentators saw as the original grapevine. Noah is reported to have cultivated the vine just as soon as he found dry land, and was the first to suffer from overindulgence in wine.

The early Hebrews, it appears, were no more and no less intrigued with wine than other peoples of the region. Their special contribution to its lore was an insistence that it be used in sanctifying the One God. Of all liquids, wine alone merits a special blessing, "You are blessed, King of the universe, who creates the fruit of the vine." And wine is used for the Kiddush (sanctification) of the Sabbath and holidays. It was also essential to the services of the Temple.

But wine was also a staple, an everyday drink for rich and poor. Neighboring peoples reserved wine for special occasions, with mead—the precursor of beer—as the common beverage. But wine remained by far the most popular drink of the Jews until the Middle Ages. The biblical list of the seven species, the agricultural pillars of the land, puts the grape third in importance, following only the food staples wheat and barley.

In biblical times and after, most wine was diluted, so that alcoholic content was negligible. The best wine, of course, was savored without dilution, and harder drinks were also developed, perhaps equivalent to brandy. It is probable, also, that other fruits and grains were fermented, too.

The various effects of different levels of intoxication are noted throughout the Bible. Among the more interesting stories is that of Hannah, mother of the Prophet Samuel, who is accused by the High Priest Eli of muttering drunkenly in the Tabernacle. Tradition credits Hannah as the first to pray silently, but it is more surprising to find the tippling housewife to be a common character more than three thousand years ago!

By the time of the Roman occupation, Judaea had become a major wine-producing nation. The Talmud, describing this era, notes many varieties of wine, recipes containing wine and other spirits, and details the therapeutic qualities of these drinks. After the destruction of the Temple in the year 70, one rabbi proposed that the Jews drink no wine, as a sign of mourning, until the Temple was rebuilt. This proposal was voted down by his colleagues; they considered wine to be more of a necessity than a luxury.

The prohibition against drinking the wine of gentiles made a Jewish wine industry imperative wherever communities formed in the Diaspora. The earliest records show that Jews were active in the founding of the great vineyards of France and Germany in the early Middle Ages. From the necessity of making wine for their own use, Jews developed an industry that served their Christian neighbors as well. Several early popes went on record to complain that, in order to obtain the best wine, Christians had to buy the Eucharist itself from Jews.

Church and state soon collaborated in forbidding the ownership of land by Jews throughout Europe. Jews, therefore, lost their preeminence as vintners. Nevertheless, they continued to be active in the distribution of wine and related products, wherever such trade was permitted to them.

The Jewish population eventually shifted to the less hostile areas of Eastern Europe. Here too, Jews continued in the wine and spirits trade. Distilling and brewing became important occupations, and Jewish women as well as men were active in them.

Tavern-keeping became one of the most important sources of income for Jews from the Middle Ages until this century. The Jewish tavern-keeper was as much a fixture of Eastern European society as the Irish bartender would become in America. Since anti-Semitic laws expelled Jews from the major cities while keeping them from owning land, tavern-keeping offered one of the few possible means of livelihood.

The taxation of spirits was controlled by the nobles, who preferred that the Jews collect this revenue. Since the Jews were not allowed citizenship, they could survive only at the nobles' pleasure. Consequently, these aristocrats could depend on the Jews to collect liquor taxes diligently. The peasants, on the other hand, who were the frequenters of the bars, were given a handy scapegoat in the form of the Jewish tavern-keeper. Their alcoholism and chronic indebtedness was conveniently blamed on the Jew who sold them liquor and extended credit. The contempt was not one-sided. "Drunk as a goy" was one of the worst insults a Jew could hurl at his fellow.

Tavern-keeping attracted only the lowest classes of Jews. Usually, this occupation meant the isolation of a family from a larger Jewish community. The tavern doubled as an inn and, on occasion, a Jew traveling on business would stay the night and eat a meal. But the regular clientele at the bar was always gentile. Tavern-keepers hired live-in Hebrew teachers to educate their children.

Even so, Yiddish literature and lore show the tavern-keeper and his family as figures of ignorance, and, despite their relative prosperity, of lower status than manual laborers. Poignant stories and poetry portray the Jewish tavern-keeper late at night, reciting the Psalms over and over, with drunken peasants lying in a stupor all around him.

As the middle class began to grow in Eastern Europe, others began to covet the niche of the Jewish tavern-keeper. Laws were soon passed to favor the entry of Christians to this field. Nevertheless Jews continued to dominate the watering holes of Eastern Europe until the Holocaust. As early as 1600 it is recorded that Jews overcame the state-supported competition by innovations such as offering musical entertainment at their taverns. Thus began the cabaret!

When the masses of Jews emigrated from Europe to the New World, they brought their skills at distilling and brewing with them. The Canadian Bronfman family founded the Seagram liquor company, which remains one of the world's largest. (Curiously, the word *bronfen* means whiskey in some regional dialects of Yiddish.) Jews were also active in other, smaller enterprises, but few resumed the trade of tavern-keeper.

The early Zionist settlers of Israel dreamed of resuming the historical wine industry that had been destroyed, with nationhood, two thousand years before. Tiny wine-making enterprises had been in operation for that entire time in Jerusalem and other centers of Jewish population. The Baron Edmond de Rothschild, however, decided to found a large-scale wine-making enterprise. In 1870 he organized the first winery in "modern" Israel. He imported vine stocks from France and taught the young pioneers the essentials of wine-making and bottling.

After more than a century of trials—wars, mass emigration, devastating plant diseases, radical changes in wine-drinking habits—the Baron's enterprise is thriving as Israel's large Carmel company. Its symbol is a rendition of the biblical report of the spies sent by Moses to Canaan—a cluster of grapes so huge that two men must carry it. The Israeli Government supports a scientific and marketing institute for wine. Clearly the potential for a greater share of the world wine market is there.

Alcoholism and the Jews

Any reader can see that alcohol abuse was no rarity in biblical times. In the first postbiblical centuries, too, drunkenness was not an uncommon problem among Jews, as recorded by the Talmud. But some time in the next millennium Jews seem to have lost their taste for quantities of liquor. When the first statistics on chronic alcoholism began to be compiled, Jews were already at the bottom of every ethnic list.

The numbers were truly staggering. Jews were not only sober compared with their traditional neighbors, the hard-drinking Russians and Poles, they even drank less than such sober peoples as the Chinese and other Asians, and less then members of religions which prohibited the use of alcohol altogether, such as Protestant fundamentalists and Moslems. Nor were the Jews simply less likely to drink. Many studies found them to be hundreds of times less likely to drink to excess than comparable socioeconomic groups. In a study of mental hospital admissions at the beginning of this century, not a single Jewish patient was found to have a complication of alcoholism. The general percentage of alcohol abuse among such patients was over 50 percent.

These facts were so significant that serious scientists undertook to find a genetic factor among Jews that might explain some form of resistance to alcohol. Their search became less meaningful as the twentieth century progressed and the incidence of alcoholism among Jews climbed steeply. Today, alcohol abuse among American Jews is still rare among the traditional. But the rate climbs with the more assimilated Jews. Among Jews who have little or no ethnic identity the rate of alcoholism approaches that of their non-Jewish socioeconomic peers.

The sobriety of traditional Jews is coming under new scrutiny as these new trends develop. It is a subject of interest to non-Jews as well, now that alcoholism has been recognized as one of the most widespread and debilitating of human diseases.

First, it should be noted that teetotaling is rare among Jews. Certainly it has no basis in the Jewish religion, which requires the drinking of wine in many ceremonies. Second, the genetic theory of sobriety may well be discounted. Even among the most homogeneous Jewish populations there is a wide diversity of both the ability to metabolize alcohol (the Talmud tells of one of its rabbis who could drink gargantuan amounts of liquor, and his colleague, who could barely fulfill the religious requirement of four cups of wine at the Passover Seder), and the desire to imbibe. (Many Jews barely wet their lips on the Kiddush cup; others, as the Yiddish saying goes, are "fond of a glass"—but never of a bottle!)

Some of the factors which led to the traditional Jewish moderation in drink include:

• Religious customs that sanctify wine and other spirits. These beverages were forever associated with holy things in the Jewish mind, so that it became impossible to consider them merely recreational. Jewish law also prohibits drunkenness during many mandatory and pleasurable activities, such as prayer or sexual intercourse. In addition, the religion gave legitimate outlets for drinking. It is a *mitzvah* to drink copiously on the holidays of Simchat Torah and Purim, and Hasidim and other mystics use alcohol abundantly, but in a regulated manner, to heighten spiritual perception.

• The Jew takes pride in intellectual clarity, a facility that is quickly obscured by alcohol. Many everyday occasions and special celebrations are marked by a display of Torah learning. A wedding guest, for example, would be deeply humiliated if he flubbed a Talmudic discussion in which he was asked to take part. He will therefore keep his drinking under control, even at such a legitimate drinking event.

• By custom, virtually all drinking is at public, happy events. "This calls for a *lechayim*," one might say after learning of an engagement or an auspicious business deal. (The correct method of toasting is to say the appropriate blessing on the drink, take a sip, raise the glass, say "Lechayim," add any other salutation, and take another sip.) Such drinking is done with the other celebrants or well-wishers, never privately. Traditional Jews never drink to overcome depression or to relax after a taxing experience.

• In Jewish culture, drinking does not have a macho image. The sites of masculine camaraderie were the House of Study and the synagogue, where men spent almost all of their leisure time. The tavern did not represent an escape from family obligations, as it did in many other cultures. Nor was mighty drinking a symbol of passage to manhood. Jewish babies are given a drop or two of Kiddush wine before they even eat solid food, and children of both sexes will take a sip of harder liquor at family celebrations whenever they are capable of doing so comfortably. An appreciation of alcohol is not considered unfeminine —the grandmother who takes a daily shot of schnapps for her "digestion," is a commonplace. Alcohol use—and abuse—is virtually evenly distributed between the sexes among all classes of Jews.

• In many countries where alcoholism is very widespread, the roots of the disease are traced to long-standing social problems, especially the unending oppression of peasant life and the boredom of rural existence and urban poverty. The peasant or laborer sees no way out other than the dulling of his pain by drink.

The European Jew had at least as hard a time surviving, but his troubles were of a different nature. He was the subject of sudden violence by the peasantry and rapacious oppression by the authorities. Unlike his gentile neighbors, the Jew's life and home were always precarious. He needed his wits about him to survive, and the habit of dulling his senses with alcohol would be extremely dangerous.

• As tavern-keepers, the Jews were in an excellent position to view the debilitating effects of alcoholism on their neighbors. They were filled with horror at the sight of violence, disease, increased poverty, psychosis, and the loss of self-respect. Worst of all, to the Jew, was the abdication of family responsibility and even the abuse of wives and children that was caused by drunkenness.

• Drinking patterns are strongly influenced by the behavior of parents. Whether this is genetic or environmental has yet to be determined. Even in the latter case, the average Jew grows up in an environment with a casual regard of alcohol as something that is not very important—neither a magic elixir nor the Devil's brew.

(An amusing bit of folklore: it is said that Jewish boys lose the desire for alcohol at the age of eight days. Immediately after the circumcision, it is customary to give the baby a handkerchief corner dipped in wine to soothe him.

Supposedly, the association of pain and drink is sufficient to modify his behavior for life!)

• In the Jewish world view, life is neither a vale of tears to be endured nor a den of pleasures to be exploited. Rather, it is a moral adventure, full of challenges to meet and ladders to climb. The worst condemnation of alcoholic overindulgence, therefore, is that it is a monumental waste of consciousness and time.

Guide to Today's Kosher Wines and Spirits

More than any kosher food, kosher wine is the butt of disparaging remarks. These snobbish putdowns are a sure sign of the parvenu. Professional wine experts will quickly point out that, while there are no kosher wines among the pantheon of greats that sell for hundreds of dollars a bottle, there is also no shortage of drinkable and delightful kosher table wines.

Curiously enough, the bad reputation of kosher wines is of American origin. In Europe the wines of Jewish vintners were considered as good or better than that of other winemakers in their regions. Then, in 1843, a new grape, the Concord, was discovered in New York State. It was a mutation of native American grapes. The Concord was immediately accepted as a luscious eating grape—it has a deliciously rich flavor and a powerful perfume. These traits are highly desirable in table grapes and other products such as grape juice and jam (Concord jelly and peanut butter are a match made in heaven). In wine, however, the Concord is excessively "foxy," that is, it is too fruity, too fragrant, overpowering, lacking in subtlety. A short acquaintance with a variety of wines convinces most people that Concord wine lacks the delicacy that is the greatest pleasure of the beverage.

Because of the nature of the grape, Concord wine is always sweet. Moreover, extra sugar is usually added so that the wine tastes like a fortified soda pop. In the early decades of Concord cultivation this was not considered a fault; a hundred years ago the world's most favored wines were sweet ones such as Madeira, Tokay, sweet Sherry, and Sauterne. Furthermore, the American market for all wines was small. The great rise in the popularity of wine is only about fifteen years old!

When significant numbers of Jews began to arrive in America at the end of the nineteenth century, concentrating in New York, they naturally took to producing Concord wine for religious purposes. This variety soon became associated with kosher wine. Today, firms such as Manischewitz and Mogen David sell almost 5 million cases of this wine per year—the vast majority to non-Jews. There are a great many people of every religious persuasion who have not had the benefit of a wine education. For them, the appeal of Concord wine is immediate and direct. So great is the world market for this wine that Israel has imported Concord vines and now produces that all-American wine for export.

THE MYTH OF "SACRAMENTAL" WINE

The requirement that wine be kosher differs from other laws of kashrut in that no special procedures or prohibitions apply to the wine itself. To qualify as kosher, wine may be made of the same grapes and by the same means as other wines. However, from the time of grape-crushing until bottling all work must be done by observant Jews. (Other kosher foods may be prepared by non-Jews, as long as an observant Jew is supervising.)

The rabbinical body of the Conservative branch of Judaism has ruled that kosher wine is required only for ritual purposes, while ordinary wine may be used at other times. This has led to some confusion about "sacramental" wine. Benediction does not change the essence of wine in Judaism, as it does in Christianity. Blessing a cup of wine does not convert a non-kosher wine to a kosher one. And every food or drink taken by a Jew must be blessed, according to the Torah.

Many believe, mistakenly, that kosher wine must be red and sweet. While some rabbis prefer red wine for ritual purposes—its royal color makes it seem more "important"—and others favor sweet wine around the time of Rosh Hashanah—as a symbol of the sweet new year to come—there is no religious reason not to recite the Kiddush over a chilled cup of crisp white wine!

PURPLE PARTY PUNCH

Concord wine does make a festive drink for entertaining.

Makes 20 servings.

1 ice mold
2 bottles Concord wine
2 bottles club soda
1 lemon, sliced thin
1 lime, sliced thin

Form an ice mold by filling a Bundt pan halfway with water and freezing. Unmold into a clear glass punch bowl (the magnificent purple color is one of Concord wine's strongest attractions). Pour the wine and soda onto the mold and stir. Float the citrus slices on top.

Kosher-wine drinkers, like other lovers of the grape, have begun to acquire French tastes—that is, a liking for drier, more subtle wines. The companies which serve this population, notably, Kedem of New York, Carmel of Israel, and many small wineries in France, Italy, Spain, and California, have responded to these changing tastes.

Kedem has increasingly turned to California as a source of grapes for its domestic wines, producing some good varietals at reasonable prices. It also imports and distributes many of the best European kosher wines.

Carmel, whose sweet wines comprised 75 percent of its total output not many years ago, now devotes the lion's share of its bottles to sophisticated dry wines. The small wineries bottle dry wines exclusively.

Kosher wines are easily found—they are better distributed than many kosher foods. Large liquor stores, even in areas with small Jewish populations, often stock a variety. Many Jewish bookstores carry wines, too. And don't overlook the wine departments of large supermarket chains, they sometimes have good kosher wines at terrific prices. If you can't get the wines you want, try contacting the local distributors of kosher wines. They may be able to get what you want and, if you buy by the case, offer good discounts, too.

If you are attempting a first foray into the world of fine wines, especially if you are weaning yourself from the sweet "sacramentals," you may find dry wines to be distressingly sour at first sip. Start gradually with a soft red wine, such as Bartenura Lambrusco (Italian) and a fragrant white, such as Carmel's fruity French Colombard.

Work your way up to the versatile table wines, including Kedem Zinfandel (red) and Chenin Blanc (white), Carmel Cabernet Sauvignon (red) and Sauvignon Blanc (white), Bartenura Valpolicella (red) and Soave (white).

For serviceable table wines at a low price, Carmel's Adom Atik, a burgundy, and Hock (white) are good choices.

To splurge, try the kosher wines of the French château bottlers. And, if you can get your hands on some, the exquisite Johannisburg Riesling, a heavenly, slightly effervescent white wine from the tiny Hagafen winery in California's Napa Valley.

For special occasions, chill a bottle of Israel's excellent champagne, The President. Less glamorous but lots of fun—as Italian wines are likely to be—is the sparkling Bartenura Asti Spumante. You can glean good tips on kosher wines from the wine column in your newspaper. Many wine experts do a roundup of kosher wines in the pre-Passover period. This is also a good time to stock up, as liquor stores have the largest variety to choose from. The High Holiday period in the fall is also a good time to shop.

Bear in mind that wines vary according to vintage. Also, some wines don't travel well and can turn into vinegar at some point between the vineyard and your table. If a wine has been highly recommended, but you thought it was awful, try another bottle the following year.

If, despite current fashion and the advice of oenophiles, you still prefer sweet wines, do try some more delicate and flavorful varieties such as: Kedem's Matouk Royale and Carmel's Chateau Richon (Sauterne), and Carmel's Kadmon (Madeira), Partom (Port), Sharir (Sherry), and Topaz (Tokay).

LIQUOR

Selection of liquors poses few problems for the kosher drinker, since most common spirits and liqueurs are kosher. The major exceptions are those liquors made from grapes, such as brandy. The minor exception is the Mexican cactus liquor which reportedly contains a cactus worm in each bottle. It is important to note that most alcoholic beverages today are made from a grain base, or include some grain alcohol, and are therefore not to be used on Passover. All potables used during Passover should be certified kosher for the holiday.

There is no kosher substitute for the noble Cognacs and Armagnacs. However, Carmel's 777 brandy is very good indeed. Try it as a pleasant change from sweet liqueurs and mixed drinks.

The Israeli liqueur Sabra is a nice blend of chocolate and orange. While many find it rather heavy sipped straight, it is excellent in mixed drinks, in cooking and baking, and as a sauce for desserts. It is a wonderful substitute in recipes calling for Grand Marnier, which is brandy-based.

A generous dollop of Sabra instantly dresses up a mundane dessert such as vanilla ice cream, fruit salad, or plain pound cake. The American importers of this drink offer a booklet of inventive recipes. Here are two others.

OLEH CHADASH (New Immigrant)

1 jigger vodka
1 jigger Sabra

Stir well and pour over ice. Garnish with an orange twist.

STRAWBERRY JEWELS

Allow two or three strawberries per person, if serving as an after-dinner treat. Or, for an exquisite gift, nestle a dozen in fancy paper in a pretty little basket.

1 pint large strawberries, with stems
Sabra liqueur
1 (6-oz.) bar of fine bittersweet chocolate

Select the best berries, those that are firm but red right up to the shoulders. Wash and dry carefully, taking care not to remove the stems and green crowns. Fill a hypodermic needle with Sabra and inject each strawberry with a few cc's of the liqueur. Melt the chocolate on top of a double boiler. Holding each berry by its stem, dip in the chocolate, leaving a little bit of red shoulder visible. Hold aloft for a few seconds until the chocolate cools and hardens.

Israel produces many amusing liqueurs, some of which are only available inside the country. One interesting export, Carmel's Liqueur des Patriarches— Abtei, is made of herbs, a possible substitute for Chartreuse, another French liqueur with a brandy base.

Arak and its many cousins, including Ouzo, is the liquor most favored in Moslem countries—where permitted—and in the Balkans. Often it is made with a brandy base. Carmel's Arak has a sweet anise scent, but don't be fooled, it packs a 100-proof punch. You don't have to be Sephardic to love it.

There are certain fruit brandies that were much beloved of Eastern European Jewry. These include slivovitz (plum brandy), palinka (apricot brandy), pear brandy, and wishniak (cherry brandy). These are not sweet liqueurs—sweet versions of these drinks are not the real thing—but liquors in which the fruit sugars are allowed to ferment completely, leaving a powerful liquor with a fruit perfume. Despite the destruction of their native Jewry and the hostility of Soviet Bloc governments, limited quantities of these liquors are produced under rabbinical supervision for export. It is doubtful that their manufacture is long for this world, so snap up these products when you see them; they will soon be heirlooms.

JUICIER MEAT

The major deficiency of kosher meat is that it is less juicy than similar cuts of nonkosher meat and, therefore, standard recipes using kosher meat, even when exactly executed, can seem off-key.

Cattle bred for the kosher market are leaner than standard livestock. Ranchers raise them this way to accommodate the Jewish taste for less marbled meat. Kosher meat will thus have an all-over lower fat content, with fewer fine veins of fat. The animals raised for kosher slaughter tend to be tougher, stringier, and more compact.

In the salting and soaking process of kashering, meat loses not only most of its blood content, but much of its other moisture as well.

In addition, many kosher diners prefer their meat very well done. Extralong cooking time dehydrates the meat even further. (Recently, in a kosher restaurant, I overheard a patron ordering a steak. He wanted it well done, and he took a deep breath, obviously wanting to explain to the waiter, in no uncertain terms, just how well done the steak should be. The experienced waiter stopped him in midsentence. "I know, I know—incinerated.")

Several steps can be taken to avoid dried-out meat and insure greater success with new meat recipes.

- Use meat tenderizer generously and according to product directions.
- Never use salt before or during the cooking of meat. Salt extracts moisture. Often less salt is needed in the dish than the recipe calls for because the meat has already been abundantly salted in the kashering process. In any event you will get more salt flavor per shake of salt if you add it just before serving. In addition, for health reasons, and because the modern diet contains excessive amounts of the mineral, growing numbers of diners are using little or no salt at the table and many are learning not to miss it.
- Increase by a fourth the amount of liquid (but not the seasonings used) in a sauce in which the meat is to be cooked. For example, if a meat-loaf recipe calls for a cup of tomato sauce, try adding another 1/4 cup. Do not change the recipe if the sauce is to be added after the meat has been cooked.
- Try searing meats (browning quickly over high heat) before they are to be cooked on the stove top. This locks in the juice.
- For meats that are to be baked or roasted, preheat the oven to 100° higher than the recipe calls for. Insert the meat in the oven, wait three minutes, then lower the oven temperature to the required degree.
- Make an effort to accustom your family to rarer meat. Every palate needs to be educated to savor subtle flavors.
- A preference for burnt meat is sometimes a way of indicating a desire for a crisp skin or coating. A shorter cooking time on higher heat (carefully monitored), and removing the cover during the last half hour or so of baking, are two ways of getting crisper exteriors and juicier interiors.
- Is it possible that an insistence on having meat practically charred masks a secret revulsion to it in the first place? Why not save money and energy by replacing more meat meals with dairy or vegetarian dishes.

MEALTIME ETIQUETTE

No discussion of Jewish cuisine is complete without considering the vast subject of proper table manners. Ideally, Jews not only eat unique foods, they eat their food uniquely.

Some general principles:

- Food must never be wasted. It is the cook's responsibility to see that leftovers are accounted for. It is literally a sin to use food as a means of conspicuous consumption, such as preparing a huge meal, most of which will have to be discarded. Bread, the chief symbol of God's bounty, is to be treated with special reverence. Bread which has fallen to the floor should be picked up immediately.

Crumbs should be saved for feeding birds. If bread must be thrown away, it should be wrapped in a paper napkin, not tossed conspicuously into the trash.

• Moderation is the path to follow in all things gustatory. Gluttony and asceticism are equally frowned upon. The Talmud, adapting and refining the manners of the Greco-Roman aristocracy, makes such fine points as the rule that one should not down a beverage at a single gulp. Rather, no more than five swallows should be taken and then the glass or cup placed on the table. The rabbis of the Talmud also make extensive comments on the socioeconomic role of food. One proverb considers the golden path in buying life's necessities. In housing, live according to your means; in clothing, dress more elegantly than you can afford; in food, eat more simply than you can afford.

In the twelfth century, Maimonides, speaking as both physician and rabbi, set down extensive dicta concerning food and health. It was his contention that virtually all noncommunicable diseases are caused by improper diet. The advice he offers to counter it is startling in its modernity. It includes the following:

• The proper time to end a meal is when you feel there is still room enough for half again what you have eaten.

• Reserve white bread for the Sabbath challah. During the week, eat whole-grain breads.

• Limit yourself to small amounts of sweets.

• Avoid heavy meals just before or immediately after bathing, exercise, sleep, or sexual intercourse.

If the ideal Jewish diet is spare, it is nonetheless far from stark. On the Day of Judgment, says the proverb, every Jew will be asked why each permitted pleasure was not tasted. One should not slight God's gifts.

Since ancient times fasting has been considered a valuable spiritual tool. But it is secondary to those other paths toward perfection, prayer, repentance, Torah study, and social action. And on occasions when celebration is called for —the Sabbath, the festivals, life's happy milestones—food, glorious food, is essential.

STYLES OF DINING

Whether a traditional Jewish meal is to be formal or informal is determined not by the luxury of the setting but according to what is being served to whom. A meal is considered formal if (a) bread is served, and (b) at least three adults of the same sex are dining together. These factors determine which blessings are to be said before and after the meal.

Of course, an informal meal can be quite elaborate and festive. An important example is the Kiddush. A Kiddush is given to celebrate any happy event. It is held on Saturday, immediately following synagogue services, in a separate room at the synagogue or at the home of the sponsor. It can be simple, including wine and spirits and cake, or elaborate, with several courses of hot foods, salads, and rich desserts available. Much depends on the budget of the hosts and the catering facilities available. If no special event is celebrated, the synagogue itself will often sponsor a Kiddush. At the Kiddush, the special Sabbath blessing is recited over wine or liquor, but no bread is served and no Grace is said. A formal meal, on the other hand, can be casual in tone. Three friends sharing sandwiches can transform a picnic blanket into a "holy altar" by reciting the blessing over bread and the Grace after meals. In the following discussion, we will treat the formal meal in its most common form, a Sabbath or festival lunch or dinner, in the company of family and friends.

Setting the Table

The tablecloth is a symbol of respect for the table and its central role in Jewish life. During the Sabbath and holidays, tablecloths cover all dining tables throughout the day. Many older Jews remember with affection the starched white linen cloth whose spotless expanse heralded the Sabbath Bride. Today, easy-care fabrics and jazzy decorator touches are more commonly seen. Nevertheless, white or pale colors are still preferred. A bare table, no matter how beautiful its finish or how lovely the place mats, will not do.

Candles form the centerpiece of the table. The lighting of the candles is the primary ritual of the Sabbath and festivals. It is done by the female head of the household, who lights and blesses at least two candles. Usually, all other adult women present also light two candles. In some places girls from the age of three light a single candle. When no women are present, candle lighting is the duty of the senior male of the household. Sabbath candlesticks are often works of great artistry in silver, brass, crystal, or other materials. They are the traditional wedding gift to a bride from her mother-in-law.

The candlesticks are not placed directly upon the table, but are set on a tray. On holidays the tray may be moved, but on the Sabbath it is not touched until after nightfall on Saturday. This means that the tablecloth cannot be replaced if it becomes soiled. Crumbs are removed from the table with a cloth or brush. If a large tray seems unwieldy, it is possible to place the tray on a sideboard or other piece of furniture clearly visible to the diners. On the Sabbath, the tray may not be moved from its position at the time of candle lighting.

Fresh flowers are delightful ornaments. They are now *de rigueur* on the Sabbath table in Israel and wherever reasonably priced blossoms are available year round. On the Sabbath and festivals, vases may be moved and fallen petals brushed from the table. However, the flowers themselves are not touched, whatever their condition, nor is water added to the vase.

The Kiddush over wine is the second important ritual of the Sabbath and holidays. A special cup is set for this purpose at the place of the male head of the household. Other adult males may also wish to recite their own Kiddush. If no men are present, the senior woman assumes this duty. Often the Kiddush cup is artistically fashioned of silver or brass. A Kiddush cup is a traditional Bar Mitzvah gift from a close male relative. Children of both sexes are encouraged to say part of the Kiddush from the time they are able to speak. Tiny Kiddush cups no bigger than shot glasses, engraved with the child's name, are a charming gift from doting grandparents.

The Kiddush cup is for ritual purposes only. Metal does not enhance the flavor of wine. If wine is to be served with the meal, each table setting should include glass stemware.

Festive breads—challah—are the third great symbol of the Sabbath and holiday table. Two breads are always used, to commemorate the two biblical commandments of the Sabbath, "Celebrate . . ." and "Remember the Sabbath to keep it holy." If two challahs seem more than your guests are likely to eat, a dinner roll or matzoh can replace one of them. However, each bread should be whole, not broken or sliced.

The challahs are placed on a board—beautiful boards of inlaid wood are available—or a platter, not deposited directly on the tablecloth. They are covered with a cloth, such as a large napkin. For generations, Jewish women put the greatest efforts of their embroidering skills into working challah covers of velvet or satin with gold stitchery and imaginative fringes and designs. Today, alas, washable materials and machine-executed designs are the norm in challah covers. A large bread knife is also set. Sometimes this knife is a special one with a handle embossed with, say, a cityscape of Jerusalem. A saltcellar is placed near the challahs. All of these ritual items are available in a wide spectrum of materials, artistry, and cost at Jewish gift shops and bookstores. It is nice, of course, to have exquisite accouterments at the table. However, you can entertain splendidly without heirlooms or *objets d'art*. Every week thousands of college students attend wonderful Sabbath meals in dormitories. They budget on a shoestring and pitch in with the preparation and the cleanup. Yet, for many, these meals touch their souls more profoundly than any synagogue service.

What are the minimal supplies for a formal Jewish dinner? Here's a perfectly passable table setting for a Sabbath camping trip: plastic cloth to cover a picnic table; tray made of several layers of aluminum foil; candlesticks made of foil-covered bottle caps; pretty wildflowers in a soda bottle; a plastic champagne goblet for Kiddush; double paper plates for the challah; a bandana or large napkin for challah covering. The Exterior Designer will provide an ambiance of fresh air, rustling trees, and sparkling stars.

Seating, Serving, and Other Questions of Honor

In Western culture the norms of etiquette are often determined by values that are absent in Judaism. One such value is that women need greater solicitude than men. That is why women receive such privileges as getting first choice from the serving platter. Another value is that, at a dinner party, each guest would prefer companions of the opposite sex, excluding the spouse. Conventional etiquette therefore arranges seating in the classic boy-girl-boy-girl pattern, with host and hostess seated at opposite ends of the table, or if more than one table is used, at different tables. These customs are rooted in the days of chivalry, when lords and ladies who cared about things like manners, were also the people whose life-style was regulated by marriages that reflected political convenience and love affairs that reflected personal attraction. These concepts of love and marriage were alien to the Jews.

In the United States democracy also had an impact on conventional good manners. One would look askance if a very wealthy or successful guest were accorded conspicuous treatment. In the same vein, children, if they are considered old enough to be seated at a dinner party, are considered the social equals of the older guests. Certain aspects of democracy have indeed affected Jewish dining habits, but in many respects the Jewish way of seating and service at table remains quite different.

At the Jewish table the hierarchy of "honor" is based on certain values, in the following order:

(a) The honor of the Law is paramount. Therefore, when the person who blesses the bread cuts slices for everyone at the table, he eats the first piece before offering any to the guests. Blessing and eating are a single religious act. What is between a person and God is not interrupted for the sake of courtesy.

(b) The marital bond is the supreme social tie. Husband and wife serve each other first. When a man blesses the wine, he takes the required drink without interruption, then hands the cup immediately to his wife.

(c) After the spouse, the parent receives the greatest honor. A number of customs underscore this point. For example, a child—including one grown to adulthood—does not sit in the usual place of either parent.

(d) Outstanding scholarship is recognized by social preference. Jewish studies are the most honored. Thus a brilliant young Talmudist would be served before an eminent brain surgeon.

(e) Age is respected. Strictly speaking, the person serving would serve guests in descending order of seniority. Today, however, Jews, like other Western peoples have a horror of old age, rather than a respect for it. Nevertheless, the elderly are served first, then the middle-aged (pretending that all between twenty-five and sixty-five are of the same age), then young adults, and so on.

(f) Guests are served before family members of equal age and status. In general, the more distant the origin of the guest, the greater the honor accorded.

(g) Children are served in strict descending order of age. It may be pointed out that little David eats only the drumstick. Should big sister Rachel lunge for the last remaining one on the platter, she can be stopped by withering glances or physical force. She must, however, be presented with the platter before her little brother.

At the traditional table, seating is arranged in the following manner. Husbands and wives are seated together, with the other dinner partner a member of the same sex. A typical seating scheme might be: Mr. A., Mrs. A., Mrs. B., Mr. B., Mr. C., Mrs. C. Host and hostess may also sit together in their usual places. However at a large party, where many of the guests do not know each other well, host and hostess may sit at opposite ends of the table to facilitate conversation and a sense of "belonging."

Seating should also take into account an important aspect of Jewish dining, matchmaking. Single people should have maximum access to each other's company, and the hosts need make no apology about segregating all the eligible guests at one end of the table.

Children are an important part of the social life of the table, and should never be obviously excluded. In traditional Jewish homes it is considered inappropriate to have a separate children's table either before or during the time the adults dine. If circumstances necessitate a late dining hour for the adults on a regular basis, the children can eat their meal earlier but still put in an appearance and eat some token food at the time of the main family meal. It is a good idea to have a regular seat for each child, and to respect his place even when guests are present, unless it is extremely awkward. A highly regarded form of conversation at the Sabbath table is the questioning of the children about their studies, especially Jewish studies. The dialogue should not be pressured; rather, it should serve as an icebreaker, allowing everyone to make a contribution on the topic.

Beginning the Meal

Several religious ceremonies precede the meal, especially on the Sabbath and holidays.

The parental blessing of children is a beautiful custom in many homes. The short blessing is bestowed at the side of the table, either immediately after candle lighting on Friday, or upon return from services, before beginning the Friday evening meal.

Also on Friday evening, a minimum of two hymns are sung at the table, with everyone standing at his place. These are "Sholom Aleichem," welcoming the angels of the Sabbath to the home, and "Eishet Chayil," extolling the virtues of the Jewish woman.

The host then recites the blessing over wine, Kiddush. On Friday night this is always done with wine, on Saturday afternoon other spirits are often substituted. While customs vary, most people stand during the blessing and sit during the drinking of the wine or liquor. It is always proper to follow the example of the host. When the person reciting the Kiddush completes the blessing, all present respond with "Amen." However, no one should speak further until having drunk of the wine or liquor.

The one who has blessed the wine should drink at least three ounces of it. He passes it first to his wife, and then, in order of "honor," to the other guests. Each takes a small sip. Wine rarely transmits disease; however, guests with bad colds, or those who are especially fastidious, may request, before the Kiddush, that they be separately served. In that case, the host says the blessing and immediately pours some of the wine from his cup into those of the guests. Alternatively, a cup of wine may be given to each guest who requests it. These arrangements must be made beforehand, however. Wine should not be poured after the blessing has been made.

All the diners now wash their hands ritually. This is not a hygienic procedure; if one's hands are soiled, one should wash them in the usual manner before Kiddush. A special washing cup is sometimes used, and these are often ornate, two-handled vessels of copper or silver. All rings are removed prior to washing. Each person fills the cup and twice pours water on each hand sufficient to rinse it completely to the wrist. The blessing "You are blessed, Lord, our God, King of the universe, who has sanctified us in his commandments and commanded us about the washing of the hands," is said while drying the hands. All return to their seats and remain silent until the bread is eaten.

When everyone has finished washing, the host lifts the cloth from the two challahs. He lifts the challahs and recites the blessing, "You are blessed, Lord, our God, King of the universe, who brings bread forth from the earth." All respond with "Amen." The host passes the bread knife over the two challahs, then chooses one challah and cuts it. He takes the first slice, dips or sprinkles it with salt, and eats a bite of it. He then cuts slices for every person at the table. In some homes it is customary to cut a slice of challah for family members who are temporarily away from home and even infants who are too small to eat bread, indicating that they are part of the family. However, this slice is not cut for married children and never in memory of the dead. This bread should not be wasted; it won't be too difficult to find someone who would like a second slice of delicious challah.

The Meal Itself

The order of the dinner service, so strictly ruled by Western etiquette, has few restrictions by Jewish custom. The most important one is the division of fish dishes from meat and poultry. The laws of kashrut permit fish and meat to be served at the same meal. The customary division of the two is based on considerations of safety. Fish, with its small bones, was long ago observed as a major cause of choking. It is always served in such a way as to permit the diner's full attention to the course.

Fish and meat are never combined in the same dish, even in indirect ways, such as seasoning meat with anchovy paste. If fish and meat are both to be served, the fish is served as the first course. It is the custom in many Jewish communities to take a drink of spirits after the fish. Today in trendier homes and at catered affairs, the French influence has caused the shot of hard liquor to be replaced with a tart ice or sherbet to clear the palate. The time during which the fish is eaten is about the only time during the meal that silence prevails— talk might cause a fishbone to lodge in one's throat. The strength of custom is such that all of these measures prevail even if the fish is filleted beforehand or is served in the form of gefilte fish.

It will come as no surprise to any who have even the briefest acquaintance with Jews that the major form of entertainment at a formal meal is talk. What passes for witty conversation? Torah erudition always ranks highest. It is customary to discuss the biblical portion of the week at the Sabbath table. While the scholar may begin the discussion, everyone has a right to be heard. Often discussants will pull books out to support an argument. It is perfectly acceptable to read the books at the table, but never to actually eat while one is reading. In Orthodox homes one or more bookcases are standard furnishings of the dining room.

Other topics are welcome too, with politics a special favorite. Controversy is as commonplace as challah in many homes. This does not mean, however, that any kind of conversation is acceptable. Business discussions are taboo, as is gossip about persons who are not present. Flirtation is considered in bad taste. In keeping with the notion that the table is a holy altar, language is expected to be more refined than in everyday use. Humor is dearly loved; it can be biting, as long as it's clean.

A hallowed custom is the singing of the Sabbath mealtime hymns. Booklets containing the verses are handed out between courses. Most of these were written during the Golden Age of Hebrew lyric poetry in Moorish Spain. However, new melodies are constantly composed, and everywhere Jews have adopted melodies from faraway communities. The same hymn may be sung to a rousing march in the Hasidic manner or a haunting ballad of the Yemenite style. A guest who brings a new melody to a Sabbath hymn is considered to have brought a special treat.

The Postprandial Ceremony

In many traditional homes, the formal meal is followed by the ritual of Final Waters. A small amount of water is passed around the table. Charming vessels are often used for this, some shaped like tiny wells or urns. Of course a simple shot glass and saucer will serve just as well. Each diner tips the vessel with the water in one hand, collecting a drop or two. He distributes the drops to the other hand and passes one hand over his lips. One's napkin serves to wipe away excess moisture. This custom is optional for women. One of the rationales for the Final Waters is that they symbolically wipe away unkind deeds and words. Convention has it that women are less likely to possess these faults.

The spiritual climax of the Jewish dining experience is the Grace After Meals. This prayer, some ten paragraphs in length, is an affirmation of many of the basic tenets of Judaism. Special booklets containing the Grace and its translation are distributed. On the Sabbath and holidays the Grace is preceded by the singing of the exquisite 137th Psalm.

If three or more adults of the same sex are present, the host (or hostess, in an assembly composed chiefly of women) honors a guest by appointing him Leader of the Grace. The following is said:

> LEADER: My companions, let us offer our blessing.
>
> OTHER DINERS: May God's name be blessed now and forever.
>
> THE LEADER repeats their words and adds: With the permission of the host and the hostess, my teachers (an honorific extended to all) and friends, let us bless the One whose food we have eaten.
>
> OTHERS (Bow slightly from the waist): Blessed is the One whose food we have eaten, and because of whose kindness we remain alive.
>
> LEADER: Blessed is he and blessed is his name.

All proceed directly to reciting the Grace, either silently or in communal song. Its conclusion marks the end of the meal.

Index